THE PRAYERS OF THE BIBLE

THE PRAYERS OF THE BIBLE

R. E. Clements

SCM PRESS LTD

© Copyright John Knox Press 1985

British Library Cataloguing in Publication Data

Clements, R.E.
The Prayers of the Bible.
1. Bible—Prayers—Commentaries
I. Title
220   BS680.P64

ISBN 0-334-02268-1

First British edition published 1986
by SCM Press Ltd
26–30 Tottenham Road London N1 4BZ

Printed in Great Britain by
Richard Clay (The Chaucer Press) plc
Bungay, Suffolk

Contents

To
The Reverend Professor G.W. Anderson, D.D., F.B.A.
Scholar, Colleague, Friend

1
Prayer in the
BIBLE

The Centrality of Prayer

The Bible is quite obviously not a "prayer book" in the more familiar way in which that expression is understood. In fact, if one proceeds to introduce the subject of the "prayers" of the Bible this might appear to intend a reference to the book of Psalms, which have formed a central body of prayer texts, either to be spoken or sung, for both Jews and Christians. The Bible contains a great many prayer texts, however, besides those preserved in the Psalter, and in addition, a great many other passages refer to spontaneous acts of prayer on the part of central biblical figures where the content of the prayer is mentioned briefly or not at all. Quite evidently turning to God in prayer, either in a situation of distress or at a time of great perplexity or simply in order to praise God, is regarded as an entirely normal action. It is regarded as the most natural, and yet also as the most intensely personal and direct way in which the benefits and privileges of a knowledge of God impinge on human lives. It is true that priestly ministrants and to some extent prophets also are regarded as experts in prayer, and there is sufficient evidence to indicate that such persons might be looked to for guidance about prayer. Yet the Bible in no way sanctions the idea of any priestly monopoly on prayer nor does it regard it in semimagical fashion as requiring any mysterious words, names, or formulas which might ensure that only those who were suitably professionally qualified might approach God. On the contrary, so far as the biblical picture of life is concerned, anyone can pray. It is a spontaneous, free, and open privilege which anyone can enjoy and benefit from.

In a study of the non-Psalmic prayers of the Old Testament, M. Greenberg (*Biblical Prose Prayer as a Window to the Popular Religion of Ancient Israel* [Berkeley: Univ. of California Press, 1983] 7) notes the presence of some ninety-seven prayer texts in the Old Testament alone and the number is significantly increased when we include the further material of the New Testament. Prayer is regarded in the Bible as the most fundamental of all expressions of religion, and it is portrayed in a great variety of forms, sometimes with extraordinary simplicity and at others with great complexity and formality.

Considerable discussion has arisen among scholars concerning the way in which the historical development of this aspect of biblical spirituality occurred. On the one hand it becomes evident from the careful use of stereotyped formulas and the emergence of rhetorical "structures" in the Psalter that a measure of skilled professional prayer composition took place during the Old Testament period. Similar formalized psalmic language can be traced even further back, most particularly in a number of lament prayers from ancient Mesopotamia. Such skilled and formalized language must certainly point to the existence of a body of professional cult-personnel who made the composition and use of such prayers a distinctive part of their own religious expertise. Although not all scholars remain agreed on the point, it can be affirmed with considerable confidence that the prayers contained in the Psalter are with few exceptions the product of such professional Psalm-writers. The Bible says very little about such professional writers of prayer, however, and instead vividly portrays prayer as everyone's privilege, which would be heard by God on account of each person's need and the loving nature of God in outreach towards humankind. Not only does it not limit the privilege of prayer to "the professionals," but it presents the essential character and value of prayer, or more pertinently the character of the God who "hears" prayer, as relatively indifferent to the literary skill or professional status of the person praying. This does not mean that God is presented in the Bible as indifferent to the content of prayers, which is far from being the case, but rather that prayer is open to all as a means of communion. Not only is prayer not a privilege restricted to professional people of prayer, but it is not even limited to those who belong to Israel in the Old Testament or to the church in the New. It is a truly universal spiritual prerogative and privilege. Although there is much that is instructive in the Bible concerning the blending of formal and informal, of spontaneous and predetermined elements in prayer, there is little reason for doubting that it is the free, spontaneous, and unstructured aspects that have the historical priority. Even in the Psalter, where the skill of generations of expert Psalm-composers has been brought to remarkable literary expression, the elements of openness and freedom have been sufficiently retained for their compositions to have enjoyed a wide use among lay persons. Nor should we doubt that whoever their actual authors were, such Psalms were intended from the outset to be voiced to God by ordinary men and women who felt themselves to be in some form of acute distress, or who were eager to utter their own private thanksgivings to God. Many Psalms have clearly been composed for a wider congregational use in a context of public worship.

If the religion of ancient Israel was one that was characterized by a remarkable freedom and openness in its use of prayer, as the Old Testament testifies to us, then this has undoubtedly been one of its foremost legacies to the respective faiths of Judaism and Christianity. So many of the characteristic features of Jewish and Christian spirituality quite understandably have their roots in the way in which the Bible itself pictures men and women resorting to prayer.

In view of the fact that so much attention has been devoted by scholars to the study of the Psalter, as in the widely acclaimed contributions of such men as H. Gunkel and S. Mowinckel, it is surprising that so little attention has been given to the study of the non-Psalmic prayers of the Bible. A number of factors indicate that such relative neglect is undeserved. These prayers are the sort that God is portrayed as "hearing," and they depict the kinds of concerns that are brought to God. They offer us some of the most deeply theological insights of the Bible. It is in reality almost impossible to separate the questions of "What is God like?" and "How should I pray?" Prayer is in a large measure theology moving into action and testing out its own understanding of the divine nature of reality. When we pay proper attention to the predominantly "story" form which the Bible adopts in its presentation of its message, we are certainly led to recognize that the theological aspects of this story form are brought home to us most directly in its prayers. So often it is the inclusion of a prayer text in a narrative that provides the biblical author with a means for expressing his or her own understanding of the theological significance and meaning of the situations and events being dealt with.

A further consideration relates very closely to this. It is a commonplace feature to note that the Bible has a great deal to say about a number of leading personalities. Although when we begin to look beneath the surface we can see that the biblical narratives are often concerned with the emergence and adoption of particular "ideas" or with the rise and fall of great religious institutions such as the temple of Jerusalem, virtually all its stories are built up around the portrayal of certain personalities. Often the real figure or personality who lies behind such narrative portrayals is very shadowy, as in the case of Aaron, for instance, where it is the origin and authority of the priesthood that is of major interest to the biblical authors. The biblical stories proceed, therefore, by a sequence of narratives focusing upon certain major figures: Abraham, Moses, David, Saul, Ezra, Jesus, Paul, and so on, to name only a few of the most important. It has been a very tempting aspect of modern study to try to capture and elucidate this aspect of the Bible by presenting these men, and in some cases women, as "great personalities." Thus, in a questionable way features that are essentially modern have become fastened on to the biblical stories. This is in no way to suggest that such persons were not "great personalities," which in large measure they must have been for the tradition to have emerged in the way it did. The truth is that the Bible has very little indeed to say about those aspects of character and personality which would make it possible for us to evaluate those qualities in their personal lives which could be classified as great and which we could emulate. In a surprisingly large measure the Bible uses its inclusion of prayers ascribed to these great figures to serve as a means of conveying their outstanding significance for their own generation and for posterity. In this way prayer becomes an interpretation of the role of the central figures of the biblical story.

In this respect questions may be raised concerning the extent which any or all of the prayers ascribed to these biblical figures can be regarded by the modern reader as authentic. It can only be stated quite frankly in regard to such questions that they are unanswerable. The questions themselves therefore are virtually pointless. Not only do we not have the means by which to deal with them adequately, but there would appear to be little gain in attempting to do so, except to satisfy a certain type of curiosity. To all intents and purposes the prayers that the Bible associates with its central figures it regards as wholly appropriate to them and illustrative of their situations. Moreover the point of such prayers is not to highlight a number of "personality characteristics" which pertained to these figures but rather to indicate their spiritual significance for their contemporaries and for those who came after them. We can therefore leave out of our discussion attempts to ascertain precisely when particular prayers were composed. So far as the biblical narratives are concerned their association with the men and women to whom they are ascribed is an important feature in their character as prayers.

In a very special way the prayers of the Bible elucidate one of its most marked distinguishing features. This concerns its understanding of God as personal, so that the relationship between God's creatures and God is established and maintained after the analogy of that between human personalities. God is an "I" addressing men and women as "Thou," and in response these men and women think of God and address themselves to God in consistently personal ways. The forms, idioms, and aims of the prayers of the Bible are drawn from the world of personal relationships, often to an extent that is rather surprising to the modern mind, with its more scientific and philosophic awareness of what the Creator of our universe must be like. Nevertheless, this is part of the biblical legacy of faith, and with its necessary limitations, it is not one with which the modern world has shown any sign of wishing to part company.

We can note three ways in which the biblical writers use the recounting of a prayer to bring out the spiritual significance of the events they are retelling. In the first place such prayers often open up a disclosure of the inner hopes of the individual whose work is being described. We come to see that there is an outer history, which the archivist and archaeologist can bring to our attention through research. Beside this stands an inner history which belongs to the realm of faith and spiritual understanding. This the prayer can reveal. Secondly we find that in some cases the inclusion of a prayer may indicate how the events being described fit into the divine scheme. The prayer becomes a kind of spiritual connective, indicating the path that God's providential purpose is following. Thirdly we can claim that it is the element of prayer, and with it the whole sense of a communion between humans and God to which it bears witness, that makes the biblical story a truly religious and spiritual one. All too easily an overpreoccupation with attempts to reconstruct the biblical history "as it actually happened" can hide from our eyes the very features which the Bible is at pains to make us see. This is the sense of the divine purpose that runs through all human affairs and of the possibility which this brings for every man and woman to recognize that all historical existence opens out into a confrontation with ultimate issues. Such ultimate issues are the face of God, divinely presented to us. Just as a skillful playwright can use the speeches which various actors make in order to uncover the plot of a drama, so does the Bible use the prayers of its central figures to show that the eyes of faith can discover a purpose in human life and history. In turn such discovery makes possible new directions and new achievements in our world and society. To study the history which the Bible narrates and to leave out the dimension of prayer which it includes would be to leave out one of the central ways by which the Bible transforms its accounts of everyday profane life into a series of encounters with the eternal God.

The Centrality of Prayer in Religion

It is a relatively easy and familiar way of approaching the Bible to contrast its own revealed ideas and institutions of religion with those of other religions where such revelation is lacking or less clearly evident. Such a perspective is certainly not to be given up, although it is often in jeopardy of being dangerously oversimplified. Prayer is a universal feature of virtually all religion, at some times appearing in very simple guise and at others in the very complex forms of elaborate liturgies. It represents a kind of universal language, so that it is not uncommon to find that even in very different religions the way in which the divine aid is sought and the ways in which people are encouraged to seek it are often very similar. Prayer is therefore, on any level of human reckoning, a remarkably widespread and persistent feature of life and an aspect of almost all forms of religion. You do not have to be an especially religious person to pray, although the more you have practiced the art of prayer the more likely it is that your prayers will be carefully formulated and directed toward worthy ends. To a quite remarkable extent this is a perspective which is very widely adopted in the Bible. Prayer is regarded as a quite natural activity for people to engage in. The nature of human existence—the risks and dangers, as well as the joys and triumphs—is that which occasions prayer. It is assumed to be quite natural therefore that the devotees of Baal should cry to him (cf. 1 Kings 18:26), just as those who worship the Lord address their cries accordingly. From the biblical point of view the stimulus to pray arises from the nature of human life. The desire to pray therefore is in no sense regarded as an ignorant or unworthy one, although there is much in the Bible to indicate that people often do pray in very ignorant and unworthy ways. Not all prayer is equally productive or worthy, and a close correlation is perceived to exist between the way in which the deity or deities are thought of, and the kind of prayer that they will deign to hear.

The recognition that prayer is a very normal human activity and the assumption made in the Bible that this activity extends throughout all forms of religion lead on to an extensive range of further concerns about prayer. Not least the very name of the god to whom prayer is addressed becomes of great importance. It is recognized that there must exist a certain degree of commonality of interest between the concerns of the person praying and the deity to whom the prayer is addressed. In some measure this "commonality of interest" is secured by the circumstances and situation of those who offer the prayer. In this regard the most poignant and memorable instance is to be found in the account of the deliverance from Egypt which forms the heart of the Old Testament portrayal of the nature of God's saving intent. When God first reveals to Moses that the Israelites will be rescued from their slavery, it is with the words: "I . . . have heard their cry because of their taskmasters; I know their sufferings"

(Exod. 3:7). It is noteworthy that when God reaffirms the intention
to Moses of delivering the Israelites, after the initial setbacks, it is
done by reasserting that the cries of the Israelites have been heard
and by linking this to a larger purpose—a covenant with the patriarchal ancestors of Israel: "I have heard the groaning of the people of
Israel . . . and I have remembered my covenant" (Exod. 6:5). In this
fashion the efficacy and significance of prayer is brought into relationship with wider features of the understanding of God and the
relationships which have already been established with those who
worship the Lord.

These features are of very great importance so far as the biblical
understanding of prayer is concerned. The way in which the character and nature of God is conceived and presented determines the
character and content of prayer. Even though the Bible makes no
narrow pretensions in respect of the exclusiveness of Israel's privilege in addressing God in prayer, it does recognize that, in lacking a
proper understanding of the nature of God, men and women will be
unable to direct their prayers worthily and intelligently. From the
biblical perspective, then, there is certainly no indifference to
the religious traditions through which prayer is undertaken and
the understanding of the divine nature and purpose that relates directly to this. All of this, so far as biblical tradition is concerned,
finds its focus and expression in the conviction that prayer is offered
in the "name" of the Lord God. The right use of the "name" of God
in prayer is therefore of the greatest importance, and abuse of this
name is a great offense (cf. Exod. 20:7). This biblical sense of the
efficacy of the proper use of the name of God, and the legacy that it
has left in the continued regard for offering prayer to God with appropriate invocational and ascriptional names and titles, is of prominent interest. There is no doubt at all that in many religious
traditions, especially in antiquity, the belief in the importance of
using the right "name" for God in prayer was treated in a magical or
semimagical fashion. In this way the deity's "name" became a kind
of formula which was thought to be particularly efficacious in ensuring that the prayer would be heard and answered. This is certainly
not the normal biblical view of prayer, however, and such ideas are
far removed from the biblical view of how men and women are

related to God and enjoy communion with the deity. It may be argued that virtually any person's religion, whether it be in ritual or in the offering of prayer, can relapse into a quasimagical approach to reality. This is not the view of prayer encouraged in the Bible, and it is evident that the intensely personal view of God that it endorses virtually ruled out such an approach. Just as other human beings could be persuaded but not coerced into action, so is a similar "personal" view adopted in all of humankind's dealings with God. Although therefore it has at times been argued that the concern for the right use of the divine name in prayer in the Bible reflects a semimagical quality, this would not appear to be the case. The evidence for this is to be found in the contents of the prayers themselves. If anything we may dare to suggest that the prayers of the Bible move in the direction of "personalizing" the nature of God to an extent that jars somewhat with the more scientific and philosophic understanding of what the divine Creator must be like. We may also carry this further in noting the ways in which the Bible relates prayer to the understanding of a providential order. Prayer is the discovery of God, and this means that how we pray and what we pray for must be guided and informed by the nature of God. It is very much this Godward dimension of prayer that makes the great prayers of the Bible so instructive and illuminating. They provide a meaningful and helpful indication of the content of what theologians have called more abstractly "communion with God." We can therefore expect that the biblical prayers will shed light on the nature and reality of God and will show how this must inform what we pray for and what we can expect prayer to achieve.

The Central Forms of Prayer

For many people prayer is simply asking God for certain things to happen or to be given to them, with little attention to questions of how the asking is to be presented. For many in fact the very informality of the requests and the simplicity of the language in which they are presented come to be regarded as pointers to the sincerity and genuineness of the person praying. For others the use of written prayers and the clothing of them in very formal, and often archaic, language is felt to strengthen their claim to be true and worthy prayers and to enhance their religious character. If we are to judge by the prayers that are recorded in the Bible there is evidence that the form of particular prayers was felt to be of importance, and, if we were to judge from the Psalter alone, we can see that in biblical times the manner of praying was undoubtedly a factor to which great attention was paid. Our concern here, however, is not particularly with matters of phraseology and formal structure, but rather with matters of content. The contention as already expressed is that behind even these details of the way in which the prayer is formulated prior questions exist about the nature and purpose of the One to whom the prayer is addressed. We cannot pray properly unless we have developed a theology—an awareness of the nature, purpose, and nearness of the Supreme Reality who has created us, and whose character we should seek to imitate in our own lives. For the Christian no book can more effectively or richly provide this knowledge than the Bible itself. When looking in the Bible at the way in which people prayed we may hope to find for ourselves an understanding of what it has to teach about communion with God.

Certainly we can begin to look at the central forms of prayer which the Bible contains by concerning ourselves with petition. "Ask, and it will be given you" (Luke 11:9), seems at first glance to sum up all that we mean by prayer. It is wholly in line with this then to find that simply to "ask" God for something becomes a basic expression for prayer. Yet such a simplicity of expression seldom stands wholly alone. Alongside it we find very prominently in the Bible the verbs "to seek" and "to inquire" of God. In a very real measure we discover that our desire to ask for divine help forces us back to question where and how this help can be found. It raises immediately issues which we can see to have been very keenly felt in Bible times. Will God be more likely to hear and respond to my request if I ask it in a special place? Or will a special day be more pleasing, or even a special form of words? When some men and women appeared to have been more successful than others in obtaining their requests to God, it must have suggested that such experts in prayer could be used or even employed in order to present the prayers of their fellow men and women also. We need not elaborate further upon this theme, since it will be evident to everyone from this prayer of petition that a whole range of questions immediately arises about who God is, and how this divine Being may be contacted. That it remains at the very heart of prayer and brings us closest to uncovering the reasons why men and women pray is abundantly evident.

It is easy to see how petition, if this alone is allowed to dominate all our praying, can become self-centered and ultimately destructive of the very growth in spiritual understanding we desire. Prayers that are simply a repetition of "Give me . . .; give me . . ." will show that we have not learned very much about the nature of God. For this reason, although it is so basic to prayer, the use of petition calls out most urgently for guidance and instruction if we are to develop a healthy attitude toward life. This is not the case with the second form of prayer which we shall have to consider, which is that of intercession. If asking things for ourselves can become merely selfish, then this is surely less likely to be the case if we ask things on behalf of others, unless we restrict these "others" to our own immediate circle. Undoubtedly a healthy measure of outgoing and self-giving is found in our being prepared to think about the needs and concerns of other people. Nevertheless, here, too, are reasons which should give us cause to stop and think, lest we rush in too forthrightly with a list of requests offered in the interests of our neighbors.

In the first place the form of intercession forces us to consider one of the most fundamental of all issues in religion and in the theology which seeks to understand and interpret this religion. This concerns the relationship of God to ourselves as persons, and with this our own individual relationships to other persons. God is very evidently a great respecter of personal freedom, since the divine will and intentions are not forced upon us. Otherwise there would be no point in praying at all. We should simply have to do what God wants! This is evidently not the case, since we have been given the dignity and possibilities which our freedom represents. We can hardly expect therefore that God will override this freedom in others, simply because we ask it. In any case we must ask ourselves whether what we are asking on behalf of others is what they really want. If it is not, is it what they really need? How do we know anyway what it is that they need, and how can we discover what their needs really are? We could go on drawing up an almost endless catalog of questions that could be asked if we are to make intelligent use of the form of intercession. If petition involves a prominent element of self-discovery, so then intercession requires of us a very marked willingness to discover the circumstances and needs of others. In the final analysis we shall soon find that it raises some of the biggest questions that our minds can contemplate. What are the best interests of other people? What is the ultimate destiny of all humankind? The extent to which these questions call upon us to think out carefully what kinds of lives other people should live, what kind of society we expect them to live in, and what kinds of help we can give to assist them in achieving these ends becomes evident. We cannot start out on a prayer of intercession without first thinking about some of the most important questions which face humankind. To discover the way in which some of the great biblical prayers give guidance and example for such intercession is one of the things that we may hope to achieve by our study.

So far the two forms of prayer which we have considered, petition and intercession, have concerned the seeking of help from God. The very fact of our venturing to seek such help, however, forces us back to the realization that we are not very suitable persons to be making such requests. We might easily begin to call out to God in an almost unthinking awareness of our own need and the urgency of our own desires, but we shall soon discover cause for questioning whether we have any proper reason for expecting God to help us. This brings us to note the next form of prayer, which is very central in the Bible. This is contrition, in which we might suitably include the element of confession. We need not spend long over the reasons why contrition has become a central form of prayer, because it is to be hoped that they are self-evident. The more we develop a convincing and spiritually informed awareness of the nature of God, the more we shall be forced to realize that the very idea of our asking anything at all in prayer is filled with a boldness and assurance which borders upon spiritual impertinence. The expectation of establishing a communion with God through prayer raises for us an extraordinary range of thoughts and notions which relate to God's graciousness, and our own unworthiness. A whole host of words appear in the Bible to deal with precisely these questions: grace, loving-kindness, steadfast love, forgiveness, justification. We need not go into them further at this point, but it is well that we should be forewarned that the form of contrition plays an important part in the great prayers of the Bible. To understand such prayers will call upon us to look at some of the most central and distinctive truths that the Bible has to offer about our relationship to God. It does not start out with the assumption that this is an "easy" or "natural" relationship, but rather assumes and argues that this is a most difficult relationship which has only become possible because of the remarkable and utterly unique goodness of God.

We can conclude our review of the central forms of prayer in the Bible by considering what, in the final analysis, should be the most important and central goal of all prayer. That is praise to God. If petition and intercession are a form of self-discovery, in which we find out what kind of persons we really are and sort out what we would like to be, and if intercession is a deepened awareness of the place of other people in our lives and in our world, then praise must surely be our discovery of God. It must open out to our minds some sense of the unlimited and unimaginable greatness of the Creator who has formed us and given us a part to play in the world. Often, in listening to the prayers presented publicly in churches, it seems as if the form of praise is merely a preamble—a suitable introduction to the real business of asking for things which are bound to follow! Yet this is a wholly unbiblical view of praise, since it appears as the highest and greatest of all the forms to which prayer can aspire. If we had done nothing more than lift our hearts to God in praise, we should have achieved the greatest goal possible for any prayer. The difficulties for us in doing this are caused because it requires so much in the way of thought and reasoned preparation, if we are to do it in a meaningful way. It is so much easier to hurry on with the thoughts and concerns we have about ourselves, with which we have become very familiar, than it is to stop and let our minds contemplate God— the Author and Source of all our lives and the One who alone knows the destiny fashioned for all creatures. In a very real sense all our theology, and not just theology but all our knowledge of the universe, is a way of learning how to praise God—to think God's thoughts. It would certainly be a great misunderstanding to suppose that praise was simply a formal and deferential introduction to the task of putting our requests to God. Still less can it be that God especially wants to hear a multitude of applauding voices. Praise is the greatest form of prayer because through it we come to a true and proper understanding of our place in the world and of the infinite possibilities which God has set before us.

2
A Prayer of
ABRAHAM

Genesis 18:22–33

Abraham the Man

Abraham appears to us as the father of the people of God and it is wholly in accordance with this that he has come to be revered as the "Father of the Faithful" in the three great monotheistic religions of the modern world: Judaism, Islam, and Christianity. The migration of Abraham from Ur of the Chaldees, via Haran, to enter the land of Canaan (Gen. 11:31-32) marks the real beginning of the story of the people of God. What has been recounted before this forms the primeval history (Gen. 1—11) and embraces the biblical accounts of creation, the great flood, the rise of the nations, and the confusion of their languages at the time of the building of the Tower of Babel. It is a story of origins, but it is also a story of decline and defection from the divinely intended order and morality. It must be read and understood more directly for what it tells us about human nature and existence than for its incidental references to humankind's geological and anthropological origins. To this extent therefore it serves more as a prologue to the story of the Bible than as a primary feature of that story itself. It pictures to us people groping in darkness, having lost sight of their divine creation and birth, fumbling to find some new way that will lead them back to God. After having thrown away the will and the desire to obey God, men and women lapse deeper and deeper into suspicion of each other and onto a path of fratricide and vengeance-seeking. Even the warnings of the flood find a response only in the attentive ears of Noah and his family. Yet even after this primordial catastrophe the story of division and defection does not come to a halt but leads only to a desire to take heaven by

storm and establish a way back to God. Certainly the account of this
remarkable primeval history impresses its message upon us, not by
the details that it gives of the fabric of the universe, but rather by its
merciless exposure of the passions of greed, suspicion, and hatred
that lie within the human heart. It portrays a violent universe, but
very remarkably traces this discord and violence back to the hearts
and minds of the men and women whom God has made. When we
ask "Why is there all this pain and suffering and bloodshed in the
world?" the biblical witness points its finger of accusation unwaver-
ingly at men and women whose disorderly ambitions have given rise
to a disordered world.

It is against the background of such a grim and shadowed world
that the story of the divine plan of salvation begins to unfold. With
the call of God to Abraham, "Go from your country and your kindred
and your father's house to the land that I will show you" (Gen. 12:1),
a new beginning has been established. Surprisingly this new beginning introduces us immediately to a feature we should hardly have
expected to find mentioned so prominently but which was destined
to become a continuing part of the unfolding story. This feature is
referred to simply as "the land that I will show you," the land that we
have come to know variously as the land of Canaan, Palestine, Israel,
Judea, or more simply as "the Holy Land." How surprising it is that
so small a strip of territory, roughly only 120 miles from its northern-
most city, Dan, to its most southerly center, Beersheba, should, since
the days of Abraham, have played so large a part in the biblical story
of salvation! Lying on the coast of the Mediterranean Sea on one
side, exposed to the influences of the great Mediterranean civilizations of Phoenicia, Greece, and Rome, its further side was open to
the East. Here the incredible cultural and technological achievements
of the ancient world had come to their earliest flowering with the
civilizations of Sumeria, Babylonia, and Assyria. The rich glories of
Persia were still in the future in the days of Abraham, whereas to the
South the remarkable brilliance and greatness of Egypt was already
old when Abraham made his momentous journey to the West. The
land promised to Abraham and his descendants was a narrow strip of
soil that lay between the edges of the desert and the sea. It also
formed a bridge between the centers of the primary cultures that gave

rise to the ancient world—Sumer, Egypt, and Babylon—and those that gave rise to the newer civilizations that took over from them—Greece and Rome. From these our western European civilization has been nurtured. Nor can we regard these geographical features as merely incidental to the biblical story and message of salvation. Certainly within any assessment of the role of the Bible upon human life, thought, and culture we are faced with the extraordinary fact that it has been able to combine the religion and spirituality of the East with the arts, thought, and science of the West. In a sense the migration of Abraham and his family from Ur to the land of Canaan was a passage from an ancient world to a modern one. In the days of Abraham we find ourselves still in a world of prehistory, the ages of which are measured by technological skill in the use of bronze and iron. Where the biblical story reaches its climax in the Roman era, when the temple of Jerusalem was destroyed by the Roman armies and Jesus of Nazareth had been executed by crucifixion outside the city, we are firmly set in the classical world.

The promise of the land to Abraham and the role this land was thereafter destined to play in the unfolding story of what the Bible describes as "salvation" presents us with two important aspects of the entire biblical message. On the one hand this message is related to human history and is vitally involved in the economic, social, and political realities which serve as the interacting forces of history. It is true that no absolutely firm and certain date can be given for the time of Abraham's migration. Perhaps none ever will be achieved with the degree of historical certainty that we should desire. Nevertheless this cannot take away from the inescapable conviction that we are dealing here with an event which shared all the factual concreteness of other such historical migrations. Men watched Abraham go and others saw him arrive! Many other such migrations had taken place before, and many more have taken place since. The need for fresh pastures for sheep, the lure of the settled land, and perhaps also the political pressures of and spiritual disenchantment with the life offered by Ur and Haran all played their part. From this point on we find the story of the history of salvation inextricably intertwined in the common stream of human history.

This leads us to recognize the second of the important aspects of the biblical understanding of salvation that is drawn to our attention by the promise of the land. The "blessings" that are promised to Abraham and his descendants as the fruits of faith and obedience are not simply mystical blessings capable of being experienced only privately and in an inner world of the spirit. It is undoubtedly true that such a dimension of salvation exists, but it is altogether more practical and all-encompassing than this. In the best sense it is a very "worldly" salvation, since it is concerned with real life. The land promised to Abraham serves as a witness to the concrete reality of what is promised by God. From this point on the people who lived on this land, their ways of establishing a living through trade and agriculture, their social organization in families and tribes, their laws and customs, even their kingship, governmental processes, and military skills, all played a part in the story of salvation. When we have set ourselves to study the great prayers of the Bible we are not thereby pressed into a study of forms of meditation and reflection appropriate to a withdrawal from the world and preoccupied with the cultivation of the interior life. We find, on the contrary, that we are thrust into a world of vital relationships involving the property, morality, and physical and social welibeing of human communities.

It is not part of our purpose in this study to sketch out the further details of the life of Abraham. Already we have established two important features of Abraham's place in the biblical story of salvation—his role as "father" of the people of God, and through that as father and guide of the faithful, and his work as leader of the migration to, and settlement in, the land promised by God. Here we find the key elements of the story of Israel's nationhood which form the main part of the subsequent story of the Old Testament. For the same reason, they provide a key to understanding the birth of the "church" in the New Testament, which is not a new people of God, but one which shares through faith an ancestry that is traced back to Abraham. Through Abraham Israel acquired its ethnic identity and its national territory. To a modern secular person these two might appear to be enough to authenticate his importance in the biblical tradition. Yet there is a third element which cannot be overlooked and which, in its own way, is inseparable from the biblical story of salvation. Abraham was a great founder-figure of religion and this finds expression through his establishing of altars in the land to which he had now come (Gen. 12:7, etc.). Abraham is, in biblical tradition, the "friend of God" (cf. Isa. 41:8). This godward side of the work of the patriarch is brought into focus through the establishment of a covenant between God and Abraham (Gen. 15:18).

The notion of a covenant involves a necessarily two-sided relationship, no matter how strongly one partner may take the initiative, and no matter how prominently that partner may appear as the senior, or stronger one. In such fashion the concept of a covenant reappears again in the Old Testament so strongly that via the Latin word *testamentum* which came to translate the Hebrew word, the whole literature of the religion of Abraham and Moses came ultimately to be described by it. The work of Abraham therefore is presented to us, not simply under the guise of ancestral father and migrant leader, but as that of the founder of a new experience of God. Since that experience was grasped at the first, it has brought to us a new understanding of God. When we come to consider the prayer of Abraham in the light of this background, we find that central to it is this awareness that God had entered into the life of the world in a new way with Abraham's journey away from Ur and Haran to the land divinely promised to him.

Abraham's Prayer

The occasion of Abraham's remarkable prayer is provided by the threat of ruin and disaster brought about in divine judgment upon the cities of Sodom and Gomorrah (see Gen. 18:16–21). The reason for this judgment is clear enough: "Because the outcry against Sodom and Gomorrah is great and their sin is very grave" (Gen. 18:20). However, Sodom was by now the city in which Lot, the nephew of Abraham, lived! The question of judgment therefore involved questions regarding the sharing of guilt and the distinguishing between those who were blameworthy and those who were not. The story of the prayer unfolds from this point:

> So the men turned from there, and went toward Sodom; but Abraham still stood before the LORD. Then Abraham drew near, and said, "Wilt thou indeed destroy the righteous with the wicked? Suppose there are fifty righteous within the city; wilt thou then destroy the place and

not spare it for the fifty righteous who are in it? Far be it from thee to do such a thing, to slay the righteous with the wicked, so that the righteous fare as the wicked! Far be that from thee! Shall not the Judge of all the earth do right?" And the LORD said, "If I find at Sodom fifty righteous in the city, I will spare the whole place for their sake." Abraham answered, "Behold, I have taken upon myself to speak to the LORD, I who am but dust and ashes. Suppose five of the fifty righteous are lacking? Wilt thou destroy the whole city for lack of five?" And he said, "I will not destroy it if I find forty-five there." Again he spoke to him, and said, "Suppose forty are found there." He answered, "For the sake of forty I will not do it." Then he said, "Oh let not the LORD be angry, and I will speak. Suppose thirty are found there." He answered, "I will not do it, if I find thirty there." He said, "Behold, I have taken upon myself to speak to the LORD. Suppose twenty are found there." He answered, "For the sake of twenty I will not destroy it." Then he said, "Oh let not the LORD be angry, and I will speak again but this once. Suppose ten are found there." He answered, "For the sake of ten I will not destroy it." And the LORD went his way, when he had finished speaking to Abraham; and Abraham returned to his place.

(Genesis 18:22–33)

The form of the prayer is that of a dialogue between Abraham and God, and in this sense it might appear to be less of a prayer than a meditation. In a very vital sense, however, its essential character as a prayer is not in doubt, since the dialogue has arisen out of a concern over the impending fate of Sodom and Gomorrah and a desire to intercede on behalf of those righteous men like Lot who remained within the cities. Out of a concern to protect the innocent therefore, Abraham begins his prayer with a question: "Wilt thou indeed destroy the righteous with the wicked?" Already the mind of Abraham was set on concern for Lot and his family. With this, however, went also a concern for the rightness and necessity of God's judgment upon Sodom. Quite fittingly then, instead of simply interceding on Lot's behalf, the patriarch comes before God with a question. One question leads to another, for the first is readily and speedily answered: "Far be it from thee!" If men, in the course of their day-to-day behavior towards one another, would not behave in such a brutal and tyrannical way as to punish the innocent along with the wrongdoers, how much more was this true of God! The nature and manner of punishments inflicted by men were different from those understood to be used by God, however, so there is added force in the second question with its rhetorical emphasis: "Shall not the Judge of all the earth do right?" Of course! How unthinkable it would be if the one who is the Ground and Guardian of all right and justice should behave in an unjust way! The very foundations of justice itself would be swept away. In this way what might so readily have begun with a very simple request that Lot and his family be spared has been lifted to a higher plane altogether because such a request raised questions about the nature and actions of God. Will not, indeed must not, God always act in a manner that is completely just and righteous? In this moment we encounter the most fundamental breakthrough in all our understanding of prayer. The roots of all our seeking of God and our crying out for divine help and intervention lie in our own experienced desires and needs. In crying out to God, though, we are not invoking some blind and unthinking force. Instead we are calling on one who possesses a will and character far above our tainted standards. Prayer and the act of praying involve us in theology—the thinking out of the true nature and character of the supreme Ruler of the Universe. We cannot bend this Ruler, and make God an agent for the carrying out of our wishes. It is we who must bend to God's will and discover God's nature and character.

Already the prayerful question with which Abraham has come before God has found an answer in the rhetorical outburst which establishes the groundwork and foundation of all our relationships with God. God, the Judge of all the earth, must by nature, do what is right. This profound recognition raises a whole series of further questions in which Abraham presses his interrogation of God. How many righteous people must be in a city if God is to spare it and forbear to inflict upon its inhabitants the punishment which their wrongdoing deserves? Must there be fifty, forty-five, forty, thirty? Or will a mere ten suffice to avert the judgment of God? Is in fact the issue one of mere numbers at all? Would not a great wrong be perpetrated if even so much as one righteous man suffered along with the guilty? Having discovered through his prayer the perfect justice of God, Abraham is now forced to reflect upon the mysterious network of relationships that make up human society.

Sodom and Gomorrah were cities whose wrongdoing created such an outrage upon earth that God was forced to inflict punishment upon those who lived there. Lot and his family lived in Sodom, though, so that even in such a place some had not been carried along with the rising tide of evil. Without a way of escape for Lot and his family, the very infliction of a just punishment upon the cities of the plain would become an act of injustice! So it is with all human actions and experiences. "No man is an island" (John Donne), and so no one individual can act without what he or she does affecting other people. The whole of humankind live in a remarkable web of relationships in which every individual action has its consequences upon others. The creation of life and the taking of life influence and act upon other people. In families, clans, tribes, and nations; in houses, settlements, villages, and cities, the actions of men and women interact with each other, and thereby human society is experienced. This was now something of which Abraham's prayer had made him fully conscious. How then could God inflict punishment upon those who deserved it without involving the lives of those who were innocent?

The resolution of the difficulty comes for Abraham in a twofold form. First, in the more immediate practical setting, it is resolved because God is able to provide a way of escape for Lot and his family. Even from the gateway to destruction there is a way that leads to salvation. The second, and more theoretical, resolution of the problem, however, is both more profound and more indicative of the whole way in which the Bible understands human existence as an experience lived in the very presence of God. Even ten righteous people may be sufficient to stay the hand of God from judgment, and so be able to bring about renewal and a new encounter with life on a path of justice and righteousness. A handful of good men and women can become a saving remnant! The way of the wrongdoer and its inevitable consequence of judgment may be turned round, and a new way of hope opened up, through the presence of righteous men and women in an otherwise hopeless situation. By his adventurous arguing with God Abraham had broken through into a new awareness of what the role of the people of God was to be throughout the centuries.

The Significance of Abraham's Prayer

We may reflect upon the significance of Abraham's prayer in three ways. In the first place the rhetorical question, "Shall not the Judge of all the earth do right?" brings us to the most fundamental of all possible reflections on the meaning and value of prayer. What can we ask of God? Judging from the prayers which we so regularly hear and may even offer ourselves, there are an endless variety of benefits and blessings which we should like to receive from God, or which we should like God to share with others. "Ask and you will receive," would appear to be a completely open-ended commitment on the part of God to give us whatever we are bold enough to seek. Why not ask God for a new car or even two new cars or why not even an airplane? The answer lies not with us nor with our faith, but with God, and with God's loving and righteous nature. If it is our sense of need and our unfulfilled desires which prompt us to the act of prayer, then it is God's nature and unwavering commitment to what is just and right that provides us with the answer. Perhaps the greatest of all the features of Abraham's prayer is precisely the way in which it calls upon us, when we pray, to develop a theology. We must think about who God is, what the divine nature is, and in what way God's nature is presented to us. If God is just and righteous, should we not be concerned first of all in our praying that we might learn to be equally as just and as righteous?

It may seem, on first reflection, to be a kind of cheating on the part of God, if, when we turn in prayer to ask for something, we are not given what we ask but instead are forced to come to terms with some new understanding of God. In reality this is not so, however, and there can be no richer way in which our prayer finds a response on the part of God than if it brings us to some fuller understanding of the divine nature. What unimagined depths of understanding lie hidden in the simple recollection of the question "Shall not the Judge of all the earth do right?" How many of our prayers would never need to have been asked, if only we had realized this truth first! Correspondingly what whole new worlds of possibility are opened up to us once that fact has taken hold upon our thinking!

The second feature of Abraham's prayer which makes it so significant for us still is the way in which it combines a great truth about God with an extraordinary social realism. We might even suggest that it has anticipated in a remarkable fashion the necessity for a dialogue between theology and sociology. God cannot act against some members of a city or any community without such an action affecting its other members also. God cannot punish a father without affecting the children. Neither can God destroy a city without it affecting the country of which that city is a part. Here we come face to face with a very distinctive and imposing aspect of the way in which the Bible teaches us about God. In fact, when we consider it as a whole, the Bible is very much more "community-conscious" than we ourselves, with our modern sense of individual responsibility, tend to be. At times this sense of social solidarity may even appear repugnant to us, when, for instance, it describes God as "visiting the iniquity of the fathers upon the children to the third and the fourth generation of those who hate me" (Exod. 20:5). Later on this awareness of the common life shared by a family living in the same home was revised and modified in the interests of a greater sense of individual justice (Deut. 24:16; Jer. 31:29–30; Ezek. 18). It would be quite wrong, however, to think of the Old Testament sense of community as out of date. On the contrary, it is as real a part of our human experience today as it was then. We are, each one, influenced and molded by the lives of those around us. In turn, we may assist in the development and formation of the lives of those who know us and depend upon us. For how long would Lot and his family have held aloof from the customs and conduct which had given rise to such a cry of outrage against Sodom? Of course we do not and cannot know, since his flight from the city renders all such questions hypothetical and meaningless. We do know, from the observation of the lives of those around us and from any honest self-criticism, that we are greatly affected by those whose lives touch ours. In home, school, work, and leisure, we are constantly being affected, and even transformed, by other lives which impinge upon our own. Such a realization gives us added opportunity for reflection upon the momentous nature of the decision which led to the separation of Lot and Abraham from each other (Gen. 13:8–13). When we consider the reasoning which governed Lot's choice: "And Lot lifted up his eyes, and saw that the Jordan valley was well watered everywhere like the garden of the LORD" (Gen. 13:10), then we may well pause to reflect that appearances are not everything! At the time when Lot "moved his tent as far as Sodom," he may well have been confident that he would not let his life be governed by the conduct of that city. For how long, though, could he maintain his innocence? Would even nine just companions be enough to enable him to keep his resolve?

This brings us to the third feature of Abraham's prayer, which, in its own way, brings us to the very heart of the biblical experience of salvation. In pressing his questioning of God to the limit of what he dared to ask, the patriarch realized that even ten righteous men in a city might be sufficient to avert t' e judgment of God. In coming to this truth, he had, in that same moment, come to the truth of the role a righteous remnant might play in the fulfillment of the divine purpose. If the society around us is in a constant state of movement and change, then there are forces at work in that society which are either pulling it upwards or downwards. It is not in a state of fixed equilibrium, but rather is in constant transformation. These changes are factors of which everyone is conscious, but which are very difficult to monitor or analyze. It is precisely because this is the case that we need professional sociologists and analysts to try to plot these changes and to understand their causes. It is also the presence of these factors promoting change that provides the need and opportunity for those small communitites—whether church or synagogue or other such group—who can function as the agents of salvation and righteous renewal. Just as Abraham came to perceive that God might spare a city for the sake of ten righteous individuals, so does that provide all the greater stimulus and incentive for adherence to a right path. In seeking what is best for oneself, one may act for the salvation and protection of a whole community.

3
A Prayer of
JACOB

Genesis 49:2–27

Jacob the Man

The preceding prayer of the patriarch Abraham introduced us to the world of Mesopotamia, with all its importance for the rise of human civilization and culture. We shall see in the next chapter, focusing on a prayer of Moses, something of the world of ancient Egypt, since the great leader and religious founder brought Israel up from that land. In the present study we are concerned with the person of Jacob, whose other name Israel shows him to have been the patriarchal founder of the Israelites and the father from whose twelve sons the tribes of Israel were named. What is striking about the world of Jacob is that he belongs so firmly to the land of Canaan itself. The places with which he came to be most closely associated were in the central hillcountry of Israel—Bethel and Shechem—and his life, character, and exploits are strongly colored by his belonging to the sheep-farming culture of the land. In this way, through the three figures of Abraham, Jacob, and Moses, we are brought face to face with the ancient peoples of Mesopotamia, Canaan, and Egypt. Probably to these we should add the name of the patriarch Isaac, even though he is less celebrated than the others, since he draws our attention to another facet of the world from which Israel sprang—that of the desert region and the importance of the oasis city of Beersheba.

Jacob was a man of Canaan, as the many stories in which he appears with his family make clear. In later times we know how much Israel came to dislike and distrust the Canaanites for their hated religion with its cult of Baal, their blatant commercialism, and not least because they represented a rival claim upon the land of Israel.

It would be wrong, however, to allow this stereotyped picture of animosity and distrust to hide from us the immensity of Israel's debt to the life and people of Canaan. The Canaanites were people in the middle, both in a literal sense and even more significantly in a figurative one. In a literal sense this was true because the land occupied by the Canaanites straddled the vital caravan routes which stretched from the Phoenician ports of Tyre and Sidon to the rich trading areas of Arabia, with all its reputation for the luxuries of gold and spices. In a different direction another of the great caravan routes of the ancient world crossed the soil of Canaan, this time from Mesopotamia to Egypt. This narrow strip of the fertile crescent provided a means by which the East came to the West. This was achieved through the Phoenicians, the seafaring sister people to the Canaanites who were settled a little further to the north in what is now Lebanon. The Canaanites too were traders who got their name from the rich purple dye produced from the shellfish found along the Mediterranean coastal strip. The cloth produced with the aid of this dye became famous in antiquity and along with this, the Canaanites too achieved fame. In some of the greatest archaeological discoveries of the twentieth century, at Ras Shamra and Ebla, the range and importance of the world of those who were close kin to the Canaanites have been set in a new light.

We may single out three ways in which the skills and culture developed by the Canaanites came to be of immense importance to Israel, and through Israel, to the emergence of the Bible. The first of these is simple, yet extraordinarily profound. It was the Phoenicians who invented the first alphabetic script, and thus the possibility of a greatly simplified and more versatile way of writing. Not only in recording business transactions, but in setting down myths, legends, and the records of historical events, writing was to become a cornerstone of human culture and achievement. Earlier forms of writing, in hieroglyphs and cuneiform, had existed for several thousand years, but never before had writing achieved the simplicity and versatility which the introduction of an alphabet of little more than twenty characters gave to it. It is not surprising therefore to discover that the language spoken and written by the people of ancient Israel, which we now know as Hebrew, was a modified and developed form of the alphabetic language of Canaan.

In a second way the Canaanites greatly influenced Israel, since they had mastered the techniques and skills of agriculture and had established a settled, urban pattern of life, made necessary by the need to protect the cultivated soil. The early ancestors of Israel had been pastoral seminomads, as was Jacob himself, rearing sheep and living from their produce. In course of time, however, the attractions and possibilities of wealth and progress offered by the skills and way of life of the Canaanites drew the Israelites into following their example. Throughout the years which marked the rise of Israel as a powerful kingdom, an important economic and cultural change was taking place among the people as they adopted the skills of agriculture learned from the Canaanites.

In a third way also Israel owed much to Canaan. This lay in its social and political organization, which was in many respects, a consequence of agricultural and urban development. Whereas early Israel existed as a collection of tribes, closely bound by loyalties to each other, but interspersed among other peoples, the Canaanites focused their lives upon cities, most of them quite small. Eventually the Israelite tribal system withered away and a more commercially self-conscious, and politically stronger, urban culture took its place. Without this transition the rise of Israel as a single territorial kingdom could not have taken place.

With the person of Jacob we encounter many of the distinctive features and values that belonged to ancient Semitic tribal society. The stories concerning him reflect the issues and ideals which molded individual families and tribes. The strong stamp of a chieftain's personality upon his clan, the rivalries that divided family from family, and the ceaseless competition to obtain the best grazing lands to survive, if need be at the expense of others, all these are themes which appear in the stories concerning Jacob. Even the story of Jacob's birth (Gen. 25:19-26) brings to light this theme of competition and rivalry. It concerns the birth of Jacob and his twin Esau, who because he was born first, acquired the privileged inheritance rights of the firstborn. From the outset the differing characters of the twins is evident: "Esau was a skilful hunter, a man of the field, while Jacob was a quiet man, dwelling in tents." From these varied characters the difference between whole communities was established.

It should not be all that surprising to us therefore to discover that in such a harshly competitive world the crafts of guile and deception played a part. Supreme among such stories is one which tells how Jacob, aided by his mother Rebekah, tricked his twin brother Esau out of the special blessing given by his father Isaac, shortly before his death (Gen. 27:1–40). The importance of such a blessing and its irreversible character are assumed as a part of the story but already the ultimate superiority and rise to nationhood of Jacob's own sons is envisaged:

"Let peoples serve you,
     and nations bow down to you.
Be lord over your brothers,
     and may your mother's sons bow down to you.
Cursed be every one who curses you,
and blessed be every one who blesses you!"
                                   (Genesis 27:29)

The stories of Jacob's guile and his special blend of industry and craftiness are brought to a climax with an account of how Jacob, while employed to look after the flocks of his maternal uncle Laban, negotiates a deal which results in Jacob's acquiring great wealth (Gen. 30:25–43). The story hinges upon Jacob's ability to induce the breeding of speckled and spotted sheep and goats which, under the terms of the agreement, are to be his. By clever tricks, Jacob ensures that he gets the stronger and healthier animals, whereas Laban is left only with the feeble ones. The storyteller sums up Jacob's success with a flourish: "Thus the man grew exceedingly rich, and had large flocks, maidservants and menservants, and camels and asses" (Gen. 30:43).

Jacob's fame does not rest with his role as chieftain and sheep-farmer, however, for like Abraham before him, he is encountered on the pages of the Bible as a great sanctuary-builder. For the sanctuary of Bethel in particular this was to be of supreme importance since in the years that followed, this famous shrine and its association with Jacob were to be of greatest importance to Israel. The story of how Jacob set up a pillar of stone at Bethel, after dreaming that he saw a

giant staircase or "ladder" at the place, has become a classic tale of
sanctuary building (Gen. 28:10–22). Not only here, however, but at
the much less well known sanctuary of Peniel we learn how Jacob
wrestled with a messenger of God—an angel—seeking to acquire a
blessing from God.

Commerce and piety are not always very comfortable companions, for the self-interest and harsh realism of the one so readily come
into conflict with the discipline and self-giving demanded by the
other. This was the world in which Jacob lived, though, and it introduces us to the many sided meanings that belong to a word which
played so large a part in Jacob's life—the word "blessing." On the
one hand it conveys a sense of prosperity, wealth, and success, while
on the other it points us to a quietness of spirit which is not easily
moved by material success or failure. We should not be surprised
therefore to discover that the great prayer which the Bible records
for us from Jacob is all about "blessing."

The Prayer

The occasion of Jacob's prayer lies in his own advancing years
and the awareness that his own death could not be long delayed. It is
interesting for us to reflect upon the importance which Jacob himself
had attached to his deceiving his father Isaac into pronouncing over
him the words of blessing which should, according to the traditional
privileges of the firstborn, have been pronounced over Esau. Now
Jacob, an established and prosperous figure and the head of a large
family, pronounced his words of blessing over his sons, and thereby
sought to invoke God's help and prosperity for each of them:

> Then Jacob called his sons, and said, "Gather yourselves together,
> that I may tell you what shall befall you in days to come.
> Assemble and hear, O sons of Jacob,
>   and hearken to Israel your father.
>
> Reuben, you are my first-born,
>   my might, and the first fruits of my strength,
>   pre-eminent in pride and pre-eminent in power.
> Unstable as water, you shall not have pre-eminence
>   because you went up to your father's bed;
>   then you defiled it—you went up to my couch!

Simeon and Levi are brothers;
   weapons of violence are their swords.
O my soul, come not into their council;
   O my spirit, be not joined to their company;
for in their anger they slay men,
   and in their wantonness they hamstring oxen.
Cursed be their anger, for it is fierce;
   and their wrath, for it is cruel!
I will divide them in Jacob
   and scatter them in Israel.

Judah, your brothers shall praise you;
   your hand shall be on the neck of your enemies;
   your father's sons shall bow down before you.
Judah is a lion's whelp;
   from the prey, my son, you have gone up.
He stooped down, he couched as a lion,
   and as a lioness; who dares rouse him up?
The scepter shall not depart from Judah,
   nor the ruler's staff from between his feet,
until he comes to whom it belongs;
   and to him shall be the obedience of the peoples.
Binding his foal to the vine
   and his ass's colt to the choice vine,
he washes his garments in wine
   and his vesture in the blood of grapes;
his eyes shall be red with wine,
   and his teeth white with milk.

Zebulun shall dwell at the shore of the sea;
   he shall become a haven for ships,
   and his border shall be at Sidon.

Issachar is a strong ass,
   crouching between the sheepfolds;
he saw that a resting place was good,
   and that the land was pleasant;
so he bowed his shoulder to bear,
   and became a slave at forced labor.

Dan shall judge his people
   as one of the tribes of Israel.
Dan shall be a serpent in the way,
   a viper by the path,
that bites the horse's heels
   so that his rider falls backward.
I wait for thy salvation, O LORD.

Raiders shall raid Gad,
  but he shall raid at their heels.

Asher's food shall be rich,
  and he shall yield royal dainties.

Naphtali is a hind let loose,
  that bears comely fawns.

Joseph is a fruitful bough,
  a fruitful bough by a spring;
  his branches run over the wall.
The archers fiercely attacked him,
  shot at him, and harassed him sorely;
yet his bow remained unmoved,
  his arms were made agile
by the hands of the Mighty One of Jacob
  (by the name of the Shepherd,
  the Rock of Israel),
by the God of your father who will help you,
  by God Almighty who will bless you
  with blessings of heaven above,
blessings of the deep that couches beneath,
  blessings of the breasts and of the womb.
The blessings of your father
are mighty beyond the blessings
  of the eternal mountains,
  the bounties of the everlasting hills;
may they be on the head of Joseph,
  and on the brow of him who was
  separate from his brothers.

Benjamin is a ravenous wolf,
  in the morning devouring the prey,
  and at even dividing the spoil."

(Genesis 49:1–27)

At first reading this does not appear to be a prayer at all but rather a prediction about the future characteristics and behavior of the tribes descended from Jacob's sons. The dividing line between prayer and prophecy was a very fine one, however, and there can be no doubt that in recording this prayer the storyteller has woven into his presentation of Jacob's "blessing" known features of the life of Israel that arose after the time of Jacob's death. For instance, we have reference to the emergence of Israel's kingship (the "scepter") from

Judah, which occurred with David. Similarly we learn of Issachar's submission to work as slave labor for their close neighbors, the seafaring Phoenicians. Yet the theme of the whole great declaration is the invocation of "blessing" upon all the twelve sons of Israel, already envisaged as growing into tribes. This is shown by the assurance given to Joseph who was to become the strongest and most prosperous of the tribes: "by the God of your father who will help you, by God Almighty who will bless you with blessings of heaven above . . ."

The occasion of the prayer is that Jacob, nearing his death, seeks to pass on to his children the prosperity and wealth which his industry and guile had brought to him. The future remained unknown to him, and just as he had now to entrust his inheritance to his children, so in turn he had to entrust these same children to the gracious mercy and goodness of God. Jacob could not determine what the future would be, he could only pray that with all their varied gifts his sons would live up to the opportunities his own prosperity had made possible for them.

The Significance of the Prayer

One feature is immediately striking about this great prayer of blessing. It is the extraordinary starkness and realism with which it describes the characters of each of the sons. By the use of skillful imagery and metaphors the virtues and vices of each of the children are brought to our attention: "Reuben . . . Unstable as water"; "Simeon and Levi . . . weapons of violence are their swords. . . . in their anger they slay men"; "Dan shall be a serpent in the way"; "Benjamin is a ravenous wolf." The most vicious and warlike features are noted along with the features of leadership, courage, and industry noted of other tribes. If "it takes all sorts to make a world," so is this true even within one family. We are all different, and one of the most remarkable characteristics of the human race is the immensity of the variety which distinguishes individuals. Brother will be different from brother, sister from sister, just as one family will differ from another. Birth within the same family does not make us all identical, even though it may give to us certain very distinct and identifiable characteristics. In a very real sense we are what we are from birth, and we each one inherit particular psychological traits and features which will remain with us until we die. To this extent we must learn to recognize that God endows each of us with a particular disposition and psychological make-up, a particular measure of intelligence and physical coordination, which we have got to learn to accept and to live with.

If, as we noted in our study of Abraham's great prayer, one part of prayer is the discovery of God, another part is certainly the discovery of our true selves. Prayer is a path of self-discovery, which can lead us on to a healthy self-awareness, and through this, to proper self-discipline. No doubt it would have been as painful to Benjamin to learn that his father described him as "a ravenous wolf" as it would have been hurtful to Issachar to have been reminded that he had sold himself to servile labor for the sake of a good "resting place." The truth is often hard to bear, and it is for this reason that we keep it locked away and hidden, even from our own selves. True prayer has to become an unlocking of this hidden realm of truth about ourselves and a discovery of who and what we really are. It is not a path of discovery which we can rush along in great haste. Only a genuine honesty and inner humility can eventually lead us to this remarkable world of self-discovery. The history of spirituality and the religious life is replete with stories of great figures who never discovered or conquered their personal vices and weaknesses. Great religious leaders and men of the spirit have often offended by their pride, their petty animosities, and their unchecked love of self-display. The evident fact is that we do not see ourselves as others see us. From time to time certain very intense religious movements and communities have sought to practice a form of "open criticism," so that we might learn in a spirit of brotherly and sisterly concern what others think about us. Even this has been fraught with difficulties and dangers, so often tending to promote the very faults and failings which it seeks to overcome. Experience would suggest therefore that the only effective path to genuine self-discovery is the path of prayer.

The Blessing of Jacob, however, when seen as a prayer to God to enrich the lives and prosper the future of Jacob's family, has something else very important to make known to us. Few words in the English language have become more vague and ill-defined than has the verb "to bless." It has largely fallen out of everyday speech, except in the almost flippant rejoinder "Bless you!" to someone who has sneezed. We keep the verb for our prayers, especially for our public prayers, and the reason for this lies not simply in its revered and honored place in the biblical tradition of prayer but in its extraordinary breadth and vagueness. We are tempted to ask God to bless us and the world around us simply because we do not know or think out more precisely what it is that we wish to ask God for. We have come to regard the verb as a convenient way by which to describe the good that we expect God to impart to men and women. Vagueness, abstractions, and broad generalities are the enemies of wise and thoughtful prayers, however. If we do not know properly what we wish to ask God for, it becomes a shabby excuse for nonprayer when we resort to undefined generalities. On this front therefore the prayer of Jacob is truly remarkable, since it begins with a frank and full recognition of the characteristic features of each of Jacob's sons. They are what they are so that, if God is to bless them, it will have to be done in and through the personalities with which each of them is endowed. In this sense, far from Jacob's "blessing" being a typical instance of vagueness in prayer, it is quite the opposite. It is a careful asking of God to make the divine power known in the life of each son, as he really is! If only we could attain to a similar honesty and realism in our own praying!

There is a further aspect still which we can note in regard to this long and intriguing prayer. To the biblical historian it has become a fascinating mine of information about the features and history of each of the tribes that made up the nation of Israel. It is quite clear that these twelve tribes were not equal and uniformly successful entities, settled in roughly equal areas of the Holy Land. Rather we discover that two tribes outstripped all the others, and between them, virtually shaped the future destiny of the entire people of Jacob. These were the tribes of Judah and Joseph. This is correspondingly recognized in the prayer of blessing through the attention that is given to each of them. Contrastingly other tribes are given surprisingly brief treatment, as we see in the cases of Gad, Asher, Naphtali, and Benjamin. All of this brings our attention back to the realism and concreteness with which the Bible understands the notion of blessing. This was not considered as a vague and indeterminate "getting on well," but was spelled out firmly in terms of fruitfulness, prosperity, and health. What God had to impart to the chosen people, and what Jacob was concerned to ask should be imparted to them, were not undefined benefits that they would be "alright," but positive expectations of whole, healthy, and fruitful lives. Perhaps before we resort again to asking God to bless us or the world around us, we should pause to think out more precisely what it is that we should like God to do. Even if we are more than a little embarrassed at the frankness and harshness with which Jacob's prayer enumerates the vices and failings of some of his sons, we could certainly benefit ourselves from bringing into our prayers a greater note of honesty and realism. What do we really seek from God for the world around us? Perhaps our vagueness is merely a "cover-up" for our unwillingness to think out more precisely what our prayers are really directed towards achieving.

4
A Prayer of
MOSES

Numbers 14:13–23

Moses the Man

Moses introduces us to the world of ancient Egypt, which is justly celebrated as a civilization and culture second to none in antiquity. Its magnificence, the range of its achievements in building, arts, and science lifted it to extraordinary levels of grandeur and importance for the entire history of humankind. We are all debtors to the ancient Egyptians, even though we may no longer be conscious of how many breakthroughs in learning, invention, and understanding we have inherited from them. The reason is that the high points of the Egyptian achievement had been reached before 1000 B.C., a time when much of Europe had scarcely thrown off the limitations and primitiveness of the Stone Age. From the period from 4000 B.C. and the rise of the Hellenistic Age in Egypt in the time of Alexander the Great, Egypt was one of the great powers of the ancient world and had invented a vast range of techniques for the betterment and enhancement of human life. Improvements in agriculture, the invention and application of a wide range of tools, architectural design and construction, and the essential foundations of engineering had all been brought about through the skills and inventiveness of the Egyptians. Quite remarkably, we seldom know the names of most of these pioneering inventors, since their achievements are largely known to us through the legacy they have left in ancient monuments and the incidental records that appear in ancient Egyptian texts.

To recover a knowledge of all the greatness that belonged to Egypt has been one of the most prominent and celebrated achievements of modern archaeological research, beginning with the age of

Napoleon. From a fame built upon its ancient reputation, Egypt has become a world that is now extremely well known through the patience and efforts of many generations of archaeologists and researchers. There is a surprising paradox in all the knowledge that we possess about Egypt, however, and in all the honor that we can properly render to it. This is because in the Bible, the writings of which only began to appear very late in the flowering of Egyptian civilization, Egypt has received a very tarnished image. It has been given, as we should say in the modern world, a "bad press." No more serious or cautionary admonition could be given to a citizen of ancient Israel than to be told: "You shall remember that you were a slave in the land of Egypt" (Deut. 15:15). Egypt's greatness had a fatal flaw, a sinister cancer that had grown up within the very citadels of opulence and power. This was the institution of slavery, for all the great buildings including the magnificent pyramids, had been built by gangs of enslaved people who had no other role in life than to serve as the tools and implements of the state. From the time of their birth until death brought them relief and deliverance, these hordes of slave workers spent their days and their life-energy in the service of a state from which they stood to gain nothing at all. For the most part they are unknown men and women, unnamed and unremembered, and even the circumstances and conditions of their lives remain largely unknown to us. The fact that from time to time some of them escaped from their misery has alone given to them the kind of recognition which merited a mention in the records of the well-ordered and elaborate machinery of the Egyptian government system. The military guardians of the state were compelled to account for any who slipped away from their control.

Nevertheless one man led a group of such slaves to freedom, and thereby this one attainment brought him a greatness and a fame beyond that of even the greatest of Egypt's pharaohs, and it stamped upon the conscience of all humankind a new respect for freedom. This man was Moses, whose very name is Egyptian (it reappears in such names as Ra-meses, Thut-moses), and who led these fugitive slaves to seek a new life in the land promised to their ancestor Abraham.

With the figure of Moses we may well feel a certain division of our loyalties, since if we value the material achievement of our human story, we must certainly give a very high rating to what the inventiveness of ancient Egypt has given to us. To live in a city of beautiful buildings, to enjoy the benefits of reading and art, to know that the food supply is secure and that a strong army is available to protect it, may reflect the very best in human skills and desires. We should be very reluctant to abandon these benefits in the interests of what may appear as an elusive and costly gift—freedom! Yet this is what Moses stood for, and the epistle to the Hebrews boldly sums up what Moses and his work represented: "By faith Moses, when he was grown up, refused to be called the son of Pharaoh's daughter, choosing rather to share ill-treatment with the people of God than to enjoy the fleeting pleasures of sin" (Heb. 11:24–5).

That Moses came from Egypt, and thereby brought into Israel's heritage that other dimension which we have already noted, is not in doubt. When precisely he was there, and under which Pharaoh he fled from the land, are not clearly datable facts, although a link with the age of the great Pharaoh Rameses II in the thirteenth century B.C. has appeared probable. The dates matter less to us, however, than the motive for his abandonment of the luxuries of the Egyptian court and the reasons which led him to seek for himself and the Hebrew slaves with which he identified himself a new life elsewhere. This has made Moses into a great religious founder and innovator and has thereby made him into a historical figure far greater than if he had simply been a leader of a slave rebellion—an early Spartacus! From the days of Moses one of the most primary confessions of who God is, and what God's innermost nature means to humankind, has been coupled with this experience of deliverance from slavery:

"I am the LORD your God, who brought you out of the land of Egypt, out of the house of bondage."

(Exodus 20:2)

All of the great religions of humanity—Christianity, Judaism, Islam, Hinduism, Buddhism—are very complex entities. Although the majority of them look to one particular person as founder and originator we know that many influences and many persons have contributed to each one of them. This is also true of Judaism and of the biblical Old Testament from which it arose. Yet Moses stands above all of the other men and women of the Old Testament as the founding father of its worship and faith. It is his person that has given authority to the five books of the law assuring us that in them we are face to face with a revelation of God. It is to Moses that the institutions of worship practiced in the ancient temple of Jerusalem and in the synagogues of Judaism look back. More than for any personal qualities of courage or piety, therefore, Moses stands out as the most important of the personalities of the Old Testament on account of his work as the revealer of a true knowledge of God. This true knowledge of God finds its central focus in the events which brought about the escape of the Hebrews from the slave-camps of Egypt, and in so doing it has brought a new word—we might even call it a new experience—into the vocabulary of religion. This word is "salvation," which in its inner essence means "freedom" and which could well be translated as such in a great many of its occurrences in the Bible.

Perhaps when we survey the history of a distinctive biblical word like "salvation" we come to recognize that such words appear to take on a life and vitality of their own. They undergo a long and surprising history as they become translated from one language to another; they take on new meanings and divest themselves of old ones; they become the private pass-words of intense religious communities, and may even pass out of common, everyday usage altogether. In the present day "salvation" has all too easily become part of a distinctive "religious" vocabulary and has become very closely intertwined with a particular set pattern of religious activities and experiences. In the Old Testament, however, and most certainly in the context of the events to which Moses bound it, the word had a breadth of meaning which we must be careful not to lose. In leading his people from the depths of misery and despair to the immense possibilities of a new existence Moses simply commanded them: "Fear not, stand firm, and see the salvation of the LORD, which he will work for you today" (Exod. 14:13). To experience the salvation of the Lord was to enter into a new freedom.

The Prayer

The circumstances which gave rise to the very special prayer of Moses stand at some remove from the momentous events which brought about the escape of the Hebrews from Pharaoh's slavery. In between those events and the occasion of the prayer there lay many experiences and a vast charter of religion delivered to Israel at Mount Sinai through the mediation of Moses. In so many ways freedom is very fragile. We can see that it has two poles, one negative and one positive. At the negative pole it indicates the absence of oppression, tyranny, and exploitation; at the positive pole it entails a commitment to justice, equality of opportunity, and an openness to all the possibilities that life brings. Freedom is, in its very essence, an open-ended social value. It can be conferred by the removal of oppressive conditions and restraints, but it can only be preserved and enjoyed by an openness to truth and to social justice which are not easily protected in the social circumstances and institutions which people need. A freedom won by daring and determination can be slowly eroded away by timidity, shallowness, and an unwillingness to accept the burdens and responsibilities which the enjoyment of freedom demands. Thus we are led to the situation which occasioned a prayer of history-making importance from Moses.

After the escape from Egypt and the revelation by God of the right way of worship, which was granted to the Hebrews who came from Egypt with Moses, a whole series of less comforting experiences began to drain away their first enthusiasms. Both in the books of Exodus and Numbers, we read of a series of trying circumstances which cast a shadow upon the exuberance with which the Hebrews had first greeted their escape. With the burning heat of the sun, the shortage of water in the wilderness brought cries of regret and self-pity from the Israelites who no longer saw the path of freedom as an easy one. Added to this were the problems of finding food, together with all the uncertainties regarding the re-entry into the land promised to Abraham which was now to become "their" land. When finally spies were sent out to reconnoiter the territory and to bring back a report on the best strategy and tactics for reclaiming it (Num. 13), the fibers of courage and perserverance which had up to this point strengthened the resolve of the Israelites appear to have snapped completely. With the spies' report, carrying its message of strong men, strong and well defended cities, and a forewarning that the task of reclaiming the land would not be an easy one, all the residue of courage and common sense appears to have drained away

from the Israelites. They regretted their boldness, which now seemed
to have been foolhardy, and pitied their plight, which they now regarded as hopeless. With words which plumb the depths of self-pity,
and a cowardly concern for self-preservation at any price, the people
wish themselves back in Egypt: "And all the people of Israel mur-
mured against Moses and Aaron; the whole congregation said to
them, 'Would that we had died in the land of Egypt! Or would that
we had died in this wilderness! Why does the LORD bring us into
this land, to fall by the sword? Our wives and our little ones will become a prey; would it not be better for us to go back to Egypt?'"
(Num. 14:2–3).

When the people begin to organize seriously to flee back into
Egypt, to surrender themselves and their families to slavery once
again, Moses, Aaron, Joshua, and Caleb remonstrate with them. It
is all to no avail, since the counsel of surrender seems certain to
carry the day. Moses hears God speaking to him: "How long will this
people despise me? And how long will they not believe in me, in
spite of all the signs which I have wrought among them? I will strike
them with the pestilence and disinherit them, and I will make of you
a nation greater and mightier than they" (Num. 14:11–12). Moses
feels himself to be standing almost alone, and the words which he
puts into the mouth of God must very fully have reflected his own
wounded feelings. He had given up the comforts of a life in Egypt
which these people had never known! He had sacrificed for freedom
a life of security and plenty! Yet they were doing all the complaining,
and wishing themselves back in Egypt! How perverse the human
spirit can be! There is even a touch of justifiable pride in his conviction that God could build an entire nation through him, rather than
struggle on, calling men and women to courage and perseverance,
who surrendered so readily in the face of danger. It is precisely this
situation, with the people poised between surrender and persistence
and Moses hovering between anger and despair, that occasions one
of the truly great prayers of the Bible:

> But Moses said to the LORD, "Then the Egyptians will hear of it,
> for thou didst bring up this people in thy might from among them, and
> they will tell the inhabitants of this land. They have heard that thou, O
> LORD, art in the midst of this people; for thou, O LORD, art seen face

to face, and thy cloud stands over them and thou goest before them, in
a pillar of cloud by day and in a pillar of fire by night. Now if thou dost
kill this people as one man, then the nations who have heard thy fame
will say, 'Because the LORD was not able to bring this people into the
land which he swore to give to them, therefore he has slain them in the
wilderness.' And now, I pray thee, let the power of the LORD be great
as thou has promised, saying, 'The LORD is slow to anger, and abounding in steadfast love, forgiving iniquity and transgression, but he will
by no means clear the guilty, visiting the iniquity of fathers upon children, upon the third and upon the fourth generation.' Pardon the iniquity of this people, I pray thee, according to the greatness of thy
steadfast love, and according as thou hast forgiven this people, from
Egypt even until now."

Then the LORD said, "I have pardoned, according to your word; but
truly, as I live, and as all the earth shall be filled with the glory of the
LORD, none of the men who have seen my glory and my signs which I
wrought in Egypt and in the wilderness, and yet have put me to the
proof these ten times and have not hearkened to my voice, shall see the
land which I swore to give to their fathers; and none of those who
despised me shall see it."

(Numbers 14:13–23)

In form this prayer is an intercession, and this is viewed in the
most striking sense such a description can convey since God has
broken off dealings with this people. They have forsaken God!
Moses alone is left in a prayerful relationship, and we can well en-
visage the subjects that might have occupied such a prayer. Moses
could have allowed his personal anger to explode, urging God to
punish such a crowd of cowardly and self-pitying people. Why
should they enjoy a freedom they had not the courage to deserve? Or
he could, with a mind to his own future, have sought from God an
assurance that he and the few men who stood by him—Aaron,
Joshua, and Caleb—would form the nucleus of a new group who
would take possession of the land and form the basis of a new and
purified nation. Moses, however, resorts to neither of these two
choices. Instead he pleads with God to forgive such people, even
mentioning and thereby in a sense recalling to his own mind a basic
liturgical confession about God's goodness and mercy (cf. Exod.
34:6–7). Although in the brevity of the biblical narrative the response of God comes back swiftly and firmly: "I have pardoned,
according to your word," we must reckon that a long period of inner

struggle and turmoil ensued for Moses. In a very real and deep sense the personal issue was not whether God could forgive the people, which might easily have relapsed into a debate about theological abstractions, but about whether Moses could be reconciled to this people. Could he accept them, when it was evidently so impossible for him to accept their worthless attitudes, and when he could in no way endorse their cowardly proposal to return to Egypt?

All too easily forgiveness is allowed to become the subject of abstract theological argument concerning the conflicting interests of God's justice and his mercy. In a deep sense, however, forgiveness has a very human and personal dimension, concerned on the one hand with living together as a community and on the other with letting go of less worthy personal feelings and resentments and seizing hold of higher and bolder ambitions. We find a number of very intriguing features coming to the surface in this prayer, all of which have a profound impact on our understanding of religion and faith. First of all, Moses begins his prayer with a long reflection on the way in which the reputation of God has become tied up in the destiny of the escaping Israelites. If God is the God of true freedom, then God must surely stand by those people who have risked their own lives in order to enjoy such freedom. There could be no turning back now without at the same time turning back the understanding of God which Moses and those who followed him had come to recognize as a revelation. Second, the idea of a divine forgiveness and the awareness of its problematic character are seen to relate to men's and women's acceptance of it. Moses can plead "according as thou hast forgiven this people, from Egypt even until now." It is not the idea of a divine forgiveness that is new but the sense that the people may have moved into a situation in which it no longer conveys any significant meaning or reality. Their problems appear to them to be beyond the scope of God's assistance. A third point is also noteworthy. God's forgiveness does not result in a "carte blanche" assurance that everything is now forgotten and the people can now return to things as they were before they expressed their alarm at the spies' report. Such cannot be, and instead there is a solemn admonition on the part of God: "none of those who despised me shall see it." People cannot possess privileges which they do not have the faith and courage to seek. An individual may have to be content to know that only his or her children will enjoy the promised land. Perhaps throughout the entire prayer we are made aware of a truth, vital to the spiritual life, that the great obstacle to the acceptance of forgiveness lies in the lack of faith and courage necessary to its acceptance.

The Significance of the Prayer

It would be hard to overestimate the significance of this prayer, both in relation to its biblical setting and in its uncovering of some of the most basic realities of the spiritual life. In biblical perspective it displays the Israelite people in a mood that is downright shocking. It does not even stretch to ameliorate this by suggesting that a few disreputable leaders were able to persuade the majority to abandon the leadership of Moses. Nor does it withhold any of the most selfish, cowardly, and unworthy expressions of ingratitude and faithlessness of Israel! The very generation that had suffered and smarted under the whips and cruelties of pharaoh's taskmasters can dare to suggest: "Would it not be better for us to go back to Egypt?" Such absurdities might be put down to the way in which people forget and time softens the bitterness of wounds inflicted long ago. This is clearly not the whole truth, however, and the biblical writer is anxious that we should perceive that this is so. It is a vital aspect of the spiritual life that we are all men and women of deep emotions. Contemplated from a distance sweet reasonableness can be an easy virtue to admire and to expect in every situation. Yet in the heat of the moment, when faced with a deep disappointment or an unexpected rebuff, men and women can behave in extraordinary ways. The very need to cope with fear and disappointment may lead to outbursts of anger, hostility, and frustration that would, at other times, have been regarded as most uncharacteristic. As so often observed, those who enjoy the high experiences of faith and hope, who walk on the mountaintops with God, often are those who also suffer deep bouts of depression and gloom. Even to hint that it is only the experience of the few to pass through such times would be to miss a central feature of the biblical story. Virtually everyone is carried away with these feelings of hopelessness and despair. Only Moses and his three courageous companions are left to withstand the onslaught of accusation and complaint. Moses alone can resolve the situation through prayer! Perhaps the most vital lesson of all that we have to learn from this, therefore, is that the fact that we have experienced great insights of faith and hope in the past does not and will not exempt us from times of doubt, fear, and depression. Perhaps the most vulnerable cf all in the spiritual life are those who have come to think, "It couldn't happen to me!"

In a further reflection it becomes clear that the freedom which comes with God's salvation is never a freedom that can be taken for granted. It can be gradually eroded away, and the causes of this erosion are feelings and failings which lie deep inside the psychological make-up of everyone. They emerge in timidity, self-pity, anxiety, and a desire not to give up accustomed comforts and securities. The freedom of God is a gift, but it is a gift that has constantly to be repossessed and reawakened. A few brief moments of faith and a few steps taken courageously may mark an important beginning, but they will not, by themselves, open up the full possibilities of a new life in a new land. Such steps must mark the start of learning to live in faith and courage, and, without constant watchfulness, these virtues can easily slip away from us. Those who know the distinction which the German theologian Dietrich Bonhoeffer made between the concepts of "cheap grace" and "costly grace" will quickly recognize the relevance which Moses' prayer has for this. Freedom can never be guaranteed simply by a decision of the past nor by a charter written long ago. Such decisions and such charters are in constant need of renewal and reaffirmation as new problems and threats emerge.

One last point may also be made concerning Moses' great prayer of intercession. It is a prayer for forgiveness, and no theme may appear to be more familiar and appropriate in our entire vocabulary of prayer. How else should we come before God, unless it is first with a request that we may be forgiven? Whether it be through private contemplation, through our response to an evangelical invitation, or through our attendance at holy communion, the theme of forgiveness is likely to be high on our prayer agenda. This very familiarity introduces its own dangers, however, for the end result is likely to be that God's forgiveness is something we readily take for granted. Its apparent certainty, even bordering on the assumption that it is necessary for God to forgive us, may hide from us the truths of which Moses' prayer is all too conscious. Forgiveness, in its concern with God's order for the world, touches upon the innermost realm of our personal thoughts, feelings, and attitudes. It may become the hardest of all facts for us to accept. Just as it would have been impossible for the Israelites to have accepted God's forgiveness and still returned to Egypt, so would it have been out of the question for Moses to have accepted its reality and still given vent to his anger and disappointment with his people. Its acceptance called for a complete inner reorientation, both on Moses' part and on that of the people. The difficulty encountered with belief in the forgiveness of God does not lie in the problems associated with reconciling God's justice with divine mercy, for in essence justice and mercy belong together. The problems lie in our own inner feelings of pride, self-esteem, and self-interest. We do not want to change our attitudes towards others to the extent that forgiveness truly requires!

5
Another Prayer of MOSES

Deuteronomy 33:2–29

The Prayer

We have already looked at the significance of Moses for Israel's history. Throughout the entire history of the people of Israel in Old Testament times no other figure played so prominent a role, or was remembered with such warmth and veneration. Whereas in later times powerful kings such as David, and great prophets such as Isaiah, were to emerge, Moses fulfilled many roles within his lifetime. He was prophet, leader, warrior, and statesman. Where Abraham and Jacob could be looked back to as ancestors of the nation, the indebtedness to Moses was greater. In his achievements he was revered as the founder of the nation. It is through this fact that we can still see in his work the prophetic creativity which made him the father-founder of Judaism. Surprisingly, however, Moses did not live to see the crowning vindication of his leadership in bringing the Hebrew slaves out of Egypt. He died before they finally entered and settled in the promised land. In a remarkable and rather poignant comment on the death of this great leader the biblical historian simply records the fact of his death in the land of Moab, and the lack of any known identification of the place of his burial: "So Moses the servant of the LORD died there in the land of Moab, according to the word of the LORD, and he buried him in the valley in the land of Moab opposite Beth-peor; but no man knows the place of his burial to this day" (Deut. 34:5–6). Thus ended the life of one of the greatest leaders in history, a man who counted freedom of greater worth than all the treasures and magnificence that ancient Egypt could offer. His role as a prophetic leader of a relatively small number of fugitive slaves afforded him a greatness which few emperors or statesmen of later years can match. He did not live, though, to see even the first efforts of his followers to set up a community and society of their own in the land that he had dared to believe would be theirs.

A very memorable tradition relates how, before his death, God took Moses to the top of Mount Pisgah and showed him all the land which would eventually belong to his people and their descendants (Deut. 34:1–4). Before this event took place, however, there is recorded a splendid prayer, the Blessing of Moses, which compares very closely in form and content to the Blessing of Jacob which we have already noted. In a sense it presents us with the "last words" of Moses, who has been remembered as a prolific lawgiver, and it sets out in irenic fashion the prayerful assurance regarding the blessings that God will grant to the chosen people. As in the case of Jacob's prayer, it is part vision, part prophetic promise, and part request that his people Israel may faithfully enjoy the benefits that God's providence has made possible:

"The LORD came from Sinai,
    and dawned from Seir upon us,
    he shone forth from Mount Paran,
he came from the ten thousands of holy ones,
    with flaming fire at his right hand.
Yea, he loved his people;
    all those consecrated to him were in his hand;
so they followed in thy steps,
    receiving direction from thee,
when Moses commanded us a law,
    as a possession for the assembly of Jacob.
Thus the LORD became king in Jeshurun,
    when the heads of the people were gathered,
    all the tribes of Israel together.
"Let Reuben live, and not die,
    nor let his men be few."

And this he said of Judah:
"Hear, O LORD, the voice of Judah,
    and bring him in to his people.
With thy hands contend for him,
    and be a help against his adversaries."

And of Levi he said,
"Give to Levi thy Thummim,

and thy Urim to thy godly one,
whom thou didst test at Massah,
    with whom thou didst strive at the waters of Meribah;
who said of his father and mother,
    'I regard them not';
he disowned his brothers,
    and ignored his children.
For they observed thy word,
    and kept thy covenant.
They shall teach Jacob thy ordinances,
    and Israel thy law;
they shall put incense before thee,
    and whole burnt offering upon thy altar.
Bless, O LORD, his substance,
    and accept the work of his hands;
crush the loins of his adversaries,
    of those that hate him, that they rise not again."

Of Benjamin he said,
"The beloved of the LORD,
    he dwells in safety by him;
he encompasses him all the day long,
    and makes his dwelling between his shoulders."

And of Joseph he said,
"Blessed by the LORD be his land,
    with the choicest gifts of heaven above,
    and of the deep that couches beneath,
with the choicest fruits of the sun,
    and the rich yield of the months,
with the finest produce of the ancient mountains,
    and the abundance of the everlasting hills,
with the best gifts of the earth and its fulness,
    and the favor of him that dwelt in the bush.
Let these come upon the head of Joseph,
    and upon the crown of the head
      of him that is prince among his brothers.
His firstling bull has majesty,
    and his horns are the horns of a wild ox;
with them he shall push the peoples,
    all of them, to the ends of the earth;
such are the ten thousands of Ephraim,
    and such are the thousands of Manasseh."

And of Zebulun he said,
"Rejoice, Zebulun, in your going out;

and Issachar, in your tents.
They shall call peoples to their mountain;
    there they offer right sacrifices;
for they suck the affluence of the seas
    and the hidden treasures of the sand."

And of Gad he said,
"Blessed be he who enlarges Gad!
    Gad couches like a lion,
    he tears the arm, and the crown of the head.
He chose the best of the land for himself,
    for there a commander's portion was reserved;
and he came to the heads of the people,
    with Israel he executed the commands
    and just decrees of the LORD."

And of Dan he said,
"Dan is a lion's whelp,
    that leaps forth from Bashan."

And of Naphtali he said,
"O Naphtali, satisfied with favor,
    and full of the blessing of the LORD,
    possess the lake and the south."

And of Asher he said,
"Blessed above sons be Asher;
    let him be the favorite of his brothers,
    and let him dip his foot in oil.
Your bars shall be iron and bronze;
    and as your days, so shall your strength be.

"There is none like God, O Jeshurun,
    who rides through the heavens to your help,
    and in his majesty through the skies.
The eternal God is your dwelling place,
    and underneath are the everlasting arms.
And he thrust out the enemy before you,
    and said, Destroy.
So Israel dwelt in safety,
    the fountain of Jacob alone,
in a land of grain and wine;
    yea, his heavens drop down dew.
Happy are you, O Israel! Who is like you,
    a people saved by the LORD,
the shield of your help,
    and the sword of your triumph!

Your enemies shall come fawning to you;
  and you shall tread upon their high places."
                    (Deuteronomy 33:1–29)

The similarity with the character and structure of the Blessing of
Jacob is quite clear. There are differences, and it is not difficult to see
that these differences make the Blessing of Moses much more like
the kind of prayers that we are used to and have come to expect. For
the most part it consists of affirmation and petition, the affirmation
being concerned with who God is and what God has done for the
people. The petition is almost entirely taken up with concern for the
welfare and prosperity of the twelve separate tribes of Israel in their
individual territorial holdings. The prayer therefore contains a considerable wealth of historical and geographical information concerning the situation of the individual tribes in their separate locations.
Yet behind this diversity of opportunity and experience there lies a
sense of a common shared inheritance and a knowledge of one incomparable, unchanging God:

"The LORD came from Sinai. . . .
  he shone forth from Mount Paran, . . .
Yea, he loved his people; . . .
Thus the LORD became king in Jeshurun [Israel]. . . ."

"There is none like God, O Jeshurun,
  who rides through the heavens to your help,
The eternal God is your dwelling place,
  and underneath are the everlasting arms."

It is only by getting back to the very foundations of faith with
this knowledge of God that the assurance for the future can be
justified:

"Happy are you, O Israel! Who is like you,
  a people saved by the LORD,
the shield of your help,
  and the sword of your triumph!"

This must surely be a basic lesson and pattern for all prayer and
petition for happiness and welfare. Who is the God who has created
these people? who has guided them in the past? what has God done
for my people? my country? for me? How rudely our assumption that

prayer is simply a matter of asking God for the protection and benefits we expect to be given is shattered by such a prayer as this. Prayer
is first and foremost a rediscovery of God and a repossession of the
knowledge of God's entry into our lives. It would be difficult to think
of any phrase which could convey more emphatically and meaning-
fully this God-centeredness of prayer than this: "The eternal God is
your dwelling place." To a people who were now becoming preoccupied with questions of territory and the reclaiming of their homeland it offers an immense widening of spiritual horizons. In this way
it presents a necessary preface to our own deep concern with possessions and material security. This is not because such practical concerns are not a legitimate subject for prayer and concern in our lives
but because they have to be set in perspective. In a very striking way
therefore the Blessing of Moses presents us with a lesson in the
theology of prayer. First and foremost our prayers, if they are to be
meaningful and truly biblical, must concern themselves with the
Being of God.

A clear balancing of concerns in Moses' prayer appears, however, between the "Being" of God and the "becoming" of God's
people. Set upon the foundation of who God is and what God has
done, a whole series of requests on behalf of each of the tribes of
Israel emerge:

> "Let Reuben live, . . ."
> "Give to Levi . . ."
> "Bless, O LORD, his substance, . . ."
> "Blessed by the LORD be his land, . . ."

By such a series of petitions there is expressed a yearning and
longing that each of the tribes might come to realize its full potential.
With poetic skill and imagination, what this potential will be is set
out by a variety of images. Sometimes this potential is linked to the
particular geographical setting of the tribe, as in the case of Zebulun
and Issachar who are to "suck the affluence of the seas" through their
association with the great maritime nation of the Phoenicians. In the
case of Levi its potential is connected with its obligation to provide
the priestly servants of Israel's worship. For this, special discipline

and self-denial is involved, demanding separation from home and family. For one tribe, notably that of Reuben, the very struggle to survive will be a major concern.

Here we come face to face with the fact that if God's people are to become what they are truly meant to be there must be diversity and individuality. Perhaps even today there is a powerful tendency in every Christian community to cast people into one specific mold. Men and women feel pressed into conforming to a particular stereotype and may even feel hurt and offended when someone else does not fit in. With God, however, there is variety and diversity, so that the fulfillment of our prayers for enrichment and benefit will not result in a drab uniformity but in an ever greater richness made possible by this God-given variety.

We have already noted that in this Mosaic prayer there is a large measure of looking forward to the life that will be lived by each of the tribes when they are settled in their own homeland areas. Some will clearly do very well, on account of the relative richness of the land on which they live and the wealth of opportunities which will become theirs. Joseph will enjoy "the choicest gifts of heaven above" and Asher will "dip his foot in oil." Many will do very well, some will do not so well, and some, like Reuben, will struggle to maintain themselves at all. We find no clearer illustration in the entire Bible of the importance of breadth, and a true "catholicity," in our prayers of intercession. It is all too easy to forget and to become indifferent to the needs and concerns of others when we become wrapped up in our own. If we are doing well, it is all too easy to let slip from our minds the struggles and difficulties of those who are less fortunate. It is through prayer that the saying of the wise finds its fulfillment: "The rich and the poor meet together, the LORD is the maker of them all" (Prov. 22:2). Nor can such prayer be a mere formality. It must remind us of our own personal obligations towards others, and it must mold our own attitude and ambitions. Prayer must become a "school of caring," bringing home to us the reasons why we must care and informing us of the needs and circumstances of those we should care for. Of this the Blessing of Moses is a splendid example.

We may conclude by noting a further feature which is quite remarkable. It must appear to give a very unfair perspective on the realities of life that, of those who came out of Egypt with Moses to find a new life of freedom and opportunity in the land of Canaan, some were to have better opportunities than others. We might have supposed that in an ideal world each tribe should have had an "equal opportunity." There is, however, in the Blessing of Moses, a frank and full realization of the diversity of opportunities there will be, and in spite of looking at the best aspects facing each tribe, a recognition that it will be harder for some than for others. In this we sense something of the honesty and realism contained in the prayer. We cannot live or pray effectively in a world of abstractions and idealized perceptions. If equality and "fair shares for all" are ideals that are worth striving for, they have to be set against the experienced facts of life that we live in a very unequal world. More than half the population of the world lives in hunger and serious poverty. Only a few will enjoy the level and range of education which the very reading of such a book as this entails! How then ought we to pray? One thing is surely certain, that God cannot be indifferent to the claimant need of those who have less than we do. When we in our prayers are concerned that we should prosper and be successful, obtaining all those desirable benefits that we believe God has in store for us, do we not first of all have to widen our horizons? Would not God's answer to our praying consist first and foremost in showing us how incredibly well provided for we really are? If the Blessing of Moses is a remarkable window which enables us to look back upon the individual opportunities that faced the tribes of ancient Israel, should not our prayers in the present offer a similar window by which we can be enabled to see the realities of the world around us? When we are tempted to think that God's heart is closed towards our requests, we need to be reminded that, most likely, it is because we have closed our eyes against the world.

6
A Prayer of
HANNAH
1 Samuel 2:1–10

The Woman Hannah in Biblical History

Between the time of Moses' death and the coming of the woman Hannah to the ancient sanctuary of Shiloh, more than a century had passed. During these years the sense of unity that had existed for the relatively small number of Israelites surrounding Moses, and which had survived during the days of Joshua, had largely disappeared. Much had been gained in a material sense; the land had been won and settled, the tribes had established themselves in their own homeland areas, and each had begun to face its own problems. Enemies had arisen, sometimes from outside the land of Israel proper, but sometimes from within, from suspicious and hostile neighbors. Perhaps most of all new dangers and problems had arisen within the people themselves as the memory of Egypt and the threat that it had posed receded into the past. With it slipped away much of the feeling of deep indebtedness and the desire for uncompromising loyalty to God. Now there appeared on the scene a woman whose gift to the biblical story was twofold, but who thereby has epitomized the gifts that women have continued to contribute to our human story. The first of her gifts was a child that she bore to her husband Elkanah, a child who was destined to transform and renew the declining spiritual and political vitality of Israel. The second of her gifts was a prayer, the Song of Hannah, which is an unforgettable expression of the transforming power and goodness of God. For sheer exuberance and a sense of the infinite possibilities which exist for those who know God, it has few equals and must properly be set alongside the prayer of her New Testament counterpart, Mary the mother of Jesus.

The circumstances in which Hannah found herself are easily explained, and are not at all untypical of the kind of misfortune that could happen to a woman in almost any age. She was married but had been unable to conceive any children, which the biblical author describes with religious rather than medical precision: "The LORD had closed her womb." The bitterness of her misery was heightened because, in an age in which polygamy was quite commonplace and accepted, a rival wife, Peninnah, had both sons and daughters. It would be quite wrong to seek to understand Hannah's prayer solely in the context of her own personal misfortune and misery. For the biblical writer her wretchedness was symptomatic of the wretchedness that had befallen Israel during these years, and the answer to her cries and distress was to prove to be simultaneously an answer from God to the cries and distress of Israel. As her pleas were to find a response in the birth of a child—as if by a miracle from God—so were the needs of Israel to be met through this same child, Samuel.

The sanctuary of Shiloh had become one of the most important, if not the most important, in Israel because the Ark of God had been taken there. The venerable and respected figure of Eli the priest had served there for a number of years until old age had begun to limit his powers and his sons had taken over an increasing number of priestly responsibilities. They greatly abused their privileges by greed and lust (1 Sam. 2:12–17, 22), however, and thereby dishonored the priesthood and all the great traditions of faith with which they were entrusted. They brought shame to a great family and provided an occasion of scandal and indifference which threatened the spiritual health of the Israelite community. The situation is certainly not an entirely unfamiliar one to those who know the history of the Christian church!

Yet even this religious crisis, important as it was, served as an illustration of an even more widespread malaise that afflicted the nation of Israel during these years. There was a massive political and military threat facing the people, which they had neither the resources nor the moral fiber with which to cope. This crisis emanated from the Philistines, or Sea Peoples as the Egyptian records describe them. They had already established themselves along the coastal strip of the land of Israel in the region that borders Egypt, with Gaza as one of their major cities. They proved to be rival claimants to the land and, over a period of years, pressed further and further into the areas settled by Israel. Not only were they land-hungry and aggressive, but, from the evidence that they have left to us, they appear to have been technically well advanced and militarily well organized. They posed a threat which only a strongly coordinated and courageously led defense could hope to counter. This was just where Israel's greatest weakness lay. Since the days of Joshua there had been little unified action and a growing indifference to the obligations which bound the twelve tribes to each other. The one factor which should have promoted unity and common concern was faith in the Lord God, yet it was precisely this which had been so seriously hampered by the conduct of the priesthood provided by Eli's sons.

By the time Hannah returned to the sanctuary at Shiloh and offered there her prayer of thanksgiving to God, joyful at the birth of her child, the situation of Israel as a whole had become serious. Within the personal family life of Elkanah and Hannah there was great cause for rejoicing, yet in the larger world around them, threatening clouds and an uncertain future faced Israel. With a sense of spiritual appositeness, however, the biblical author has seen in Hannah's prayer an expression of faith and conviction which exactly fitted Israel's need. Its theme is simple, repeated, and set out with vigorous poetic imagination: God changes things!

The Prayer

The occasion for the prayer is the return of Hannah to the sanctuary at Shiloh where she had first entreated God that she might give birth. This time, however, all is joy and happiness, for the prayer has been answered: "For this child I prayed; and the LORD has granted me my petition which I made to him" (1 Sam. 1:27). In bringing her thanks to God, Hannah also presented a promise that her son would be dedicated to God's service throughout his life: "Therefore I have lent him to the LORD; as long as he lives, he is lent to the LORD" (1 Sam. 1:28). Her outpouring of thanks to God then follows:

"My heart exults in the LORD;
   my strength is exalted in the LORD.
My mouth derides my enemies,
   because I rejoice in thy salvation.

"There is none holy like the LORD,
   there is none besides thee;
   there is no rock like our God.
Talk no more so very proudly,
   let not arrogance come from your mouth;
for the LORD is a God of knowledge,
   and by him actions are weighed.
The bows of the mighty are broken,
   but the feeble gird on strength.
Those who were full have hired themselves out for bread,
   but those who were hungry have ceased to hunger.
The barren has borne seven,
   but she who has many children is forlorn.
The LORD kills and brings to life;
   he brings down to Sheol and raises up.
The LORD makes poor and makes rich;
   he brings low, he also exalts.
He raises up the poor from the dust;
   he lifts the needy from the ash heap,
to make them sit with princes
   and inherit a seat of honor.
For the pillars of the earth are the LORD's,
   and on them he has set the world.

"He will guard the feet of his faithful ones;
   but the wicked shall be cut off in darkness;
   for not by might shall a man prevail.
The adversaries of the LORD shall be broken to pieces;
   against them he will thunder in heaven.
The LORD will judge the ends of the earth;
   he will give strength to his king,
   and exalt the power of his anointed."

                                        (1 Samuel 2:1–10)

Immediately one sees that this is not a prayer which asks anything. It is rather "descriptive praise of God," setting out a picture of who God is, what God is like, and what God has done in the past. We could describe the prayer as concerned with the rediscovery of God and with a reappropriation of this divine reality in the world and in our lives. We can see from this that it is made up of a series of word-pictures of his activity, of which one only is related most directly to Hannah's personal situation: "The barren has borne seven," and even here it indulges in a touch of exaggeration!

The theme of the prayer is one that is consistently carried through and expresses one basic conviction: God changes things! If it were not for the richness of the poetic imagery and the grandeur of such an idea, the very repetition of this theme might appear monotonous. What we have in fact is a series of illustrations of the changes that God brings into the lives of people:

> He kills—he brings to life;
> He makes poor—and makes rich;
> He brings low—and also exalts.

This terrifying and remarkable power of God is then traced back, in a picture that combines poetry, theology, and the cosmology of a prescientific age, to the conviction that our world is entirely set under the controlling purpose of God: "For the pillars of the earth are the LORD's and on them he has set the world." These "pillars" were believed to be the supporting foundations on which the world was set, much like the "pillars of Hercules" of ancient Greek mythology. What such a picture expresses is the assertion that our world, and all the forces which control it, are set under the guiding and controlling power of God. All the extraordinary variety of powers and forces which are at work in our world—in nature, in history, and in the individual lives of men and women are simply the visible signs of this creative divine power. When we contemplate the infinite range and scale of the divine activity which we daily see to be at work, then we become aware how incredibly venturesome an act of prayer is! To call upon One whose energies and forces are so vast is to recognize that our individual selves are open to possibilities which can transform them in exceptional ways. God becomes the source and ground of an unlimited range of new possibilities for what we may become and what we may achieve.

For Hannah these life-enhancing possibilities had become realized through the birth of a child—the boy Samuel—whose arrival had evidently altered completely the domestic scene of Elkanah's family. No longer need Hannah feel an unwanted failure, unable to achieve her ambition and dream of motherhood. For the author of the biblical story, however, the significance of the child extended beyond this domestic world, since Samuel was to provide a new quality of vigorous spiritual leadership and was destined to introduce a new institution—that of the kingship—which would overcome the menace of the Philistines.

The Significance of the Prayer

For all our enjoyment of the vibrant spiritual enthusiasm which permeates Hannah's prayer, there is an element which inevitably occasions profound doubts and questions for the Christian. Not only does the prayer affirm God's power to enrich and exalt but also God's ability to bring down, to abase, and to punish. Since it hints, in a rather gloating fashion, at the humiliation of the rich and the proud, it gives voice to a note of vindictiveness which the Christian cannot endorse. This is a feature which we have to face frankly, not only in connection with many of the prayers of the Old Testament, but also in regard to the Old Testament more generally. Only with the life and work of Jesus of Nazareth is the biblical revelation of the love of God complete. We have always to be concerned therefore to retain this wider perspective in our reading and use of each part of the Bible. However, we certainly should not let the fact that Hannah's prayer was written many centuries before the coming of Jesus, the Christ, lead us into neglecting its spiritual richness. In many ways the very sharpness of its contrasts between the varied results of God's activity in the world serves, in poetic fashion, to highlight the range and power of God's work.

The fact that this is a prayer of praise, and that it does not, in its content, offer any special request to God, brings to our attention again one of the most central aspects of all prayer. Prayer is the discovery, or perhaps more truly rediscovery, of God. Such repeated acts of reawakening and rediscovery recall to our attention the immense possibilities that exist for our lives. We never exhaust them all, and the realization of the many potentialities which our very existence brings becomes in its own way an intimation of immortality. We never develop our full potential, for an inescapable part of living a human life is that we become aware that we cannot achieve all the goals that we should like to; we cannot become all the many persons that we sense God has made it possible for us to become. God offers an infinite range of possibilities for our lives, and a vital aspect of prayer is that it can open the way to the discovery of these new potentialities. Hannah's situation was a simple illustration of the way in which the God-given gift of a child could disclose this life-transforming power. Hannah's eyes had been opened by what had happened to her to see that this constant process of change and transformation is going on in the world all the time. It is we who become static and fixed, which often leads us into a sense of frustration and even resignation. Yet life is not fixed and static, but open-ended and full of possibilities. Time and again it is only when we regain a sense of God and of the endless chain of creative energy which God's activity in the world displays that we rediscover that these possibilities exist.

Hannah's prayer marks, for the biblical author, a turning point in the story of Israel, so that the writer can, after telling us that Hannah went on to bear three more sons and two daughters (1 Sam. 2:21), let her slip gracefully from the story. The account of Israel's further fortunes is then developed by focusing upon the figure of her child, Samuel. From this point on the providential remedy for Israel's spiritual and political ills is traced through the remarkable charismatic leadership provided by this person. Part priest, part prophet, and part king-maker, Samuel was destined to be the leading figure in the years that followed and occupies a central place until the rise of King David.

This reveals a further and exceedingly important feature of the theology that underlies Hannah's prayer. Its language is bold and assertive about the power and presence of God in our world. It is not, however, speaking about miracles in the sense that such a title conveys in our modern world where the laws of physics and the workings of the natural order are more scientifically understood. So far as we can tell there was nothing physically or medically abnormal about the way in which, after a near desperate time of waiting, Hannah was ultimately able to conceive and bear a child. For her it was the answer to prayer, so that the son who was born was a very special and precious gift from God. He was, in an unexpected fashion, also an answer to the frustrations and disappointments of the priest Eli, whose sons had proved such disreputable heirs. Even more remarkably the child Samuel was to prove to be in his later years a central figure in the defense of Israel against the Philistines and in introducing great changes in the political life of the nation. Whether we think in terms of the natural or the historical order none of these developments which emanated from Samuel was miraculous in the sense that it implied some divine disturbance of the normal flow of life. This is undoubtedly of greatest importance for the whole biblical understanding of prayer, which certainly does not claim that answers to prayer are generally miraculous. Nor for all its exuberant language does Hannah's prayer assert this to be the case. For the Bible miracles serve only as rare and exceptional signs of God's work and presence. Prayer therefore neither requires nor expects that its answers will come through totally unexpected miraculous interventions of God. Prayer belongs to a natural order, which is also part of the divine order and works in it and through it.

We may pause for a final reflection on this memorable and exciting prayer. It is highly unusual in its biblical setting on account of its ascription to a woman. Not until we turn to the New Testament, to the prayer of Mary, the mother of Jesus, do we encounter a similar prayer of such length and theological depth ascribed to a woman. In general we are forced to admit that the broad pattern of cultural and social life in which the Bible originated allowed women only a very limited and rather repressed role to play in religious and social life. It is all the more remarkable therefore when this conventional pattern is broken through, as in the cases of the prophetess Deborah (Judg. 4:4ff.) and the prophetess Anna (Luke 2:36ff.). Nor is it difficult for the historian to see that in its attitude towards women the Old Testament reflects a feature that was very widespread in antiquity. Only in much more recent times, with the emergence of new ideas and new social and economic freedoms, has this rather restricted role which society has accorded to women been significantly broken through. While there are undoubtedly many points at which, in principle and sometimes in practice, the Bible challenges and resists this restriction to the place of women, we cannot deny that it exists. Against such a background the splendor and freshness of Hannah's contribution shines out all the more remarkably, and we can see in her superb prayer the breaking through of every kind of barrier. God does indeed change things, and just as her position in the family of Elkanah was radically altered by the birth of her child Samuel, so through her prayer have the spiritual gifts of women been accorded a new place of honor in the Bible, and in consequence, in both Jewish and Christian tradition.

7
A Prayer of
DAVID

2 Samuel 7:18–29

David the King in Biblical History

When we consider what the word "government" conveys to us in the modern world, we become aware that it can arouse very mixed feelings and responses. On the one hand a good and effective government is the single most important factor affecting the quality of a nation's life and the freedom of opportunity which it offers to each individual. On the other hand governments can become ineffective, favoring only a small section of a community, and they can be centers of corruption and greed. They may pull down a country, instead of building it up. What is true in the modern world, so far as governments are concerned, was even more true in the ancient world where governmental power was centered in an institution—that of kingship—which concentrated power in the hands of a single individual and his family in a remarkable way. Kings could become great world-figures, like the Babylonian King Hammurabi or the Egyptian Pharaoh Rameses II or they could become brutal despots, like Herod the Great. In many cases they were an enigmatic combination of greatness and excess, which makes any broad and general assessment very difficult to reach. It is not at all hard to see therefore why so much that has been written in antiquity and about antiquity has concerned itself with the duties and institution of the kingship. This is certainly true so far as the Old Testament is concerned, for the writers came to see in the role of the king a very powerful and potentially good institution, which might also become corrupted and prove disastrous. So far as the good and beneficial qualities of kingship are concerned, these came to be summed up in the life and figure of King David, the founder of Israel's greatest royal dynasty.

It is here that we see a link with the Song of Hannah, which occasioned one of the most memorable prayers of the Old Testament. The story of God's saving work, which the birth of Hannah's child Samuel began, continued with the disappointments over Israel's first king, Saul, and led on to his replacement by David. One point needs to be made clear immediately in considering the many stories that deal with the persons of Saul and David. These are not "character biographies" in the manner that has become fashionable in modern times, but are themselves designed to bring out the many-sidedness of the institution of kingship. They forewarn of the excesses (e.g., 1 Samuel 8:10–18), as well as praising the virtues of the better and more honorable holders of this high office (e.g., 2 Kings 22:2). Even here it is necessary for us to look closely to see what it is in the actions of a particular king which elicits the biblical writer's praise, since it is all too easy to suppose that it was basically a matter of personal piety and good intentions. Usually a far wider range of political, social, and religious issues can be seen to have been at stake.

Nowhere is this need to look closely at the whole range of duties and achievements of a king more necessary than in the case of King David, who was by any reckoning the most important of all the men of ancient Israel who held this authoritative position. Failure to do so can only lead to moral confusion, since it is evident that David was very much a man of his times, and he could be exceedingly brutal (e.g., 2 Sam. 8:2), lustful (2 Sam. 11:2–5), cunning (2 Sam. 11:14–27), and even spiteful and calculating (e.g., 2 Sam. 6:20–23). It would certainly be wrong to suppose that God was somehow indifferent to these facts when the Bible describes David as "a man after his [God's] own heart" (1 Sam. 13:14). David could also be resourceful (1 Sam. 30:26–31), as well as being deeply loyal and concerned for his soldiers who displayed immense loyalty to him (e.g., 2 Sam. 23:13–17). The many stories in which David is involved, and in general the very extensive coverage which the Old Testament accords to his career, all help to bring out the many-sidedness of the character of David—a matter of respect and interest to the people of ancient time, just as it is for us. He was a figure who appeared to be more than "life-sized," whose exploits had changed the entire history of Israel and who thereafter left a legacy which made the very memory of his name of the very greatest importance. He may not unreasonably be compared with such men as Alexander the Great, Pompey, and Julius Caesar. David became for Israel the pattern king—the "ideal"—the founder of the most important and long lasting of Israel's royal dynasties, and the type of the hoped-for, coming, divine Deliverer—the Messiah.

How are we then to understand David? Was he really a saint with a few warts, as a number of would-be, modern biographers have endeavored to describe him, or was he rather a villain—a ruthless and self-seeking man whose reputation rests on the flattering and one-sided accounts of him recorded by his courtiers and heirs? Neither of these views is properly fair to the biblical evidence, which was clearly at pains to preserve the truth about this man, else there would have been no reason at all for recalling several of the less worthy episodes of his life. Nor is it true that the Old Testament itself seeks to invest him with a devoutness and moral excellence which he so obviously did not possess. Rather it seeks to show how important was the office of the king for Israel's life and political stability, and more especially, how important was the bond which tied the people of Israel to the family of David through the principle of dynastic succession. So much in fact that is written in the Old Testament about David must be viewed as a kind of political theology, intended to draw the reader's attention to the important contribution that the family of David, and not least David himself, had made to the health and strength of Israel. We must bear in mind that the absence of good government is anarchy when as in Judges "every man did what was right in his own eyes" (cf. Judg. 17:6; 21:25). Similarly, even under a system of monarchy, when the kings are weak men, and when governmental power is achieved through plots and asassinations, the consequences for a people are disastrous. We do not have to look very far in the modern world to see how deeply valid are these truths of which the biblical writers were very fully aware.

When we come to look at the prayer of David that is our immediate focus. It is not at all hard to see how strongly present are these questions concerning the social and political significance of the king. The description of David as "a man after God's own heart" is essentially a reference to the way in which David had achieved certain things that were important and necessary for the divine purpose relating to Israel rather than being intended as a piece of personal commendation of his piety.

In turning to this prayer therefore we should first bear in mind some of the achievements that David had brought to Israel which contributed to the memory of his life and work as setting a kind of standard by which later ages and later kings were to be judged. In the first place there was one factor to which almost every story relating to David bears witness, either directly or indirectly. His military success was such that he brought peace and put an end to a succession of wars, tribal raids, feuds, and threats of invasions which had marred the life of Canaan for at least two centuries. When David appeared on the political scene no strong figure controlled the land, and Saul's kingship, for all the partial remedy which it brought, was still not strong enough to secure firm borders and internal security. Neither Egypt in the south nor the Syrians and Phoenicians in the north were sufficiently strong to establish control in Canaan. As a consequence the peace which David secured by his defeats of the Philistines and other neighboring nations, was the essential prerequisite of all other improvements in the quality of Israel's life. When the sword ruled the land in such an arbitrary and chaotic fashion, no one was secure and no trade could flourish. In this sense David was more truly the founder of the political nation of Israel than was Moses. His skill and accomplishments made possible a nation in which justice and security could properly begin to be established.

In a further development, David laid new foundations for Israel, since it was he who sought to weld the various tribes and ethnic groups into a unity. With men and women originating from a multiplicity of backgrounds and racial affinities David began to promote a sense of unity and to form the nucleus of an administration which treated all such groups equally and which sought to show that the welfare of each was bound up with the welfare of all. Instead of pulling itself apart, as we read in the book of Judges, David saw that the nation of Israel must begin to pull itself together. It was to this end that David brought the Ark of God into Jerusalem, and for this purpose that he established a central capital in this city. It was certainly also in the pursuit of this goal that David was so staunchly zealous to promote the worship of the one Lord God of Israel. The people could only be one people when there was truly one religion for all.

It is also clear that in a yet further way David greatly altered the entire situation of the Israelite tribes. This was in bringing to them a fame and international prestige which they had not previously enjoyed. He accomplished this first by defeating the Philistines who threatened Israel, then by subjugating the neighboring peoples where constant border fighting had weakened the safety and security of the tribes. Finally, by establishing treaties with the more distant peoples of Phoenicia and Syria, David lifted the Israelite tribes to a position of great prominence in the region of the eastern Mediterranean. A great many consequences were to follow from this, since it established new contacts and new opportunities for trade and cultural exchange. However indefinable the concept must remain, Israel's "reputation" among the nations of the world undoubtedly owed a great deal more to David than may at first sight be apparent. After David's death, Solomon sought more aggressively to promote and enhance this reputation, yet it was clearly David who laid its foundations. This too provides a significant background for an understanding of David's prayer.

The Prayer of David

The most important initial point to note in regard to David's prayer is that it was presented in response to a message from God brought by the prophet Nathan. This figure was almost certainly a court prophet whose task it was to provide religious guidance for the major affairs of state, and it is entirely in line with this that we discover that what Nathan had to disclose to David was an assurance of divine support for his kingship. The scene is set by David's intention to build a temple for the Lord God. Nathan's message counters this by a refusal to give David divine permission for such a task and the giving of an assurance that David's son Solomon is to build the temple (2 Sam. 7:12–13). Nevertheless, before coming to the point

of making this assurance regarding the temple, Nathan gives the even
more important message that God will build a "house" for David (2
Sam. 7:11). In fact so important are the political and social implications of Nathan's message to David that it is worth noting them in
full:

> "Now therefore thus you shall say to my servant David, 'Thus says the
> LORD of hosts, I took you from the pasture, from following the sheep,
> that you should be prince over my people Israel; and I have been with
> you wherever you went, and have cut off all your enemies from before
> you; and I will make for you a great name, like the name of the great
> ones of the earth. And I will appoint a place for my people Israel, and
> will plant them, that they may dwell in their own place, and be dis-
> turbed no more; and violent men shall afflict them no more, as formerly,
> from the time that I appointed judges over my people Israel; and I will
> give you rest from all your enemies. Moreover the LORD declares to
> you that the LORD will make you a house.'"
>
> (2 Samuel 7:8–11)

We can readily perceive the far-reaching implications of what is
promised here, not simply for David and his dynasty, but for the
entire people of Israel under a Davidic ruler. David is to achieve a
"great name," and the people of Israel are to be assured of a country
of their own to live in, of peace and security, with an end to the
depradations of "violent people." What we have here is in fact a
promise about kingship itself, drawing attention to all the benefits
which an honorable king can bring. It is in reality "political theology" of a very significant kind. We can also see that a subtle play of
words is introduced between the "house" that David was proposing
to build for God, in the form of a temple, and the "house" that God
would certainly build for David, in the form of a royal dynasty. The
temple and the royal dynasty of David are linked together in the
prophet's eyes.

On the basis of this prophecy from Nathan we can see how later
generations of citizens, both among David's own tribe of Judah, and
more widely of all Israel, came to attach the greatest trust and hope
in the benefits and security which the kingship of the house of David
would bring. It could so easily be interpreted as a divine guarantee
that, while a Davidic king ruled, all would be well for Israel, whatever the circumstances and the situation. God does not give uncon-

ditional political assurances of this kind, however, and it is precisely in order to make this point clear that David's prayer is offered. The prayer is then a prayer about human responsibility, and especially about the responsibility of those whose task it is to govern others.

> Then King David went in and sat before the LORD, and said, "Who am I, O Lord GOD, and what is my house, that thou hast brought me thus far? And yet this was a small thing in thy eyes, O Lord GOD; thou hast spoken also of thy servant's house for a great while to come, and hast shown me future generations, O Lord GOD! And what more can David say to thee? For thou knowest thy servant, O Lord GOD! Because of thy promise, and according to thy own heart, thou hast wrought all this greatness, to make thy servant know it. Therefore thou art great, O Lord GOD; for there is none like thee, and there is no God besides thee, according to all that we have heard with our ears. What other nation on earth is like thy people Israel, whom God went to redeem to be his people, making himself a name, and doing for them great and terrible things, by driving out before his people a nation and its gods? And thou didst establish for thyself thy people Israel to be thy people for ever; and thou, O LORD, didst become their God. And now, O LORD God, confirm for ever the word which thou hast spoken concerning thy servant and concerning his house, and do as thou hast spoken; and thy name will be magnified for ever, saying, 'The LORD of hosts is God over Israel,' and the house of thy servant David will be established before thee. For thou, O LORD of hosts, the God of Israel, hast made this revelation to thy servant, saying, 'I will build you a house'; therefore thy servant has found courage to pray this prayer to thee. And now, O Lord GOD, thou art God, and thy words are true, and thou hast promised this good thing to thy servant; now therefore may it please thee to bless the house of thy servant, that it may continue for ever before thee; for thou, O Lord GOD, hast spoken, and with thy blessing shall the house of thy servant be blessed for ever."

> (2 Samuel 7:18–29)

When we look into this prayer more closely we find that it brings to light some of the most perceptive and fascinating insights the Old Testament has to offer concerning the divine promises to the house of David. In form the prayer is a simple petition to God that God "confirm for ever the word . . . spoken concerning thy servant and concerning his house" (2 Sam. 7:25) and that it may please God "to bless the house of thy servant" (2 Sam. 7:29). It is essentially a prayer of petition asking God to keep the word already promised through the mouth of the prophet Nathan to David and his family! It would appear then, superficially at least, to be an entirely unnecessary prayer—asking God to honor a promise already given! Yet when we look in detail at what it contains, we see that it is in reality the most necessary of prayers, since it recognizes the mystery and reality of human frailty and that the divine word can only be fulfilled through fallible human beings. It is, as we shall examine more closely later, a prayer concerned with the way in which the divine grace and purpose can only be realized through erring and disobedient human beings. In one swift stroke therefore it strips away entirely the whole mythology which surrounded kingship in the ancient world, exalting the king as a semi-divine being, the "son of God," endowed with power and insight above ordinary individuals. Instead it recognizes that even David, the greatest and most successful of Israel's kings, was a mere human, subject to error and pride like others. David himself might stray from God's chosen path. If this were true of such a king, how much more would it be true of those sons and heirs who would succeed hm in the unknown years that lay ahead. Even the constitutional principle of establishing a royal dynasty which retained the kingship within a single family could not provide a guarantee that circumvented the dangers inherent in all human freedom. Bearing this overall insight in mind, we can see immediately why the prayer contains the particular affirmations that it does and why its petitionary element is so necessary.

The opening section of the prayer begins with a strong assertion of the weakness and unimportance of David and his house apart from God—"Who am I, O Lord GOD." This is not a mock display of humility on the part of an established man of greatness, but a genuine recognition that even the greatest of humans remains only a human. Even David cannot escape from the human condition. Against this the prayer sets the greatness of God, who is not comparable with any other being (2 Sam. 7:22). The whole of verses 19–22 are concerned with showing that the essential greatness that belongs to David and his achievements is not due to the king himself but rather to God and the promise that God has made. Here we are face to face with the experience of divine grace working in a human life!

The next section is concerned, in verses 23–24, with the greatness of Israel. This evidently has a twofold purpose. It establishes the primary point that the issue of a dynastic kingship which lies at the heart of the prayer is first and foremost concerned with the welfare and prosperity of God's own people Israel. Secondly, it shows that the high office of the king is not a private aggrandizement for one man and his family, but a heavy public responsibility. This would be true in any nation but all the more is it seen to be the case for Israel, which is viewed as uniquely the people of the Lord God. To be responsible for governing them is a very high and demanding office indeed! We discover here too that, although in its form the prayer appears to be concerned with the relationship between God and David, it is more broadly bound up with the larger question of the continuing welfare and success of Israel. The kingship provided by the house of David is seen as one of many gifts which God has granted to this people.

The final section of the prayer (2 Sam. 7:25–29) then contains the more overtly petitionary element in which David asks that God's word be fulfilled and the promise of blessing for the house of David kept. Set against the background it has been given, such a request to God now makes excellent sense: in the light of human weakness, from which not even kings are exempt, and in view of the high responsibility which is entailed by the government of a nation like Israel, may God grant the fulfillment of what has been promised. In this way we discover that prayer is a way by which God's promise may be realized. There are no unconditional guarantees, even from God, which would override and nullify the fact of human freedom. We must pray to become what we are. Thus the Davidic kingship has been given a powerful beginning through the person of David himself. The principle of a dynastic succession of kings has further been established through the promise made through the prophet Nathan ("the LORD will make you a house"). Neither of these factors can of themselves, however, override the reality of human freedom and the necessity for each succeeding ruler to remain faithful to God and to seek afresh to fulfill the divinely given responsibilities. In such fashion we discover that prayer becomes an indispensable means of communication whereby the promises of God can be confirmed and realized in each human life. We learn that it is necessary to pray with full sincerity: "Confirm . . . the word which thou hast spoken"!

The Significance of the Prayer

When we look across the broad sweep of the Old Testament we find that it evidences a kind of love-hate relationship to the institution of kingship. On the one hand it is viewed as a beneficial gift from God, without which people sink into anarchy and brutal conflicts. On the other hand it is so evidently a dangerous situation in which individuals acquire great power with which they may "do what is evil in the sight of the LORD." Not only will they then go astray themselves, but they will carry with them scores and maybe even thousands of other men and women who will follow their lead. A good king therefore was seen as a vital and life-protecting gift from God. Such a king was David, whose essential "goodness" lay not in his personal piety but rather in his military skills and political strength to establish peace and to make an orderly and secure life possible for Israel. In the later story of Israel as it unfolds through the pages of the Old Testament we find that very few of the kings who succeeded David came anywhere close to matching his achievements. For some the principle of allegiance to the dynasty of David seemed of the utmost importance, whereas for others the need for abandoning this in the interests of a wider choice became the guiding principle (cf. 1 Kings 12:16–20). When we look in detail at the history of Israel when it was under the rule of kings, we perceive how deeply this conflict of views regarding the principle of dynastic rule and of allegiance to the house of David has affected the way in which the story has been told. Eventually the true lordship over Israel was found in one who was greater than David (cf. Mark 12:35–37).

Not only does this prayer illuminate so much that would otherwise be difficult for us to understand and appreciate in the way in which the Bible writes about kingship and the house of David, it also brings us close to some vital issues concerning the working of God's grace. In a perfectly intelligible sense the great truths of faith appear as the great certainties of life. The Word of God appears sure and unassailable, and it is the words of men which appear to be changing and insubstantial. Divine grace must work through human beings, however, and the word of God has to be realized and fulfilled through fallible individuals. If it were otherwise then certainly the history of the Christian church would have been a great deal different. Just as the kingship of the house of David proved to be both blessing and failure, so may all such major institutions. No priest, no pope, no minister, no rabbi, nor yet any president or prime minister, can escape the limitations and temptations that belong to the human condition. We can only pray that God's grace and power may be evident in spite of, and even at times through, such human frailties and limitations. The perfect grace of God has to work, and to be seen to work, through erring and imperfect men and women.

It would not be difficult to use the many instances that come to light, both in Christian history and in our modern world, to claim that the grace and power of God are somehow impugned and nullified by such limitations, yet this is not so. Perhaps the greatest of all the marks of God's grace is in the respect that is shown to our human freedom. God does not turn persons into artificial robot figures whose individuality and freedom have been taken away. Always the heart of our praying must be that we may live up to our high calling, and that far from losing our humanity, we may achieve the full potential of what it means to be human by the imitation of God. Divine grace and human responsibility are not mutually exclusive of each other. On the contrary they are complementary, so that we may hope to realize the full measure of our human freedom and responsibility by surrendering ourselves fully to the grace of God. The prayer of David that God may "confirm his word" is therefore a prayer that may be echoed in every human life.

A further reflection may bring to a conclusion our consideration of the prayer of David. Within it lies the request that God would "confirm *for ever*" (italics added) the word spoken concerning David and his sons. Such longing that good and proven institutions, which had shown their worth, would last forever has been a frequently repeated feature of human history. We find that many people have prayed that not only royal dynasties but also cities, temples, nations, and empires would last "forever." In the course of the trials and upheavals of human history they have never done so. They have been swept aside in the torrents of war and social change, and in their passing they have appeared to carry with them so much of the hope and confidence that men and women have placed in them. All too often revolution and social change have mocked at the loyalty to and trust in human institutions that seemed destined to last forever. It is understandable that not only David himself therefore, as an individual person, but also many of the citizens of Israel and Judah should have believed that the royal house of David would provide "forever" a ruler to sit upon the throne in Jerusalem (cf. Ps. 132:12). All the greater was the shock when this hope was finally frustrated by the Babylonian armies who removed Zedekiah from his royal office in 587 B.C. (cf. 2 Kings 25:7). Something and someone irreplaceable appeared to have been taken from the life of the people of Israel. In the course of God's mysterious providence, however, this too was a necessary step towards the realization of that hope of a king and a kingdom which was "not of this world" (cf. John 18:33–38). The eternal reality of God, revealed to men and women clothed in the garments of truth, beauty, and goodness, is not limited to any one single family, building, or institution. Everlasting values may be experienced and discovered within the ever changing human scene, but such values are not themselves inevitably tied to the forms and figures which that scene reveals. Hope itself must learn to fasten its assurances not upon things that are necessarily temporal, but upon those which are eternal.

8
Another Prayer of DAVID

1 Chronicles 29:10–20

David and the Temple

This further prayer of David   is presented in the Chronicler's history of David's reign and must be reckoned among the most beautiful and impressive of all the biblical prayers. In order to appreciate its proper significance it is necessary to bear in mind the particular reasons and interests which have influenced the much revised and expanded picture of David's reign that the Chronicler has given. The reader of the story of David's life set out in 1 and 2 Samuel is left in no doubt at all that the two most enduring features of this king's achievements were to be found in his establishing of a dynasty of kings, and in his preparation for the building of a temple for God in Jerusalem (2 Sam. 24:18–25). We have already seen that the question of the continuance of the Davidic line of kings is made a central concern (2 Sam. 7:18–29). During the period of Babylonian rule over Judah (604–538 B.C.), however, with Zedekiah's capture and removal to Babylon in 587 B.C., both the reign of the Davidic dynasty was broken off and the temple of Jerusalem was deliberately destroyed. In one disastrous action the Babylonian soldiers appeared to have overturned the vital political and spiritual foundations of Israel's life. It was part of the Chronicler's purpose, writing after these events, to show that this was not so and that although these were major catastrophes the true foundations of spiritual life and hope lay elsewhere than in purely external institutions. The spiritual life was based on loyalty, obedience, and trust, and above all on a willingness to give of one's own most precious possessions for the service of God. It is this theme that provides the central focus of this further prayer of David. Giving to God, even to the point of sacrifice, not only makes all things possible for the work of God, but reveals the innermost secrets of trust in God.

It has long been noted by scholars that the portrait of David presented by the Chronicler in his revised account of Israel's past history differs a good deal from that given earlier in the books of Samuel. Nor is it difficult to see why this was so. That earlier record had been deeply concerned with the military and political attainments of David, since these had appeared to be the most enduring and essential aspects of his legacy. The passage of time and the ravages of the imperialistic control over Judah by Assyria and Babylon had left little of those attainments untouched and unaffected, however. It would have been all too easy, in consequence, to relegate David to a gallery of past heroes, no longer meaningful or relevant. The Chronicler shows that this was not in fact so, and that when rightly understood, the figure and work of David provided valuable guidance and lessons for the present. In a quite unique fashion what David had achieved in planning and preparing for the building of the temple had brought to light the most fundamental features of the spiritual life. These were to be found not in territorial acquisition nor in elegantly cut stone and timber but in the inner virtues of obedience, steadfast loyalty, and wholehearted giving to God. In order to bring out these points, and thereby to show that David had the greatest significance for the problems that were facing the Jewish people after the catastrophe of their exile in Babylon, the Chronicler recounts in dramatic fashion the situation that had faced David in his days:

> David assembled at Jerusalem all the officials of Israel, the officials of the tribes, the officers of the divisions that served the king, the commanders of thousands, the commanders of hundreds, the stewards of all the property and cattle of the king and his sons, together with the palace officials, the mighty men, and all the seasoned warriors. Then King David rose to his feet and said: "Hear me, my brethren and my people. I had it in my heart to build a house of rest for the ark of the covenant of the LORD, and for the footstool of our God; and I made preparations for building. But God said to me, 'You may not build a house for my name, for you are a warrior and have shed blood.'"
>
> (1 Chronicles 28:1–3)

Instead of David building the temple, which would have been appropriate since he was the founding-father of the royal dynasty, the task had been delegated to Solomon (1 Chron. 28:9–10). Even at this initial planning stage, when the preparations for the temple were only just beginning, the Chronicler recognized that it was a time for the searching of hearts and the questioning of motives, before there was any requirement to call in architects, draftsmen and engineers. The possibility of a temple for God had to begin with a serious and heart-searching self-examination, before site surveys were attended to and plans prepared:

> "And you, Solomon my son, know the God of your father, and serve him with a whole heart and with a willing mind; for the LORD searches all hearts, and understands every plan and thought. If you seek him, he will be found by you; but if you forsake him, he will cast you off for ever. Take heed now, for the LORD has chosen you to build a house for the sanctuary; be strong and do it."
>
> (1 Chronicles 28:9–10)

What is strikingly emphasized here in David's address to the Israelite officials and Solomon, in regard to the building of the temple, is that it could only be a worthwhile and successful venture if it were made the expression of a wholehearted and sincere love for God. We can, with a reasonable degree of confidence, go on to suggest reasons why this inner spiritual aspect of the great temple building project should have come to the fore in the time of the Chronicler. Most of all we must bear in mind that the greatest of the achievements of the community in Judah after the Babylonian exile had been the complete restoration of the Jerusalem temple between the years 520–516 B.C. (Ezra 5:2; 6:13–15). This had not been an easy task, and it encountered a good deal of opposition from certain sections of the community (Ezra 4:1–3). From the correspondence that is cited in Ezra 4—5 it appears that it took a good deal of patient and careful negotiation in order to obtain the approval and support of the Persian imperial authorities. Furthermore, the work of the prophet Haggai reveals that there was a surprising amount of indifference to the question of rebuilding the temple, doubting whether it was worthwhile at all, and especially insisting that the adverse economic situation required that it should be left until a more favorable time. At the period

when the Chronicler was writing his history, therefore, it is understandable that he should have been very conscious of the spiritual
climate in which he wrote and also very concerned to use his knowledge of the past in order to bring to light truths that he saw to be in
danger of neglect. It is in this regard that he deals at such length with
David's role in the building preparations for the first temple. That
age had been every bit as burdened with economic, political, and
military problems as was the present community, yet Israel's greatest
king had recognized the need for a great spiritual focal point—a
national shrine which would serve as a perpetual reminder to the
generations to come of the spiritual foundations of life and the necessity for a right attitude to the Lord God.

We can sense too the kind of objection that was being raised in
the Chronicler's time to the commitment of so much time and so
much of the community's hard won material resources to the rebuilding of the temple. In the first place it could not be denied that the
temple had lain in ruins for more than half a century. No doubt the
site was visited and used for acts of worship of a kind (cf. Jer. 41:5),
but there had been no proper building and no adequately organized
program of worship. A great many people had evidently become
used to regarding the temple area as a ruined site and had become
accustomed to thinking of the building as a feature of the past, belonging to an age of former national greatness. Certainly too there
were some who had associated the power and blessing of God so
closely with the temple that its destruction had appeared to mark
God's disowning of the people and their sanctuary (cf. Lam. 2:7). To
rebuild the temple therefore seemed to such people to be a return
to a false and discredited view of God and even to be attempting to overturn God's own verdict (cf. Isa. 66:1).

Even without such radical views however, it is evident that the
situation created by the Babylonian exile had brought about a very
changed attitude to the temple. It had brought into existence the
Jewish Dispersion (Diaspora), the process of scattering which was to
go on spreading and expanding until it was to spread the Jewish
people among all the nations of the earth. What meaning could a
temple in Jerusalem have for such people as these who, no matter

how loyal they wished to be to their faith, would seldom, if ever, have an opportunity for worshiping in the temple?

A third factor may also have been present. We know from Ezra 4:1-3 that opposition to the rebuilding of the temple threatened to become a divisive issue behind which we can readily sense the difficulties that were being experienced in reconciling the aims and interests of those who had been in exile in Babylon and had now returned with those who had remained. It was a real danger that by restoring the temple, instead of reconciling these differences and creating a new sense of unity in Jerusalem, the work on the temple might actually make the situation worse. Only by ensuring that there was a right understanding of what the temple was for, and by looking beyond it to the spiritual and moral values that it represented, could this bold new project succeed. It is these issues that are raised with such force in this further prayer ascribed to David and that have made it such a memorable expression of an inward spiritual sense of God and God's service.

The Prayer

In order to appreciate the prayer it is important to bear in mind the situation in which it was offered. Between the time of announcing the plan to build a temple and the offering of the prayer, David had brought together the materials and gifts that were needed for the task and the people of Israel had responded in similar fashion by a massive show of devotion and self-denial in bringing their contributions (1 Chron. 29:1-9). Now David was in a position to give thanks to God for all that had been brought together, to seek God's blessing upon it, and to show the importance of the spiritual values that such giving for God's work enshrined. All of this gains considerably in significance when we reflect that the Chronicler was very aware of the need for similar acts of generosity and devotion in regard to the rebuilding of the temple, an event which was relatively recent for him:

> Therefore David blessed the LORD in the presence of all the assembly; and David said: "Blessed art thou, O LORD, the God of Israel our father, for ever and ever. Thine, O LORD, is the greatness, and the power, and the glory, and the victory, and the majesty; for all that is in

the heavens and in the earth is thine; thine is the kingdom, O LORD, and thou art exalted as head above all. Both riches and honor come from thee, and thou rulest over all. In thy hand are power and might; and in thy hand it is to make great and to give strength to all. And now we thank thee, our God, and praise thy glorious name.

"But who am I, and what is my people, that we should be able thus to offer willingly? For all things come from thee, and of thy own have we given thee. For we are strangers before thee, and sojourners, as all our fathers were; our days on the earth are like a shadow, and there is no abiding. O LORD our God, all this abundance that we have provided for building thee a house for thy holy name comes from thy hand and is all thy own. I know, my God, that thou triest the heart, and hast pleasure in uprightness; in the uprightness of my heart I have freely offered all these things, and now I have seen thy people, who are present here, offering freely and joyously to thee. O LORD, the God of Abraham, Isaac, and Israel, our fathers, keep for ever such purposes and thoughts in the hearts of thy people, and direct their hearts toward thee. Grant to Solomon my son that with a whole heart he may keep thy commandments, thy testimonies, and thy statutes, performing all, and that he may build the palace for which I have made provision."

Then David said to all the assembly, "Bless the LORD your God."

(1 Chronicles 29:10–20)

A number of features about this prayer are immediately striking. In the first place the language is beautiful and clearly reveals a long and rich tradition of public prayer which sought to express some of the deepest truths of faith. Secondly the element of petition to God is focused upon two specific requests: "Keep for ever such purposes and thoughts in the hearts of thy people, and direct their hearts toward thee"; "Grant to Solomon my son that with a whole heart he may keep thy commandments." These two requests are clearly of different kinds, the first concerned with a very broad feature of the quality of piety desired for Israel and the second directed more specifically to the temple. We can readily see how the two were linked together, because the temple was to be a continuing vehicle and symbol of such piety. For the rest of the prayer is replete with a long introduction showing precisely who the Lord God is and how weak, dependent, and short-lived are the men and women who may grow to worship God. By this means the prayer establishes a basis of self-understanding and is concerned with setting a proper perspective for all life by showing that this requires some awareness of the Lord and

Giver of life. Without this men and women think of themselves as the owners and masters of the world, dispensing life and death as they wish, instead of recognizing that they are only stewards of the God who has first fashioned every thing and every person.

We may note how the prayer falls into four well-defined sections. The first of these (1 Chron. 29:10–13) is entirely devoted to defining who God is. By heaping up words describing all that is great, good, and powerful the worshiper's mind is first alerted to the fact that any true and worthy prayer, adequate to describe who God really is, is quite impossible. God far transcends even the richest and grandest concepts that our minds can frame. God's Being exceeds our mental capacity to grasp, or to understand. All that we can hope to do is to recognize that God exists and that all our sense of greatness and grandeur points us toward the fact of this existence but is unable to reveal it fully to us. In turn our own human condition is a gift to us from God, who has not simply launched us upon the sea of life, thereafter to find our own way, but constantly touches and directs us. In this light the aim, the mystery, and the power of all true prayer are only to be found when we learn to give thanks and praise to God. Far from such praise being a needlessly repeated act of congratulation to our maker, it is the ever necessary and totally inadequate discovery of our true selves in the wonder of life that God has made possible. Constantly we realize that our perspectives have become foreshortened and our sense of wonder dulled by our failure to recall the infinite miracle of God and the majesty and variety of life. The element of praise is the essential beginning of this prayer, since it provides the indispensable foundation for the further elements which follow.

The second element in the prayer (1 Chron. 29:14–16) consists of a meditation on the theme "Who am I, and what is my people?" We should certainly have expected to find here some recollection of the special calling and destiny of Israel and the special purpose within this that God had declared for the house of David. Instead we find neither of these things, but rather a recognition of the creature-liness of all human beings and the frailty and shortness of life when compared with the eternal nature of God. "Our days on the earth are like a shadow, and there is no abiding." With such a thought the prayer contrasts the weakness and uncertainty that belongs to our human existence with the greatness of God. Nor are we really in a position to give anything to God, for everything comes from God, and we are merely giving back some of what has been given to us. The language is beautiful and rich in its imagery, but we should be very careful not to let it hide from us the depth of its theological insight. Our awareness of God, our sense of need to learn more about God, our concern to frame some mental picture of what God is like, all find their origin in our own awareness of life. The questions "What is man?" and "Who is God?" are not distinct from one another, since it is when we begin to search out the frontiers and limitations of human life, that we become conscious of the mystery that has given this life to us, and in turn of the Ultimate Source of all life.

In particular the imagery used that we are "strangers before thee, and sojourners," draws upon a unique aspect of ancient Israelite society. Those who were "strangers" were those who were foreign citizens, owning allegiance elsewhere, who lived in the community for a time without taking up permanent residence. Such persons were merchants and foreign officials. The "sojourner," however, was a person from another community who had left it and had taken up permanent residence in one of the towns or villages of Israel. The sojourner now lived among this people, although the fact that his or her roots originally lay elsewhere could not be hidden nor entirely forgotten. This is how David's prayer envisages our human existence. It has no permanency, since we remain conscious of when it began every time we celebrate a birthday, and we know that it must one day come to an end, so that we can never fully and completely "belong" to the world. Set in such a light, the offerings that are made to God are simply a way of returning such things as God has given us to use for such time as we need them.

It is in the third section of the prayer (1 Chron. 29:17–18) that it turns to the highest point of spiritual intensity, turning from praise and reflection into active petition: "keep for ever such purposes and thoughts in the hearts of thy people, and direct their hearts toward thee." As a preface to this plea, however, we are reminded that God knows the innermost thoughts of the human heart, and takes pleasure in its integrity and generosity of spirit. From this perspective what matters most to God, in regard to the wealth of giving displayed by David and the people in making ready to build a temple, is that it has provided an opportunity for demonstrating such genuineness in their love for God. It has revealed in an outward and practical fashion the inner feelings and thoughts that the people have about and for God. It is this inner feeling and love of God that provides the impulses and reasons of all true worship. We are here brought very close to that world-transforming insight declared by Jesus to the woman of Samaria: "God is spirit, and those who worship him must worship in spirit and in truth" (John 4:24). By such an understanding all the institutions and apparatus of worship are penetrated into their most secret inner shrines. In the light of such a truth the purpose, meaning, and historical importance of the temple of Jerusalem become plain. This was not a building that would last forever, since it would be subject to the ravages of decay and war, as is every other human edifice. As a sacred building, however, it would express and enshrine a genuine love for God that could live on "for ever" in the minds and hearts of those who had learned to worship through its agency.

The concluding section of the prayer (1 Chron. 29:19) concerns itself directly with the figure of Solomon, whose life and work we shall have opportunity to consider more fully in examining two of his prayers. In the present context the content of the request concerning this king must be regarded as of a deliberately broad character: "Grant to Solomon my son that with a whole heart he may keep thy commandments." Clearly it represents no small or unworthy desire on the part of a father for his son and heir. Here it must be seen as intended less in a purely private and family context than in one concerned with the nature of the royal office and with the whole range of public and civil administration. Much about Solomon's life and work was to leave a tarnished and unpleasant memory in Israel. More even than his brash and arrogant successor, Rehoboam, Solomon's reign engendered the resentment and hostility which led to rebellion during his reign and the break-up of the united Israelite empire after his death. It mattered very much to the Chronicler therefore, in presenting this prayer at a time when there was no longer any king ruling in Israel, to show that David had not envisaged that his sons and successors should rule as irresponsible and unrestrained despots.

More also, it mattered greatly to show that the first and foremost of
the king's duties was to attend to the needs of public and national
worship by the building of the temple. As we have seen, this was an
achievement that had been emulated in the post-exilic age by a more
distant heir of David, Zerubbabel, who never attained to re-
establishing the royal throne in Jerusalem. He, and his supporters,
however, by restoring the temple, had effectively fulfilled one of the
prime responsibilities of the monarchy. In this fashion the long-
established and highly regarded bond which associated the temple of
Jerusalem with the family of David had not been altogether broken.

The final injunction from David to all the assembly: "Bless the
LORD your God," was not merely an appropriate conclusion to the
prayer, but an important way of involving the people as a whole in
its requests. Public prayer involves a unique triangle of interests between the leader, the people, and God. Its reality and effectiveness
are closely tied to the extent that all three interests are adequately
expressed.

The Significance of the Prayer

Reflection upon the true nature and purpose of worship presents
us with a number of strangely ambivalent and even apparently con-
tradictory features. On one side we cannot but be conscious that it
has, throughout the entire history of human civilization, given rise
to the most magnificent buildings. Travel where we will across the
world, we encounter in every country immense and costly temples,
monasteries, and sanctuaries, built through the skill and ingenuity of
mostly unknown architects and engineers, who sought to build
"something beautiful for God." Many of the most magnificent of
them have long since fallen into ruin and decay, so that what we can
now see is only one small part of the costly sacrifice and devotion
which made them possible. To the buildings themselves we should
need to add the rich traditions of ritual, sacred dance and song,
priestly ministry, and service which go to make up the outward forms
and institutions of worship. To the eye of the undiscerning tour-
ist and onlooker such worship has all the marks of costly
extravagance and outward pomp. In explaining and justifying this
extraordinary phenomenon of human endeavor, however, we should

be compelled to turn to inner feelings and spiritual impulses in order to interpret its importance. It is not, in the last analysis of theological evaluation, the architectural design nor the costly extravagance of marble and precious metal that makes these buildings so vital an expression of men's and women's belief in God. It is rather the inner conviction that only the greatest and most beautiful creations of human skill can be adequate to symbolize the greatness of God:

> Give all thou canst; high Heaven rejects the lore
> Of nicely-calculated less or more;
>> (W. Wordsworth, "Ecclesiastical Sonnet 43")

In a manner that is extraordinarily bold and consistent, this prayer of David sees in the preparations for the building of a temple for the Lord in Jerusalem, the opportunity for men and women to show the genuineness of their worship. The high expense of the building and the elaborateness of the design will not be simply an expression of Israel's new-found prestige among the nations of the world, but a genuine mark of its devotion. The outward form will be a sign of the inner intensity of its faith and gratitude.

In recognizing this need to match outward form and beauty with inward sincerity and love of God, the prayer brings together this essential two-sidedness of worship. External symbol and internal devotion are to belong together so that the one may be the stimulus and constant reminder of the need for the other. It is almost as if the building itself is to go on saying to each succeeding generation of men and women in Israel: "Keep for ever such purposes and thoughts in the hearts of thy people." In turn another, contrasting problem would one day arise when, with torches and battering-rams, the soldiers of Nebuchadnezzar, King of Babylon, would raze the building to the ground. Would that then not appear to mark an irreversible defeat for God? The answer implicit in this prayer of David's is clearly that it would not. The significance and worth of the building would lie only in the love and piety that it made possible. In turn that same love and generosity of spirit could make another temple possible, or it could become evident in a multiplicity of other ways. The destruction of a building would not be the end of worship but only the occasion for finding new ways of expressing it.

In reflecting upon the scale of human endeavor to build temples and shrines for God throughout the ages, it could readily suggest to our minds that this has been a fruitless and ultimately futile quest. This is in reality not so, and we can, armed with the insights of David's prayer, go on to see that the greatness of this endeavor lies in the way that it has passed on from one generation to another the vision of a great Creator, who desires to be worshiped through creative energies and costly devotion of his creatures.

9
A Prayer of
SOLOMON
1 Kings 3:5–15

Solomon the Man

David had brought to Israel a vitally important gift in the form of political stability and a relative measure of peace. From a situation in which Israel had been seriously threatened with being swallowed up by the nations which surrounded it, it had instead become the strongest nation in the region. Above all the threat posed by the Philistines had been removed. Yet the internal security of the Israelite tribes was a far from settled question, as the record of the two major revolts against David's rule shows. First Absalom had led a rebellion against his own father which had forced the king to flee from Jerusalem. Then the Benjaminite Sheba had led a revolt against David (2 Sam. 20), undoubtedly drawing upon much of the resentment felt by the Benjaminites against the eclipse of the royal family of Saul. For all that David had achieved therefore by way of increasing the military strength and international reputation of Israel, an important role remained for his successor to fill as a conciliator and administrator. The person upon whom these responsibilities fell was Solomon, the son of David by Bathsheba, and the first of his prayers that we are to consider is centrally concerned with these issues. First of all, however, it is important that we should look at the circumstances which brought Solomon to the throne, and some of the unresolved questions which surround them.

David had several wives in his royal household, and consequently a large number of sons who might potentially have been regarded as his heirs. He himself lived to a good old age, leaving apparently the question of who was to succeed him unresolved. The prayer of David that we have looked at in 2 Samuel 7:18–29 focused upon the divine assurance that he would be the founder of a long dynasty of kings, without defining which one of his sons would be his immediate successor. The stories that are preserved in 1 Kings 1—2 show that, in the event, even before David's actual death the transition to the rule of Solomon was not achieved without conflict. This led ultimately to Solomon's execution of Adonijah, his elder brother and chief rival, and to the putting to death of Joab, David's now aged military commander. In fact the period of changeover to the new king was not complete until a good deal of blood had been shed, including that of Shimei, to whom David had sworn an oath of protection (1 Kings 2:8–9, 36–46). These actions certainly cannot have been looked upon with indifference by the population, and they undoubtedly served to inflame old rivalries and to reopen old wounds, which David had endeavored with some success to reconcile and heal. Like a new and brash commander determined to impress his personality and resolve upon his wavering troops, Solomon came to the throne with all the vigor and ruthlessness which he regarded as necessary to hold his kingdom together. The final consequences of his actions are far from easy for the critical historian to assess. Of more immediate concern for an understanding of the first of Solomon's prayers is the recognition that the new king's tough and ruthless policies brought fear and dismay to his subjects. It is true that he succeeded in holding the kingdom together, and thereby in preventing the break-up of the unity of the various tribal factions, and also in gaining for them a certain international prestige for his culture and learning. Old sores were reopened, however, and the heavy taxation and slave labor service which his projects demanded led to further understandable rebellion. It is not difficult for us to see, therefore, that Solomon himself contributed in no small measure to the disaffection which led to the break-up of his united kingdom after his death. From that point onwards Israel and Judah were to pursue separate political roads for two centuries, before the imperialistic expansion of Assyria brought an end to the Northern Kingdom.

It would be easy, at a first consideration therefore, to dismiss Solomon as just another oriental despot, who has had many peers and emulators at other times. Yet he had held the kingdom of Israel together, and when the threat from Assyria emerged later, the small kingdom of Judah fared better, and survived longer, than did the Northern Kingdom which had turned its back on the house of David. It is not altogether surprising then that the later historians of Israel, whose work has preserved for us in the Old Testament virtually all that we know about Solomon, should have viewed him in a strangely mixed fashion. On the one hand he was the heir of David—tough, assertive, and ruthless—yet on the other he was seen to have disregarded some of the most essential requirements of a just king. It is quite appropriate therefore that Solomon's prayer should be concerned with the question of the wisdom that is necessary for good government.

The setting for Solomon's prayer is an occasion of worship, offered, rather surprisingly in view of the newly enhanced importance of Jerusalem as Israel's capital and central religious shrine, at the ancient sanctuary of Gibeon. Already before this event, however, the reader is alerted to two facts which were later seen to be connected with each other. The first of these (1 Kings 3:1) is contained in the report that Solomon had contracted a marriage alliance with Egypt by his marriage to one of the daughters of the Egyptian pharaoh. This was certainly a remarkable indication of the new honor and prestige that the kingdom of Israel had acquired, and Solomon had no doubt sought such an arrangement precisely for this purpose. It was a requirement for Israel if its kingship was to be esteemed like that of the nations round about (cf. 1 Sam. 8:5). At the same time such actions, especially when contracted with so eminent an international figure as the Egyptian pharaoh, demanded certain concessions which ultimately had religious repercussions. The biblical historian could therefore regard such marriages with foreign women as a major factor in the ultimate break-up of Solomon's kingdom after his death (cf. 1 Kings 11:1–8). The second fact concerns the continuance of worship by Israelites at the older shrines outside Jerusalem, because the temple had not yet been built there (1 Kings 3:2). Prominent among these older sanctuaries was that at Gibeon, situated not far from Jerusalem and particularly important to the tribe of Benjamin who still felt deep resentment at the passing of the kingship from the house of Saul. Why Solomon should have singled out this shrine situated on a hill-top, and should have been so lavish in his worship at it—"Solomon used to offer a thousand burnt offerings upon that altar" (1 Kings 3:4)—is not made clear. The historian is content with the explanation that no proper temple had yet been built in Jerusalem. At any rate it was this shrine which provided the occasion for Solomon to engage in a prayerful meditation before God, which the Old Testament records as transpiring "in a dream by night" (1 Kings 3:5).

The Prayer of Solomon

The practice of spending a whole night in a sanctuary in order to receive some illumination or answer from the God who was present there is widely known in the ancient world. It has a special name as the rite of incubation. Quite evidently the story in which Solomon's prayer is incorporated envisages the king taking part in such a rite and receiving the answer to his prayer very much in a manner analogous to the oracular response which such a practice of incubation sought. Furthermore, the general tone of the story is highly favorable to Solomon. Not only is this the case in a broad sense, but it is especially noteworthy that it commends Solomon for possessing precisely the virtue and skills which many in ancient Israel, especially those living under this ruler's tough measures, would not have admitted to be true. It is important to the historian therefore to bring the story to the reader's attention at the beginning of the account of Solomon's reign in order to make it clear that, in spite of the many aspects of his reign which were oppressive and distasteful, God had nonetheless been with him and worked through him. In other words the story could be described in modern terms as a piece of royalist propaganda. We shall need to look at this feature of the story later. The currency of stories of this kind, intended to praise the virtues and office of the king, is found elsewhere in the ancient world, and particular instances are well known from ancient Egypt. It is not on this account, however, that the story most concerns us but rather for what it has to teach about the purpose and value of petitionary prayer. We may therefore consider the prayer primarily in this light:

> At Gibeon the LORD appeared to Solomon in a dream by night; and God said, "Ask what I shall give you." And Solomon said, "Thou hast

shown great and steadfast love to thy servant David my father, because he walked before thee in faithfulness, in righteousness, and in uprightness of heart toward thee; and thou hast kept for him this great and steadfast love, and hast given him a son to sit on his throne this day. And now, O LORD my God, thou hast made thy servant king in place of David my father, although I am but a little child; I do not know how to go out or come in. And thy servant is in the midst of thy people whom thou hast chosen, a great people, that cannot be numbered or counted for multitude. Give thy servant therefore an understanding mind to govern thy people, that I may discern between good and evil; for who is able to govern this thy great people?"

It pleased the LORD that Solomon had asked this. And God said to him, "Because you have asked this, and have not asked for yourself long life or riches or the life of your enemies, but have asked for yourself understanding to discern what is right, behold, I now do according to your word. Behold, I give you a wise and discerning mind, so that none like you has been before you and none like you shall arise after you. I give you also what you have not asked, both riches and honor, so that no other king shall compare with you, all your days. And if you will walk in my ways, keeping my statutes and my commandments, as your father David walked, then I will lengthen your days."

And Solomon awoke, and behold, it was a dream.

(1 Kings 3:5–15)

It is evident immediately that the story is, by its very design, couched in a form that is very favorable to Solomon. Not only does it imply that he was a very wealthy and honorable ruler, but it affirms that he loved and sought wisdom more than wealth or honor and that it is for this wisdom that he should be most remembered. We may begin a more detailed consideration of the prayer itself by looking at what it consists of. It opens with a strong affirmation of praise to God for three things God has done (1 Kings 3:6–9). The Lord God had made David a very great king, so that behind his great achievements and victory we can discern the great achievements and victory of God. High in the list of these great achievements is God's making of David the founder of a royal dynasty, so that in the situation by which Solomon had become king there appeared an element of divine confirmation for David himself: "thou hast kept for him this great and steadfast love, and hast given him a son to sit on his throne this day" (1 Kings 3:6). The concern here is with the principle of a dynastic monarchy and the hopes for social and political stability which that would bring. The second element in the thanksgiving to God relates to Solomon having become king, although he was "but a little child." This was evidently meant metaphorically rather than literally, since we have already been given a full account of the circumstances in which Solomon attained to his father's throne, and these are certainly not indicative of a very youthful or immature person. Rather this note of royal innocence and self-deprecation was intended to contrast the great wisdom and knowledge possessed by God with the inevitable limitations of the insight and knowledge possessed by any human. In spite of his famous father and his privileged office he remained a mere man! The third element of the thanksgiving turns its attention to consider the greatness and size of the people of Israel, over whom Solomon is to reign. Who would be equal to such a task as this? As so often in the biblical prayers that we have considered we find that a major part of it is concerned with the offering of praise and thanksgiving to God. This is certainly not the primary purpose of the prayer here, which is genuinely petitionary in its character. Nevertheless the words of praise to God establish the framework of ideas and theological perspective which alone can make the element of petition truly meaningful and effective.

The petition proper is then presented with a stark and simple dignity: "Give thy servant therefore an understanding mind to govern thy people, that I may discern between good and evil" (1 Kings 3:9). What is meant by an understanding mind, capable of discerning between good and evil, is then very skillfully and wittily illustrated by the story of the conflicting claims of motherhood of the two harlots, which follows in verses 16–28. Wisdom, as understood in this fashion, is not then mere learning that could be acquired by gathering facts and committing them to memory. Rather it lies in shrewdness of judgment—insight into the hidden motives and desires that lie behind the words and actions of men and women. It is, in a broad sense, knowledge of life itself and of the ways of people. In a special way it involved the ability to make just laws and to administer them wisely.

From the perspective of a study of prayer, the petition offered here is a very pertinent one. Prayer is closely related to desire, so that whatever form of words we use, what we most deeply and privately desire is what we are actually praying for. Yet our desires and longings need to be guided and directed in the best and most healthful ways. We have to learn to pray in a right fashion by directing our petitions towards the most worthy goals. This is indeed part of the very purpose of prayer and is the reason why we can often learn so much from the prayers of others. Do you sincerely want to be rich? Do you sincerely want to be famous? Solomon's prayer frankly and fully recognizes the fact that, whether we admit it to ourselves or not, these are likely to be high on the list of our innermost desires. However, it values one gift from God higher than these: that of wisdom to govern well and to discern the difference between good and evil. In this way Solomon's prayer points to a central factor in all petitionary prayer which calls for careful reflection and theological caution. If petitionary prayer is no more than the presentation to God of a list of things that we would like to receive or to have done for us, it makes a nonsense of all prayer, because it sees God as no better than a weak and indulgent parent. Since God is loving and righteous by nature, the gifts conferred through prayer must be loving and righteous for use in the world. Prayer is not a means by which we can become the spoiled children of God!

We have already touched upon the fact that this prayer occurs in a story concerning Solomon which is intended to present the king in as positive and praiseworthy a light as was possible. Nor is it difficult to see that the reputation and memory of Solomon became a very tarnished one so far as Israel was concerned in biblical times. The Old Testament is faithful in preserving many of the details of the controversial reputation Solomon had left. His ambition, his extravagance in immense building projects, and his own lavish lifestyle exceeded those of any other ruler of ancient Judah or Israel. He was the heir of David, however, and when the northern tribes rebelled after his death, they found themselves with rulers who were no better, and in most respects much weaker, than Solomon had been. It is in this light that the historian, writing at a time when the Northern Kingdom had been lost to the Assyrians and when Judah also was seriously threatened and weak, saw new interest in this story of Solomon's plea for wisdom. Taken by itself it drew fresh attention to those values which alone can make a kingdom great. Beyond this, it enabled the biblical writer to reassert his own conviction, still zealously kept and guarded in his own day, that God had never abandoned the house and family of David. In his time there were still sons of David, who might yet bring greatness to the throne of their revered ancestor, and it is with this hope in mind that he endeavored to show that even the person of Solomon, whose reign had caused such bitterness, had not been devoid of those values and insights for which the kingship of David stood.

The Significance of the Prayer

The most interesting and challenging feature of this famous prayer of Solomon lies in the extraordinary openness of the offer which came to Solomon in a dream: "and God said, 'Ask what I shall give you.'" It is only in our prayers and meditations that we can become as free and as open as this with ourselves. What is it that we want more than anything else in the world: riches? fame? wisdom? Each of them presents its own possibilities and attractions. Most probably, however, we are never as honest as this with ourselves, and we are, if we are Christians, likely to be very sensitive to the dangers that lurk in the nursing of ambitions that can become too dominant and ultimately destructive. At various times certain religious orders and groups have practiced a form of "open" confession in which its members have looked into their own hearts in order to discover their innermost being and their most secret faults. How difficult and at times dangerous such a path can be! Perhaps the value and significance of our own private prayers would be greatly helped if we paused and imagined God saying to each one of us: "Ask what I shall give you." What would we choose to seek from God? Would not such an imagined situation expose immediately the self-interest that is present in so much of what we ask God for and compel us to a new thinking out of our religious priorities. According to ancient tradition those who visited the oracle at the famous Greek shrine of Delphi would be given the injunction "Know thyself!" Does not the divine offer made to Solomon in his dream amount to a very similar directive? The difficulty that presents itself time and again when we endeavor to pray some familiar and worthy petition to God is that we do not mean it. Would not the value of such a prayer be entirely transformed if we could first discover for ourselves that we do not mean it? Such prayers represent only the surface world of what we think the religious situation demands that we should ask of God. We are thus compelled to go on praying the same prayer day after day until at last we can come to a point where we may dare to trust that we are beginning to offer it "in sincerity and truth."

The biblical portrait of Solomon does not present him as a figure of very great piety and we have already drawn attention to the way in which the accounts of his reign point out serious blemishes in his character. The vaunted splendor of his court and the extravagance of his lifestyle were bought with the blood and sweat of his subjects, who were ultimately provoked into rebellion by his excess. Even several of the stories concerning his wisdom associate it with a certain wit and cleverness with words rather than with any very deep appreciation that the foundations of a kingdom have to be laid with justice and fairness. This aspect of the biblical tradition finds further confirmation in the later ascription to him of writings such as the Song of Songs and the Wisdom of Solomon (in the Old Testament Apocrypha). There is a certain paradox therefore in the story concerning Solomon's prayer to God that he might be given wisdom above any other divine gift. Yet we must not dismiss the story on this account, nor suppose that the biblical writer did not himself sense the tensions that his many-sided picture of Solomon's character and achievements presented. We are all subject to inner conflicts and turmoil in which we can only establish any spiritual priorities with great difficulty. That we may, in moments of insight and reflection, come to recognize the need for a very high and noble ideal for living is highly probable. That we shall thereafter be able to live up to these ideals with a steadfastness and directness of aim is much less likely. The need is to set a clear standard for our lives through prayer and then to go on reminding ourselves of that prayer and of our commitment to its goal. Immediately this will show up the dangers of two extremes. If the standard is set so high that we have no hope of attaining it we shall readily slip further and further down the slope of unreality. The gap between what we are and what we want to become will be so great that we shall either not notice or not be concerned to correct the difference between our real selves and our ideals. There is contrastingly the possibility of falling into the other extreme, whereby we content ourselves with our spiritual honesty and unpretentiousness, not realizing how much it implies the abandonment of any really high or worthy ideal. It is not difficult to see that, in presenting his picture of Solomon, the biblical writer has tried to be faithful to the two-sidedness of Solomon's character. That there was in Solomon's achievements a touch of greatness and a nobility of ambition could not be ignored; yet at the same time there was no need to hide the dissensions and divisions that his ambitions aroused. None of us will achieve all that we set out to do. Solomon's prayer, however, is a worthy and challenging reminder that we shall not achieve anything worthwhile at all if we do not set some clear priority for ourselves.

10
Another Prayer of SOLOMON

1 Kings 8:22–53

The Building of the Temple

   The visitor to present-day Jerusalem is struck by the appearance
of one building above all others in that historic city. Against a skyline
of modern buildings appears a remarkable edifice which is self-
evidently a sanctuary of some kind. This is the Haram esh-Sherif, the
Noble Shrine, which, with its beautiful golden dome and ornate tiled
exterior, is one of the most sacred buildings of Islam. Tradition associates it directly with Muhammad himself and a heavenly dream
vision which he experienced there. The site, however, was a sacred
one long before the rise of Islam, and forms part of the temple area
of Judaism where Herod the Great erected the great Jewish temple
which figures prominently in the New Testament. Earlier still a
temple had been built on the site by the returned Jewish exiles from
Babylon under the leadership of Zerubbabel in the sixth century B.C.
This was the most eminent of their achievements in reestablishing
their religious life after the destruction of much of Jerusalem by the
Babylonians. Before this a temple had been built on the location by
Solomon, whose name, perhaps more than that of any other, has
come to be associated with the historic religious site. It must be
regarded as virtually certain that, even before the days of Solomon,
the location had been used as the setting for a religious sanctuary of
some kind, and a primary reason for believing this is not hard to find.
The Haram esh-Sherif houses a remarkable and enormous outcrop of
natural rock, which clearly invited veneration and which has acquired during the known history of the site symbolic associations as

the very foundation stone of the Earth. This rock was probably at one time in use as an altar.

All of this adds up to a story of great religious interest, since this famous location has been in almost continuous use for more than three millennia as a place of central religious importance. It has witnessed great religious transformations—Canaanite, Israelite, Jewish, Roman, and now finally Muslim usage. Significantly too it figures very centrally in the controversies within Judaism which witnessed the birth of the Christian church. Twice within the biblical period the temple buildings which stood there suffered deliberate and massive destruction at the hands of foreign conquerors, first by the Babylonians (587 B.C.) and secondly by the Romans (A.D. 70). The sense of tragedy, humiliation, and divine judgment associated with these events, still annually remembered within Judaism as a national day of mourning (9th Ab), and the offering of prayer at the "Wailing Wall"—a surviving part of the wall of the Herodian Temple—have become meaningful rituals in Jewish life. In all respects therefore the site of the Noble Shrine in Jerusalem, now especially sacred to Islam, forms one of the most famed and sacred religious sites in history. Uniquely too it forms a central meeting place for the three great monotheistic world religions—Judaism, Christianity, and Islam. To learn something of the history of this one small space on the earth's surface is to discover some of the deepest and most central truths regarding the religious aspirations of humankind.

It is necessary here, however, to pause to consider a certain paradox in the recognition that this should be so. To the modern mind religion is about ideas, cultural values, and moral and spiritual aspirations. It appears more than a little strange that a particular place, the more prominent feature of which was nothing more than a massive and unusual outcrop of rock, should have become so inseparably and passionately linked with the understanding of God. Many have died defending the place, and in the destruction of the temples that have stood there many have felt that their honor, their hopes, and even their God, experienced terrible defeats.

Certainly it is not difficult to recognize that religion, not simply Jewish and Christian religion, has always been deeply concerned with places and buildings. People have visualized and symbolized their experience of God in the erection of monuments, altars, and ultimately elaborate temple buildings which have given outward expression to this sense of the "presence" of deity. From the remarkable ancient step-towers—the Ziggurats—of ancient Sumeria to modern cathedrals, synagogues, and mosques, religion has been as much and often more a concern of architects and pilgrims, as of the philosophizings of the human mind. In his book, *The Idea of the Holy*, Rudolph Otto sought to describe this characteristic feature of religion as a sense of the *mysterium tremendum*—an awesome sense of wonder and mystery—which pervades certain places and buildings. In its earliest manifestations, of course, such a sense of fearful wonder was linked with natural phenomena and events—storms, mountains, eclipses of the sun and moon—but later came to be associated with buildings and rituals which were the work of men and women. It is not difficult to discern a rather paradoxical element in this which has continued to excite religious thought and to provoke profound reflection. In a very real sense religion is about what is given to us; it comes from God and impinges on our lives as an awareness that God exists before us and comes seeking us through our experiences. Religion is also a human part of life, concerned with buildings, activities, and ministries all of which are the work of people. We can even carry this further in noting that religion is ultimately a very private, inward, and personal experience, in which we sense that we are, in the last resort, alone with God. Yet before this very spiritual and inward side of religion can reach us, it must be preserved, proclaimed, and communicated by a vast range of outward forms and ceremonies. Religion is God-given, therefore, and yet made by humans; it is also very visibly formal and external, yet essentially very private and internal. We may even go on to press these striking paradoxes further, since religion is first and foremost a revelation from God, yet also it is necessarily a seeking and a discovery on our part. In a remarkable way all of these contrasting features are touched upon and highlighted by the magnificent prayer of dedication for the temple of Jerusalem delivered by Solomon. In one sense it is very markedly a prayer about a very specific building and a very specific tradition associated with it; yet it is also one of the most searchingly reflective prayers in the whole Bible regarding the

nature of religion. It is very conscious of the physical and external
side of religion, epitomized by the majestic and expensive edifice
which Solomon's initiative and the accumulated skills of many
craftsmen had erected. It is aware that such dedicated expertise and
devotion would become pointless and without meaning if the worship of the temple and even the knowledge of its mere existence did
not evoke a truly inward and spiritual response in the hearts of men
and women. It was to be a "house of prayer," not only in the sense
that prayers could be offered within it, but that it would be a constant
reminder of the possibility and power of prayer.

The Prayer

The prayer itself is a very long one—one of the longest of the
entire Bible—and it begins with a recollection of who God is and
how God's past goodness has enriched the life of people. It is also
very strikingly aware of the impossibility for men and women to
comprehend God (cf. 1 Kings 8:27) and of grasping the full understanding of God's being and power. In this context prayer can never
be a claim upon God but must rather be a way by which men and
women can broaden and deepen their understanding of life and
thereby open their lives more fully to the fact of infinite possibility
God means for them.

> Then Solomon stood before the altar of the LORD in the presence of
> all the assembly of Israel, and spread forth his hands toward heaven;
> and said, "O LORD, God of Israel, there is no God like thee, in heaven
> above or on earth beneath, keeping covenant and showing steadfast love
> to thy servants who walk before thee with all their heart; who hast kept
> with thy servant David my father what thou didst declare to him; yea,
> thou didst speak with thy mouth, and with thy hand hast fulfilled it this
> day. Now therefore, O LORD, God of Israel, keep with thy servant
> David my father what thou hast promised him, saying, 'There shall
> never fail you a man before me to sit upon the throne of Israel, if only
> your sons take heed to their way, to walk before me as you have walked
> before me.' Now therefore, O God of Israel, let thy word be confirmed,
> which thou hast spoken to thy servant David my father.
> "But will God indeed dwell on the earth? Behold, heaven and the
> highest heaven cannot contain thee; how much less this house which I
> have built! Yet have regard to the prayer of thy servant and to his sup-
> plication, O LORD my God, hearkening to the cry and to the prayer

which thy servant prays before thee this day; that thy eyes may be open night and day toward this house, the place of which thou hast said, 'My name shall be there,' that thou mayest hearken to the prayer which thy servant offers toward this place. And hearken thou to the supplication of thy servant and of thy people Israel, when they pray toward this place; yea, hear thou in heaven thy dwelling place; and when thou hearest, forgive.

"If a man sins against his neighbor and is made to take an oath, and comes and swears his oath before thine altar in this house, then hear thou in heaven, and act, and judge thy servants, condemning the guilty by bringing his conduct upon his own head, and vindicating the righteous by rewarding him according to his righteousness.

"When thy people Israel are defeated before the enemy because they have sinned against thee, if they turn again to thee, and acknowledge thy name, and pray and make supplication to thee in this house; then hear thou in heaven, and forgive the sin of thy people Israel, and bring them again to the land which thou gavest to their fathers.

"When heaven is shut up and there is no rain because they have sinned against thee, if they pray toward this place, and acknowledge thy name, and turn from their sin, when thou dost afflict them, then hear thou in heaven, and forgive the sin of thy servants, thy people Israel, when thou dost teach them the good way in which they should walk; and grant rain upon thy land, which thou hast given to thy people as an inheritance.

"If there is famine in the land, if there is pestilence or blight or mildew or locust or caterpillar; if their enemy besieges them in any of their cities; whatever plague, whatever sickness there is; whatever prayer, whatever supplication is made by any man or by all thy people Israel, each knowing the affliction of his own heart and stretching out his hands toward this house; then hear thou in heaven thy dwelling place, and forgive, and act, and render to each whose heart thou knowest, according to all his ways (for thou, thou only, knowest the hearts of all the children of men); that they may fear thee all the days that they live in the land which thou gavest to our fathers.

"Likewise when a foreigner, who is not of thy people Israel, comes from a far country for thy name's sake (for they shall hear of thy great name, and thy mighty hand, and of thy outstretched arm), when he comes and prays toward this house, hear thou in heaven thy dwelling place, and do according to all for which the foreigner calls to thee; in order that all the peoples of the earth may know thy name and fear thee, as do thy people Israel, and that they may know that this house which I have built is called by thy name.

"If thy people go out to battle against their enemy, by whatever way thou shalt send them, and they pray to the LORD toward the city which thou hast chosen and the house which I have built for thy name, then hear thou in heaven their prayer and their supplication, and maintain their cause.

"If they sin against thee—for there is no man who does not sin—and thou art angry with them, and dost give them to an enemy, so that they are carried away captive to the land of the enemy, far off or near; yet if they lay it to heart in the land to which they have been carried captive, and repent, and make supplication to thee in the land of their captors, saying, 'We have sinned, and have acted perversely and wickedly'; if they repent with all their mind and with all their heart in the land of their enemies, who carried them captive, and pray to thee toward their land, which thou gavest to their fathers, the city which thou hast chosen, and the house which I have built for thy name; then hear thou in heaven thy dwelling place their prayer and their supplication, and maintain their cause and forgive thy people who have sinned against thee, and all their transgressions which they have committed against thee; and grant them compassion in the sight of those who carried them captive, that they may have compassion on them (for they are thy people, and thy heritage, which thou didst bring out of Egypt, from the midst of the iron furnace). Let thy eyes be open to the supplication of thy servant, and to the supplication of thy people Israel, giving ear to them whenever they call to thee. For thou didst separate them from among all the peoples of the earth, to be thy heritage, as thou didst declare through Moses, thy servant, when thou didst bring our fathers out of Egypt, O Lord God."

(1 Kings 8:22–53)

It is not difficult to see that the prayer has been very carefully constructed to include various situations of need which inevitably arise in the normal course of the life of Israel. In turn, each such major occasion of distress comes within the purview of the prayer with the request that God may indeed hear the cries of people when they are in trouble and respond accordingly, delivering them from the cause of their misfortune. No doubt many such prayers, presenting a "catalog of needs," had been formulated and used, not only in Israel but from all kinds of people in various different religious traditions. It is not on this account, however, that Solomon's prayer is so remarkable and memorable. Rather it is because it is a highly reflective—we should probably say theological—composition, in which all the attention is focused upon the understanding of God, the importance that a specific temple and city (Jerusalem) might have for God, and the way in which God can be approached by men and women and respond. To this extent Solomon's prayer is not simply an act of dedication for the temple in Jerusalem but rather an act of dedication for all human worship, since it is concerned to declare in what terms prayer is possible for human beings who are setting themselves to call upon One whom even earth and sky together could not possibly contain. Why and how is prayer then possible at all?

The Significance of the Prayer

It would be very hard indeed to overrate the importance of this prayer of Solomon within the development of Jewish and Christian spirituality and of the whole of humankind's religious quest. In the first place it sets prayer in the very forefront of religion so that the most beautiful and elaborate temple which Solomon had built in Jerusalem with all its rituals and sacrificial offering is viewed as a means through which Israel may learn to pray effectively. Religion is thereby remarkably enriched beyond any wooden or rigid understanding of what may be achieved through formal acts of worship. The outward form is seen to be essentially a means towards an inward goal. This inward goal is achieved through prayer, which is the truly personal form and realization of communion with God. The outward building is thus made the symbol and sign of inward experiences of seeking God, of repentance, of accepting forgiveness, and finding meaning and direction. We are already here at the threshold of the recognition that "God is Spirit and those who worship him must worship him in spirit and in truth" (John 4:24).

It is in this centrality accorded to prayer in religion that Solomon's words achieve their exceptional impact since they recognize so fully that theology and spirituality belong intimately together. All too easily the study of the nature and being of God can become a formal, external, and relatively detached, intellectual exercise. Prayer, contrastingly, can be looked upon as a very private, unpretentious, and intellectually undemanding, personal communion with God. Yet these two aspects of religion belong essentially together and cannot properly be separated. All too readily modern individuals have frowned upon the Judeo-Christian tradition as too speculative and philosophically oriented to satisfy the inner needs of the human spirit. In consequence the elaborate traditions of spirituality of the

East have appeared more attractive and less vulnerable to the intellectual stresses and speculative ambitions of the West. Spirituality and prayer are indissolubly one, as Solomon's prayer so forcibly asserts. Who God is relates inseparably to who we are and how it can come about that we can seek, find, and enjoy communion with God. Theology begins when we pause to reflect upon why we say prayers and what use such praying may have. In fact it is hard to find a more clearly presented argument for the necessity of theology than Solomon's prayer. God is omnipresent and utterly transcendent to the visible world—"heaven and the highest heaven cannot contain him"; he is omniscient—"for thou, thou only, knowest the hearts of all the children of men"; he is utterly and impartially righteous—"condemning the guilty . . . vindicating the righteous." We can find in this prayer most of the essential theological formulations concerning the being and attributes of God which are familiar from later and more systematic expositions. All of this is needful if we are to make any sense of prayer at all. If God is great enough to have created such a world as ours, is it not likely that God would not be bothered with mere human requests? If God is so all-knowing, as to be able to see into the hearts of every living person, does this not, of itself, make unnecessary any attempt to tell him of our needs? If he is so just and righteous that before him no living creature can be wholly innocent and free from sin, does this not render futile any expectation that God would deign to offer help to needy men and women? All of these questions are raised and dealt with in this magnificent prayer.

Perhaps as much as any of these questions, however, we see the essential theological richness of this prayer in its very awareness of the nature of God as one who is more than just a "presence" that men and women can seek. When we look at religion as reflected in the Bible we become very conscious that it was throughout beset with the question "Where can God be found?" Everywhere there were temples, shrines, sacred rocks, sacred trees, and a host of other signs and symbols which were believed to manifest the "presence" of a deity. Whether such shrines were natural features or whether they were made by individuals; whether their sacred character was believed to be assured because of visions or special manifestations which had been experienced there; whether the deity was believed to visit the shrine or in some way to be resident there, the multiplicity of such "holy places" was the most prominent feature of the religious aspirations of humankind. God or the gods were to be sought and found through the place or places where they had ordained their presence should be revealed. God was thought of, therefore, in very direct and often very physical terms. It is easy for us in the modern world to "modernize" our understanding of this aspect of ancient religious life by offering a spiritual and psychological interpretation of what it was that constituted the sense of the "presence" of deity. For the men and women of those ancient times, however, such a separation between the "symbol" and the reality which it was thought to symbolize was an intellectual distinction which was seldom made or explored. Even to describe such sacred shrines and structures as "symbols" of a divine presence introduces a level of theological reflection and understanding which those who participated in such religion did not share. It is at the very heart of Solomon's prayer, however, that such a distinction should and must be made. God exists beyond and above our normal sense experience, though both our senses and the forms and traditions of worship which have been established enable us to find the divine power. We can never identify God's full and essential nature, however, with any single earthbound form which expresses it. Even the great temple in Jerusalem, the glory and proud achievement of Solomon, which meant so much to the life of ancient Israel, was not to be identified with God. In time this temple would suffer decay and stand in need of repair; in time it would be plundered and vandalized by hostile armies; in time it would, as later events were to demonstrate all too horrifically, become an object of deliberate destruction. In a most vivid prophecy Jeremiah was to disabuse people of their illusions that the temple could provide them with an indestructible security (cf. Jer. 7:1–15, especially vs. 4). Perhaps with a note of even sharper severity, the prophet Ezekiel foresaw that, when the time of judgment came, it would be necessary for it actually to begin at the house of God (Ezek. 9:6,7). Constantly the temptation exists for people to identify God with the forms and fixtures to which they have become attached as the means by which the divine presence is made known. A time comes when it may be necessary, then, not simply to recognize that men and women will have to learn to do without the familiar artifacts of religion but that it may be necessary for their own spiritual good that they should do so (cf. Isa. 66:1). It is small wonder then that centuries after Solomon's time, when new buildings, new priestly elaborations of ancient rites, and a thousand years of history in which the temple of Jerusalem had played so large a part in Israelite-Jewish religion, the Christian martyr Stephen should have come to see it as a most formidable obstacle to the true understanding of God (Acts 7:47–51). The tragedy is that, with so rich a prayer as that of Solomon   for the dedication of the temple, it should have been necessary for Stephen to die for its lessons to be learned.

11
A Prayer of
JONAH

Jonah 2:2–9

Jonah the Prophet

Although the book of Jonah appears in the Bible among the
Prophets, it is essentially a story about a prophet rather than one
which contains a collection of his prophecies. The link with prophecy is a very important one, since the account of what happened to
Jonah and of his reaction to this experience provide one of the most
important insights which the Bible has to offer about the way in
which prophecy is to be understood. A prophet Jonah is referred to
in 2 Kings 14:25 as having prophesied during the reign of Jeroboam
II (786–746 B.C.) in the Northern Kingdom. This would make Jonah
a near contemporary of Amos and Hosea, perhaps preceding them
by twenty years. Moreover the story in the book of Jonah, which
was certainly written very much later and concerns Jonah's preaching
against the great Assyrian city of Nineveh, is indirectly related to the
circumstances and events of Jeroboam II's reign. It is important to
begin a study of Jonah's prayer therefore by looking at what the Bible
has to tell us about Jonah's preaching:

> He [Jeroboam II] restored the border of Israel from the entrance of
> Hamath as far as the Sea of the Arabah, according to the word of the
> Lord, the God of Israel, which he spoke by his servant Jonah the son
> of Amittai, the prophet, who was from Gath-hepher.
>
> (2 Kings 14:25)

The biblical historian then does a very unusual thing in giving a
reason for this period of great political and military success of Israel,
which was certainly achieved at the expense of neighboring nations,
including Judah:

> For the LORD saw that the affliction of Israel was very bitter, for there
> was none left, bond or free, and there was none to help Israel.
>
> (2 Kings 14:26)

Jonah then was an ardent and patriotic prophet who had foretold the expansion and greatness of the Northern Kingdom of Israel in the days shortly before the appearance of Amos and Hosea.

Such political success on the part of Israel not only contrasted strikingly with the grim and ultimately catastrophic days which followed soon after Jeroboam II's death but was in itself thoroughly undeserved, since Jeroboam II was a harsh and godless ruler: "he did what was evil in the sight of the LORD; he did not depart from all the sins of Jeroboam the son of Nebat [i.e., Jeroboam I], which he made Israel to sin" (2 Kings 14:23). Why then had God allowed events to take such a turn, and what was the meaning of the appearance of such a prophet as Jonah in the midst of these affairs? The answer to these questions that is set out in such an interesting and oblique way in the book of Jonah provides us with one of the most important of all biblical insights into the way in which God's providence works.

Before we can investigate this further we must look a little more closely at the circumstances of Jeroboam II's reign and its aftermath. During the latter years of his long period on Israel's throne the prophets Amos and Hosea came on the scene foretelling doom and ruination for this ruler's dynasty and kingdom. Amos probably appeared first and his message is unmistakably clear:

> The high places of Isaac shall be made desolate,
>   and the sanctuaries of Israel shall be laid waste,
>   and I will rise against the house of Jeroboam with the sword.
>
> (Amos 7:9)

In the case of Hosea the prophet's message is expressed rather more indirectly, but its content is essentially the same, foretelling a violent and terrible end to the kingdom and dynasty of Jeroboam II. It is set out in the form of a name, actually a place name Jezreel, given to the first of Hosea's children:

> And the LORD said to him, "Call his name Jezreel; for yet a little while, and I will punish the house of Jehu for the blood of Jezreel, and I will put an end to the kingdom of the house of Israel."
>
> (Hosea 1:4)

The essential clue which shows that the name "Jezreel" is intended as a warning of divine punishment and ruin coming upon Jeroboam II's kingdom is to be found in 2 Kings 10:11, which tells how this king's ancestor, Jehu, came to the throne of Israel by a fearful massacre at Jezreel. Although Jeroboam II survived to die peacefully in his bed, his son, Zechariah, was murdered after only a brief six month's reign (2 Kings 15:10). Not only was such an event disastrous in itself, but it effectively marked the end of the period of Israel's greatness. Within twenty-five years the independent political and national life of Israel was finished off by the Assyrians, a tragedy which is reflected extensively in the book of the prophet Isaiah and which is reported and explained very fully by the Old Testament historian (2 Kings 17). Some of the longer term consequences of this will be noted when we come to study the prayer of the Judean king Hezekiah. What is important in the immediate concern is that Jonah's prophecy and the period of Israel's expansion to which it was related were a kind of peaceful interlude before the days of ruin and catastrophe came. Many historians have come to write of "*la belle époque*" in Europe in the two decades before the disastrous year 1914 put an end to its easy-going illusions. In a way we could very well describe the age in which Jonah lives as "*la belle époque*" of Israel, with the prophet himself being a very ardent and patriotic supporter of it.

The opening part of the story of Jonah (Jon. 1—2), in which the prayer is set, is sufficiently well known for it to need little retelling. Jonah was called by God to go to Nineveh to warn the city that God's judgment would come upon it soon. Rather than obey God Jonah ran away by ship, but was thrown into the sea in a storm and swallowed by a large fish. It is from inside the fish that his prayer to God is offered, after which he is vomited out on the dry land. The account is full of humor, irony, and a significant measure of symbolism, which undoubtedly appears very noticeably in the prayer itself. Subsequent to Jonah's remarkable escape God called him a second time to go and prophesy against Nineveh. This time Jonah obeyed but was then angry and thoroughly displeased to find that, after all his trouble, no judgment befell the people of Nineveh, because the people had repented in sackcloth and with fasting. Only by a symbolic gesture involving a gourd was Jonah then made to realize that such repentance was the true purpose of his prophecy. Far from his prophecy not being fulfilled, after all the pains and trouble he had gone to to proclaim it, it had been most truly fulfilled by the repentance it had brought forth.

Jonah's Prayer

Although Jonah's prayer has frequently been thought by scholars to have been added to the original book, it has certainly now become an important and intrinsic part of the whole story. Through his experience of God in prayer Jonah himself undergoes a profound change of heart and comes to discover the grace and goodness of God in a new way. Later he is upset and infuriated that God shows a similar merciful goodness to the people of Nineveh, on whose account this prophet from Gath-hepher had been put to so much trouble. Throughout the story the feature of exaggeration, irony, and a highly pictorial use of word symbolism are prominent. It is important to keep this in mind in examining the prayer, since it is the pictorial imagery of the language which conveys so much of its meaning. This symbolism, and probably the actual words of this prayer, did not originate with the author of the story of Jonah, but were part of a very much older tradition of worship in Israel. Although Jonah was a real historical figure therefore, it is really to misunderstand the story to question whether the "fish" was actually a whale and whether Jonah could have survived his ordeal of being swallowed by it. These features are all part of the irony and symbolism which belong to the story. We can proceed then to look more closely at Jonah's remarkable prayer:

> "I called to the LORD, out of my distress,
>   and he answered me;
> out of the belly of Sheol I cried,
>   and thou didst hear my voice.
> For thou didst cast me into the deep,
>   into the heart of the seas,
>   and the flood was round about me;
> all thy waves and thy billows
>   passed over me.
> Then I said, 'I am cast out
>   from thy presence;

how shall I again look
   upon thy holy temple?'
The waters closed in over me,
   the deep was round about me;
weeds were wrapped about my head
   at the roots of the mountains.
I went down to the land
   whose bars closed upon me for ever;
yet thou didst bring up my life from the Pit,
   O LORD my God.
When my soul fainted within me,
   I remembered the LORD;
and my prayer came to thee,
   into thy holy temple.
Those who pay regard to vain idols
   forsake their true loyalty.
But I with the voice of thanksgiving
   will sacrifice to thee;
what I have vowed I will pay.
   Deliverance belongs to the LORD!"
                  (Jonah 2:2–9)

The distinctive character of the prayer is provided by its use of the symbolic language of "the depths" as a portrayal of human distress and despair. Just as in a Psalm the pain and grief-stricken worshiper can cry out "all thy waves and thy billows have gone over me" (Ps. 42:7), so the same language concerning "the deep" and "the heart of the seas" is employed here. With a wry touch of humor it fits the picture of Jonah inside the fish, but it is clear that the language did not originate there but belongs to the imagery of all the many kinds of misfortune and trouble which could befall a person. Whether caused by illness, personal enemies, or a wider mood of depression and fear of death, the "depths" describe the antechamber to death and the grave. This is the meaning of the reference to "Sheol" and "the Pit" set out in Jonah's prayer.

In a time of trouble Jonah, like any other distressed citizen of ancient Israel, was able to put his cries and fears into words, made meaningful and reassuring through their use over a long period of time. Through such an established form of prayer the sense of despair and alienation from God was brushed aside in a new discovery of God, no matter if it seemed too late for God's intervention to be

of any help. The New International Version tellingly renders the first
line of Jonah 2:7: "When my life was ebbing away, I remembered
You, LORD." In spite of all appearances, and even in the face of
the guilt and futility which had followed upon Jonah's attempt
to flee from God, the most wonderful realization was that God
was still there! Instead of running away from God, Jonah now discovered that there was nothing that he wished for more than to be able
to get back to God: "how shall I again look upon thy holy temple?"
(Jon. 2:4).

The symbolism of "the depths" and of Jonah's being cast into the
sea to find a watery grave has another dimension, however, which is
equally important if the meaning of the book as a whole is to be
grasped. Hidden within this pictorial language many commentators
have very plausibly recognized a portrayal of the fate of Israel as a
nation cast out from the presence of God into the miseries of exile
(cf. especially Jon. 2:4). This is all the more telling if, as we have
claimed, the book is to be read against the background of the mention
of Jonah the son of Amittai in 2 Kings 14:25. The years that followed
upon Jeroboam II's death were the years of Israel's ruin and devas-
tation, brought on primarily by the Assyrians, which culminated in
the experience of exile. Many must certainly have felt that they had
been cast out from the presence of God, never to see Jerusalem or its
temple again. No wonder that such men and women saw in the words
of the prophets Amos and Hosea, forewarning of their ruin, a sen-
tence of punishment and national death from which they could never
escape. It is all the more interesting therefore to discover that the Old
Testament historian, immediately after his reference to the prophet
Jonah, offers the reassuring comment: "But the LORD had not said
that he would blot out the name of Israel from under heaven"
(2 Kings 14:27). To be thrown into "the depths," to experience hopelessness and despair, and for Israel to be scattered among the nations
as exiles are all tied together in the symbolic language of Jonah's
prayer. That prayer is not a crying out into the darkness but a rediscovery of God, and with this a renewed awareness of the Source
from whom all true hope and all new beginnings can flow. "Deliverance belongs to the LORD" (Jon. 2:9).

The Significance of Jonah's Prayer

Jonah's prayer is particularly important, not simply for the way in which it presents to God cries of grief and despair "out of the depths," but because it makes such cries a vehicle of repentance and a way to the rediscovery of the reality and presence of God. Just as the book as a whole is about repentance as of paramount importance for an understanding of the way in which the providential care of God impinges upon our lives, so is this brought out in the prophet's prayer. From the hopeless despair which cries out "I am cast out from thy presence; how shall I again look upon thy holy temple?" (Jon. 2:4), it carries us through to the confident affirmation: "But I with the voice of thanksgiving will sacrifice to thee" (Jon. 2:9). This rediscovery of the grace and goodness of God is splendidly brought out in the way in which the New International Version translates verse 8:

> Those who cling to worthless idols
> forfeit the grace that could be theirs.
> (Jonah 2:8)

Jonah's whole life and his prophetic ministry were thereby transformed by a new awareness of the extent of God's mercy. He discovered this for himself, yet he remained unwilling afterwards to extend this understanding of God's goodness to the citizens of Nineveh, and more pertinently to the way in which prophecy, including his own prophetic warnings against Nineveh, should be understood. He still felt that God's word, once it had been declared by a prophet, should be a fixed and final verdict upon the people to whom it was addressed. After so much trouble and difficulty, once he had pronounced his warnings to the men of Nineveh, he thought this should be an end of the matter. All that was needed for the prophecy to be fulfilled was the confirmatory act of judgment and overthrow upon the Assyrian city. God's attitude toward this city, however, and his prophetic message to it were touched with the same mercy that had brought back Jonah from the depths. So far as the matching of Jonah's personal experience with his subsequent teaching and attitude are concerned, some very pertinent lessons can be learned. Jonah's involvement in his special prophetic ministry had brought him personally through a most profound spiritual experience. He had passed through the "depths" of despair and depression, after which he should have been very much better equipped to understand and to show compassion towards the men and women of Nineveh. In the development of his story, this experience had paradoxically worked in the opposite direction. It had convinced the prophet that he and his preaching were so special that they could not possibly fail to prove effective for the people of Nineveh. Within forty days Jonah was convinced that Nineveh would be destroyed. What he was so slow and reluctant to realize was that his prophetic preaching was proving effective but in a manner and with consequences that he had not truly allowed for in his thinking.

The concluding episode of the story, concerning the growth and decay of the plant (RSV margin "castor oil plant"), is filled with a wry and penetrating humor. Jonah was capable of experiencing feeling and compassion, like any other normal human being. He had not allowed his thinking and his understanding of God, however, to direct and educate his feelings in a worthy and logical fashion. He was capable of becoming more upset and distraught over a plant than he was over the ruination and death of a city. He was like those men and women of other ages who have shown greater grief over the outcome of a ball game or the loss of a personal treasure than over the death and mutilation of people in war and violence. We are all, like Jonah, capable of feeling very deeply about things, but we have to instruct and educate these feelings to ensure that they are related to situations and experiences of genuine importance.

As a story, the tale of Jonah the prophet is very telling and memorable. It has lessons about divine love and mercy which stretch across all national, racial, and confessional barriers. It presents a challenge to any view of life and human history which regards any nation or group of men and women as unredeemable, and therefore, beyond the range of God's mercy! It is also a very profound and searching theological comment upon the nature and reality of human history and of the way in which God's providence is to be seen at work.

Within the writings of the Old Testament the books of the proph-

ets occupy a very honored and profoundly respected place. From the
time of the eighth century B.C., when the threat from Assyria (Nineveh) had first begun to be felt in Israel, men like Amos, Hosea, and
Isaiah had appeared revealing the purpose and intention of God.
Theirs was not a message that was at all "comfortable" for Israel and
Judah, since it exposed wrongs and spoke of judgment and punishment. Like many other prophets since, their threatening words had a
very disturbing effect, so much so that, after the Assyrian and Babylonian invasions of Israel had passed, many had come to read and
ponder the words of the prophets with the deepest awe and wonder.
Had these prophets not shown that God was a God of terrifying
justice and righteousness who might sweep away the whole earth in
a flood of vengeance against men's and women's wrongdoing? Such
words of threat and judgment had provided an important key towards
understanding the years in which Israel and especially the citizens of
Jerusalem had been cast into the depths of destruction and exile.
These warnings were not the whole truth about God, nor were they
the whole truth of prophecy, which rather was concerned to show
that, in each age, every man and woman comes face to face with
God. For those who rightly understood the message of the prophets
the truth about God was not that each generation inherits an unbear-
able burden of guilt and punishment from the past but that each
generation is free to respond in its own way to the grace and goodness
of God. Jonah was faced with a "credibility gap" which he could not
bridge—an inability to believe that there was any virtue or worth at
all in the people of Nineveh whose destruction he had proclaimed.
His own experience of having refused the call of God to prophesy
and of finding himself drowning in the midst of the seas should have
taught him that even when "his life ebbed away" he could "remember
God" and rediscover a whole new avenue of hope and reassurance.
In this sense he already believed through the words of his prayer, a
truth which he was unwilling to apply to the citizens of Nineveh.

The book of Jonah must therefore certainly be understood against
a background of thought in which the men and women of Israel,
many of whom were already scattered among the nations, were increasingly falling victim to a pessimistic fatalism. Whatever they
did, wherever they turned, however hard they tried, had not God,

through his prophets, declared that an inevitable doom awaited Israel? Were they not suffering on account of the sins of their ancestors and had not such men as Amos foretold that the children of Abraham must suffer exile and scattering among the nations as a punishment? In such a way prophecy itself could be read and interpreted in a negative fashion as the revelation of an unalterable fate. The book of Jonah counters such a view firmly and decisively by showing that all individuals, in every generation, stand freely before God and are free to make their own individual response to God. Even the word of prophecy is not the disclosure of an unalterable fate, but a call from God to repentance and new beginnings. In the context of the story we should also accept that the people of Nineveh appear as a kind of "worst case" instance, in view of the notorious cruelty and barbarity with which the Assyrians had treated Israel. If the men of Nineveh could be spared when they repented, then how marvelous and life-transforming a venture must repentance be! Since it is the prayer of Jonah which marks the turning point of the story so far as he is concerned, then it becomes clear that prayer is understood as a revolutionary experience. Jonah's prayer became the point of his discovery of the fullness of his own freedom. It became the moment of realization that he was not a prisoner of the past, locked in a chain of circumstances which held him irretrievably bound. For us, too, prayer becomes the time of discovering our true freedom and with this the openness of the future that confronts us. The "will of God" of which theologians speak is not an arbitrary destiny, preordained for each of us. It is rather the entering into the full freedom and responsibility of our humanity when God created us "in his image." To engage in prayer like Jonah therefore is the very opposite of surrendering to the restraints of the past. It is discovering a path to an open future.

We may pause for a concluding thought regarding the prayer of Jonah. In the New Testament the "sign of Jonah" becomes a very important witness to the hope of the resurrection of the dead, and a special testimony to the resurrection of Jesus (Matt. 12:39–40;16:4). In association with this, so also does the repentance of the men of Nineveh become an important anticipation of the repentance and turning to the gospel on the part of the nations: "The men of Nineveh will arise at the judgment with this generation and condemn it; for they repented at the preaching of Jonah, and behold, something greater than Jonah is here" (Matt. 12:41). Jonah's experience in the fish has become a sign of the death and resurrection of Jesus, and similarly the repentance of the men of Nineveh has become a sign of the new life that awaits the nations of the world through the gospel. Jonah's prayer is thus a prototypical prayer of the possibilities of new life that belong to those who discover the grace of God. Even in the modern world it remains true:

> Those who cling to worthless idols
> > forfeit the grace that could be theirs.
> > > (Jonah 2:8 NIV)

12
A *Prayer of*
HEZEKIAH

Isaiah 38:10–20

Hezekiah the King

Hezekiah was a singularly important king of Judah and accordingly an appropriately lengthy section of the second book of Kings is devoted to the events of his reign (2 Kings 18:1—20:21). Besides this a great many of the prophecies in the book of Isaiah relate to major events of Hezekiah's reign, so that the prayer ascribed to this king is found preserved in this prophetic book. In order to appreciate why he was so important it is necessary to understand events that had taken place since the days of Solomon. This latter king's ambitions had brought a great deal of dissension within Israel and had given rise to a marked difference of attitude toward the heroic figure of David and the dynasty of kings that sprang from him. When Rehoboam succeeded Solomon to the throne in Jerusalem, the tribes of the north broke away and formed an independent Northern Kingdom. Only Benjamin, in whose territory Jerusalem lay, remained tied to Judah and so only this southern kingdom remained loyal to David and his dynasty. It becomes very evident from the way in which the biblical tradition has remembered Solomon that it was especially the issue of the kingship, and in particular the question concerning commitment to the dynasty of David, that provided the focal point of contention. In other respects the geographical, cultural, and historical ties which bound together the tribes of Israel and Judah—the Northern and Southern Kingdoms—served to prevent the uneasy relationship between the two breaking out into open war. This has had two consequences for the reader of the biblical story, since it explains on the one hand why the books of 1 and 2 Kings narrate the story of the years that followed as though Israel were still ideally one people. It also explains why the two kingdoms did not resort to open conflict with each other but maintained in general an uneasy alliance. This lasted until the middle of the eighth century B.C., the period in which the prophet Jonah appeared. It was also the time when the prophets Amos, Hosea, and then Isaiah and Micah appeared, and therefore clearly a time of the greatest importance for the emergence of the prophetic literature of the Old Testament.

The last quarter of the eighth century was covered by the twenty-nine years of Hezekiah's reign (2 Kings 18:2), yet the first signs of danger and threat began a quarter of a century earlier still, during the long and influential reign of Jeroboam II of Israel (786–746 B.C.). This king extended the borders of Israel far down into the south, to the shores of the Dead Sea (2 Kings 14:25), and so enlarged his kingdom, partly at Judah's expense. Shortly after his death, assassination and murder brought civil war to the Northern Kingdom (2 Kings 15:8–16) and eventually a wider realignment of loyalties brought strong and bitter conflict between Israel and Judah (2 Kings 15:37). This gave rise to what has become known as the Syro-Ephraimite war, which provided an important historical backdrop to the prophecies of both Hosea and Isaiah. Its details need not concern us, since it was over before Hezekiah came to the throne of Judah, probably in the year 725 B.C. It was of the utmost importance, however, not only because it marked the end of the uneasy alliance between Israel and Judah but because it brought both kingdoms to the attention of Assyria, which was eagerly expanding its sphere of imperial control in the Levant at this time. Hezekiah's predecessor, Ahaz, had treacherously sought to use the Assyrian interest to his own advantage by sending a substantial gift to the Assyrian king (2 Kings 16:5–9). The temporary advantage won for Judah by this act of betrayal was short-lived, and marked a further step in the decline of the two kingdoms, which had once been united under David and Solomon.

When Hezekiah came to the throne of Judah, therefore, he inherited a kingdom embittered by conflict and reeling under its subservience to Assyria. Much of the inner turmoil, both in religious and political terms, which this engendered is illuminated from the prophecies of Isaiah. It was left to Hezekiah to heal the deep wounds which held Judah apart from what remained of its sister kingdom of Israel, and at the same time to avoid any overt act of disloyalty to Assyria. It is this situation which explains the character and special interest of the prayer of Hezekiah, since it is a prayer about sickness understood both literally in reference to an illness which befell the king but also metaphorically of the unease and spiritual confusion which had stricken his kingdom.

The precise time in the king's reign when he became seriously ill is not mentioned, but a clue is provided by the divine promise to him that fifteen years would be added to his life (Isa. 38:5). This would, if it were literally fulfilled, put the illness in the year 711 B.C., which is quite possible. This is complicated by the note that the king's recovery from illness is directly associated with the deliverance of Jerusalem from the attack and siege by Sennacherib which occurred in 701 B.C. In any case this major event is recounted earlier in Isaiah 36—37. However, it is almost certain the historian has made this connection between Hezekiah's recovery from a serious illness and the deliverance of Jerusalem from the clutches of Sennacherib's army. In reality the precise chronology and sequence of events has little, if any, bearing on the spiritual and theological issues that are raised by Hezekiah's illness and his accompanying prayer. It is, however, necessary to gain some understanding of the political situation in Judah during these years if the purpose of the biblical writer in recording this prayer is to be fully understood. In a quite striking fashion it conveys a double level of meaning in which the king's illness is used to convey a sense of the spiritual and political disorder of his kingdom.

During the entire period of his reign Hezekiah was a vassal-king, exercising his power under the imperial authority of three successive Assyrian rulers. During this time various attempts were sponsored among Israel's neighbors to break free from the grip of Assyria, with its heavy exactions of tribute. Most of all such acts of rebellion were encouraged and sponsored by Egypt, which had reason enough of its own to want to keep the Assyrians away from its own frontiers. So it was that in the period 713–711 B.C. Judah was tempted to join in a plan for the withdrawal of allegiance to Assyria, a temptation which

Hezekiah appears ultimately to have resisted (Isa. 20). In the year
705 B.C., the powerful Assyrian ruler Sargon died and this appeared
to provide the opportunity for a concerted act of rebellion among the
Levantine provinces, backed by Egypt, which might just succeed.
This time Hezekiah joined the rebellion, even though the prophet
Isaiah strongly urged him against doing so (Isa. 28—31). The fact
that some considerable interval elapsed before Sennacherib, the new
Assyrian king, was able to put down the rebellion suggests that the
calculations which had led to the rebellion were not entirely misconceived. The fear, tension, and uncertainty which then befell Jerusalem are not difficult to imagine. After a brief preparation for siege,
Hezekiah was forced to surrender and to pay a heavy indemnity to
the Assyrian king (2 Kings 18:13–16). Whether the report which
follows in 2 Kings 18:17—19:35 refers to a separate incident involving Hezekiah and Sennacherib, or is simply a variant and fuller report
of the same occasion has been much discussed by scholars. Probably
the latter is the likely truth, but it serves to bring out the fact that the
escape of Jerusalem and Hezekiah from an ultimate military catastrophe was seen and interpreted as a providential act of divine deliverance. What duress may have been felt by Sennacherib in explanation
of his apparent leniency toward Hezekiah is not fully known.

All of this has an important bearing on the understanding of Hezekiah's prayer since the biblical writer, seeking to trace the way in
which the hand of God had been at work in the life of this Judean
king, saw a mysterious connection between the king's recovery from
illness and the deliverance of his chief city and kingdom from the
power of Sennacherib (see Isa. 38:6). The mystery of suffering and
evil was such that the fate of the king and the fate of his city and
people were inextricably intertwined. Perhaps, however, we should
put this in a more positive and personalistic fashion: the virtues and
qualities of the king which brought about the deliverance of his kingdom were also the qualities which brought about the mercy of God
in his recovery.

The Prayer

We are not told when precisely Hezekiah became ill, nor is there
anything other than a rather meager reference to "a boil" (Isa. 38:21)

to show what form the illness took. No doubt the author of the narrative had access to the royal chronicles of Judah, which would have recorded significant events in the life of the king. It is then quite likely that it is the author's own reflection which has seen the connection between the king's recovery from illness and the range of political events with which it has become associated, culminating in the escape of Jerusalem from Sennacherib's armies (Isa. 36—37). It is probable also that the biblical writer has seen a connection between the story of how the king was healed and the story, with its threatening implications, of the visit of the delegation from Babylon told in Isaiah 39. What this connection was we can consider later, after examining the prayer.

The prayer itself is in two main parts, a lament expressing grief and bitterness at the imminence of death (Isa. 38:10–15) and a plea for healing with a consequent assurance that this either has already come, or is sure to come, in Isaiah 38:16–20. This twofold division is slightly puzzling, since we need either to assume that the two parts belong to separate times in the experience of the illness, with the note of assurance being added later, or that it was offered, as verse 9 suggests, after the recovery had actually taken place. We should note also that the precise translation at a number of points is far from clear, although the major English translations have achieved a remarkably felicitous rendering:

I said, In the noontide of my days
  I must depart;
I am consigned to the gates of Sheol
  for the rest of my years.
I said, I shall not see the LORD
  in the land of the living;
I shall look upon man no more
  among the inhabitants of the world.
My dwelling is plucked up and removed from me
  like a shepherd's tent;
like a weaver I have rolled up my life;
  he cuts me off from the loom;
from day to night thou dost bring me to an end;
  I cry for help until morning;
like a lion he breaks all my bones;
  from day to night thou dost bring me to an end.

Like a swallow or a crane I clamor,
　I moan like a dove.
My eyes are weary with looking upward.
　O LORD, I am oppressed; be thou my security!
But what can I say? For he has spoken to me,
　and he himself has done it.
All my sleep has fled
　because of the bitterness of my soul.

O LORD, by these things men live,
　and in all these is the life of my spirit.
　Oh, restore me to health and make me live!
Lo, it was for my welfare
　that I had great bitterness;
but thou hast held back my life
　from the pit of destruction,
for thou hast cast all my sins
　behind thy back.
For Sheol cannot thank thee,
　death cannot praise thee;
those who go down to the pit cannot hope
　for thy faithfulness.
The living, the living, he thanks thee,
　as I do this day;
the father makes known to the children
　thy faithfulness.

The LORD will save me,
　and we will sing to stringed instruments
all the days of our life,
　at the house of the LORD.

(Isaiah 38:10–20)

There can be little doubt that, although this is a type of prayer
that was at one time formulated for use in public worship, its impact,
and its emotional intensity are altogether private and personal. Any
one who has witnessed and tried to comfort a person who has just
received news that he or she is suffering from a very serious illness
will recognize in the opening verses the sense of shock, fear, bitterness, and anger which such a situation arouses. The telling imagery
is unforgettable—human death is likened to a shepherd's tent suddenly removed from its familiar place and to the deft cut of a weaver
suddenly cutting off his cloth from the loom. In line with the general
biblical perspective the prayer assumes without question that it is

God who has caused the illness—"He himself has done it"! This remains important in regard to any discussion about the nature and purpose of disease and suffering, since it recognizes that, whatever may be regarded in a medical sense as the scientific cause of illness, any understanding of God's sovereignty indicates that ultimately God is responsible. It is God who has so fashioned our world, with all its possibilities of freedom and development, in which human suffering and premature death can occur.

This may at first appear to point to a cruel and harsh God, which it is difficult to reconcile with the picture of the loving and caring nature which elsewhere plays so important a part in the biblical revelation. As real and deep as the tensions may become in personal experience, the problem of evil is in no way softened, let alone resolved, by claiming that God is not ultimately responsible for the world in which it exists. Nor should we be misled into shutting our eyes to all the evidence and experience which reveals to us the loving nature of God. This too is a real and assured aspect of our experience. What this remarkable prayer of Hezekiah's shows is that God's love and care may nonetheless place demands upon us and test the reality of our love in very difficult and unexpected ways. From the outset therefore one of the most striking, probably we should say *the* most striking feature of this entire prayer is the way in which the king is portrayed as willing to leave the matter, with its possible fatal outcome, in the hands of God. In spite of the understandable reactions of grief, agony, and deep spiritual shock, this willingness to leave the issue in God's hands is never abandoned. This feature is even more forcibly brought out in the dialogue which took place between Hezekiah the king and Isaiah the prophet when the illness first occurred:

In those days Hezekiah became sick and was at the point of death. And Isaiah the prophet the son of Amoz came to him, and said to him, "Thus says the LORD: Set your house in order; for you shall die, you shall not recover." Then Hezekiah turned his face to the wall, and prayed to the LORD, and said, "Remember now, O LORD, I beseech thee, how I have walked before thee in faithfulness and with a whole heart, and have done what is good in thy sight." And Hezekiah wept bitterly. Then the word of the LORD came to Isaiah: "Go and say to Hezekiah, Thus says the LORD, the God of David your father: I have

heard your prayer, I have seen your tears; behold I will add fifteen years
to your life."

(Isaiah 38:1–5)

Here in this prefatory experience and prayer on the part of the
king we are introduced to some of the most striking insights which
the Old Testament has to offer concerning prayer. First of all, when
news was brought to Hezekiah of the likely fatal outcome of his
illness, we find no angry complaints against such a fearful destiny
nor any self-pity or remorse. Alongside his natural expression of
grief and tears the king indulges in no false self-deprecation nor in
any expression of false guilt. He can surrender himself wholly to the
will of God as he has done "in faithfulness and with a whole heart"
throughout his life. Prayer requires sincerity, and yet it is precisely
this degree of sincerity that is most hard to achieve when we sense
that God has sovereign power, and we can only be debtors and beg-
gars before him.

A second point stands out immediately in regard to the situation,
for although the prayer contains no overt petition as such but merely
expresses submission to God, it is viewed as magnificently effective.
After the initial gloomy forecast of impending death, the king re-
ceives an assurance that he will live, and that a full fifteen years will
be added to his life. Moreover, not only will the king receive this
personal deliverance, but his city Jerusalem is to be saved from the
hands of the Assyrian king Sennacherib (Isa. 38:6). Clearly it is the
narrator who has discerned a connection between the royal submission to God and the healing of Hezekiah, together with the deliverance of his royal city Jerusalem. Such are the intertwined
complexities which hold together a kingdom and its faith!

The Significance of the Prayer

Probably a number of the Psalms preserved in the Psalter were
originally composed for us in time of illness. At least this is strongly
suggested by the similarities of form and language between Hezekiah's prayer and several Psalms. Altogether they highlight the fact
that the Old Testament does not say a great deal about the types and
treatment of illness, even though this must have been a painful and
commonplace feature of daily life. In biblical times medical knowl-

edge was relatively rudimentary, and a person stricken with illness could do little except to look to the ministrations of priest and prophet. God was the author of the necessary powers of healing, as several biblical incidents make clear.

If the Bible is relatively uninformative about the causes and cure of disease, however, it is contrastingly richly furnished with guidance and help regarding the spiritual and psychological impact of illness. All those responses of shock, fear, despair, bitterness, and hope which inevitably accompany any serious experience of illness, both for the victim and his or her friends and family, are fully brought out in the Old Testament literature. Nowhere is this more fully evident than in the instance of Hezekiah's prayer. All the more is this so because, in company with most of the Old Testament, there is no alleviating resort to thoughts of an enriched life beyond the grave. Death, in whatever form it comes, is viewed as an enemy. It is in this area that Hezekiah's prayer is so instructive. It manages to articulate real feelings and human emotions without artificial and illusory ones. It naturally assumes that illness is unwelcome and feared and that the danger of premature death is a cause of grievous shock and bitterness of heart. Hope and prayer for recovery are held together, however, with a realistic sense of the ultimacy of God's will which no one can escape. Nor does the prayer fall into the trap of supposing that healing *must* be God's ultimate will and that faithful pleading and piety can wrest this healing from the hands of an unwilling God. It teaches submissiveness without any touch of fatalistic despair and hope without any sense of an illusory optimism.

A further point is brought out very fully in the rich language of the thanksgiving element in Hezekiah's prayer. Through the experience of illness, unwelcome as it is, an enhanced appreciation of life can emerge. The strength of the assertion is in fact quite remarkable: "Lo, it was for my welfare that I had great bitterness" (Isa. 38:17). The realization that the time may have come to set all one's house in order, to reflect on the relative priority attached to things and persons, and to count up what is really of value and importance, can have a very salutary effect. The sheer possibility of enjoying a normal day with work and friends, with responsibilities and pleasures, with soundness of body and mind can come to be seen as an inesti-

mable privilege. Familiar scenes and familiar faces can come to be
viewed as irreplaceable sources of joy and happiness, once the realization has been faced of possibly saying farewell to them forever.
Suffering and disease are features of life that we feel we could well
do without, and yet it is undoubtedly true that life would be surprisingly different without them. They can have a beneficial effect and
be seen, ultimately, to work for our welfare. What is perhaps so
regrettable in our world is that there is so much wasted suffering,
when nothing is learned from it and when life's values are not enriched by it. If Hezekiah's prayer can teach us one supreme lesson it
must surely be connected with the phrase "O LORD, by these things
men live." (Isa. 38:16). Through the experience of illness our vision
can be restored to see what the really important features of life are.
If so much of what we get out of living is concerned with questions
of perspective, then it is not difficult to see that illness, as interpreted
by such a prayer as this, can contribute to a fuller and more sensible
perspective by which to see ourselves and our world.

A further reflection is appropriate at this point. We have already
pointed out that the biblical narrator has seen a connection between
the piety brought to light in Hezekiah's prayer and the deliverance of
Jerusalem from the besieging forces of the Assyrian King Sennacherib. Such could be no more than a hint put forward tentatively and
without any final authoritative assertion. It was an important point
which later generations of Israelites and Jews were to reflect upon
that Jerusalem, virtually alone among the cities of Israel, had been
spared the ravages of the armies of Assyria. Such was not the case a
little over a century later when the Babylonian besieging armies appeared at the gates of the city. It was natural enough then, in trying
to understand why God had not upheld the defense of the city a
second time, to look for special reasons which might explain the
situation. Among such reasons there naturally appeared the unique
piety of King Hezekiah, which had stood firm in the face of fear and
threat, both personally and nationally. It would be too simplistic a
view to suppose that the personal piety of one individual could save
an entire kingdom from superior hostile forces. Historical situations
are never so clear-cut as to rule out the vital transforming influence
of personal courage and steadfastness, however. It was no vague

clutching at straws therefore which led the biblical narrator to see in Hezekiah's prayer the expression of a whole-hearted trust in God which was bound to have the fullest repercussions in the affairs of his kingdom. By such things in fact men and women live, and kingdoms are renewed. We might, in the modern world, be happier to ascribe such qualities and achievements to factors of morale or personal courage, but in biblical times it was natural that they should be clearly located in the realm of faith. It is a remarkable nobility of faith that comes to expression in Hezekiah's royal prayer.

13
A Prayer of JEREMIAH

Jeremiah 32:16–25

Jeremiah the Man

Tradition has painted a picture of Jeremiah as a sad and tearful prophet, grieving over the misfortunes of his people and unable to do more than comfort them. He was a prophet of hope in a quite special way, however, since it was out of the very depth of misfortune and tragedy which overtook Israel during the prophet's lifetime that he came to the realization of this message of hope. Perhaps more important, it was the revelation that this hope was grounded on nothing more—and nothing less—than the reality and presence of God. As the man who saw, with remarkable suddenness, the falling away and collapse of all those institutions, assurances, and supports which had hitherto provided a basis of hope for his people, Jeremiah was forced to recognize that there was nothing left to trust in save God. Far from this being a kind of "last resort"—the final desperate refuge of a despairing people—he discovered that God is in reality the ground and source of all hope. Outside of God there is no hope, and in a very real sense all other reasons and bases for hope are secondary to this one fact that God means hope, so that all our possibilities for life and for the future derive from God. Jeremiah's prayer therefore is a prayer about hope, but it is also a prayer about tragedy, suffering, and despair, since it is in the face of these painful experiences that it reveals the true nature of hope in God. In a very real measure Jeremiah's prayer of hope anticipates the cross of the New Testament since it recognizes that the path to the resurrection glory can only be through the agony and grief of the cross. Admittedly Jeremiah did not discern the full redemptive value that such suffering might possess, but he discovered that without such agony and suffering the true meaning of hope in God could not be understood. Moreover it is Jeremiah who brings to our attention what we might call the "inner world" of suffering—the loneliness, despair, and intellectual turmoil in which the realities of life appear destructive of all those values and ambitions which make life worth living. By such means he discovered the true ground of hope as something far greater than a mere optimism and the cheerful assumption that somehow, in the end, things will "work out alright."

In order to understand the significance of Jeremiah's prayer it is necessary to know something of the times in which he lived, for his prayer is set as the response to a quite specific and extraordinary situation. When Jeremiah first received his call to be a prophet in the year 727 B.C. (Jer. 1:2), the king, Josiah, was still a young man, having come to the throne in Jerusalem as a mere boy of eight. His father had been assassinated, but the assassins had themselves been put to death and the legitimate heir to the throne installed (2 Kings 21:23–24). The intrigues and politics which lay behind such moves are not fully known to us, although it is clear that the major change that was affecting the entire area of the Middle East was the steady decline of Assyrian imperial power. It was this fact which lay behind the great reform of worship which took place in Jerusalem and Bethel five years after Jeremiah had begun his prophetic activity (2 Kings 22—23), when Josiah had been on the throne for eighteen years (2 Kings 22:3).

We have few prophecies from Jeremiah preserved for us from these years of Josiah's rule, however, and this undoubtedly reflects the sense of mounting tragedy and disaster which belongs to the later years of Jeremiah's work. In the face of the heady and enthusiastic hopes of the people of Judah that Josiah would prove to be a "new David," restoring the ancient borders of the kingdom of Israel and giving to it a new prosperity, peace, and independence, the reality proved to be quite otherwise. Egypt too was expanding and seeking to secure its frontiers now that Assyrian power had weakened, and Josiah died tragically and futilely trying to prevent the passage of the Egyptian king Necho through his territory (2 Chron. 35:20–24). After a brief three-month reign of Jehoahaz (2 Kings 23:31), this ruler was deposed and Jehoiakim made king in his place (2 Kings 23:34). However, soon the armies of Babylon were in the region, effectively filling the power vacuum left by the departure of the Assyrians and imposing their will in the entire region as far as the borders of Egypt. Jehoiakim became a vassal to the new power but rebelled after three years, inviting inevitable punishment (2 Kings 24:1–17). Jehoiakim died before Jerusalem finally fell to the besieging Babylonian armies, leaving his son Jehoiachin to face the wrath of the king of Babylon. Jehoiachin, with his family, was taken to Babylon, apparently as a kind of royal hostage, along with many leading citizens of Jerusalem. A new king, Zedekiah, also of the Davidic house and uncle of the deposed ruler, was placed on the throne. The confusions and tensions within Judah were not simply caused by the clash of personalities, however, but reflected deep-rooted uncertainties about the nature and right political ordering of the people under Babylonian imperial domination. All too readily and enthusiastically many were asserting that God's purpose for Judah must entail freedom and independence, with the removal of the imperialist yoke of the king of Babylon. Such was the advocacy of the prophet Hananiah (Jer. 28:10–11), and it is not difficult to see how readily such an apparent message from God would have appealed to a people who so dearly wanted this to be so. Although there are many indications of vacillation and uncertainty in the mind of king Zedekiah, he eventually aligned himself and his kingdom with the cause of rebellion against Babylon yet again, and invited further punishment and ruin as a result. The Babylonian king Nebuchadnezzar then sent his forces to lay siege to Jerusalem a second time, with Zedekiah determined to resist, in spite of strong and angry protestations from Jeremiah. The eventual outcome was as tragic as it was inevitable. Jerusalem was captured after a long siege and terrible suffering caused by disease and starvation; Zedekiah's sons were killed before his eyes, and he himself was blinded and taken prisoner to Babylon. Jerusalem was systematically burned and destroyed, and many more citizens taken as prisoners (Jer. 39—40). A terrible end came in this way to the surviving part of the once great kingdom of Israel, bringing an end to the two great institutions—the temple and the Davidic kingship—which had remained such symbols of hope

and assurance that God was with the people and would never forsake
them. With their downfall hope itself appeared to have been eclipsed,
as the anguished cries of the book of Lamentations show.

It was during the last months of Jerusalem's resistance to the
besieging Babylonian forces, however, that an incident happened
which came to be seen by Jeremiah as a message of hope from God,
and which provided the basis for his prayer. The incident is recounted
for us in Jeremiah 32, when a cousin of the prophet named Hanamel
came to him while Jerusalem was under siege to offer for sale a plot
of land in Anathoth. Both social tradition and family obligation
looked to Jeremiah to make such a purchase in order to preserve the
family's estate, even at a time when circumstances gave little reason
to believe that Jeremiah would ever benefit from such a purchase
(Jer. 32:1–15). Jeremiah responded to the situation by honoring his
obligations and making the purchase, and in doing so, he discerned
that the very message of God had been given to him:

> "For thus says the LORD of hosts, the God of Israel: Houses and fields
> and vineyards shall again be bought in this land."
>
> (Jeremiah 32:15)

The prayer of Jeremiah follows directly from this action and discovery of the word of God (Jer. 32:16–25), and in turn it is extended
to a further reflective meditation on God's message contained in the
opportunity to purchase the field in Anathoth (Jer. 32:26–44). In the
face of a situation of growing terror and despair Jeremiah had found
in a simple business transaction, which on the surface appeared both
futile and pointless, a sacrament—a disclosure of the being and reality of God!

The Prayer

We have already learned enough of Jeremiah's situation to see
how intimately his prayer is bound up with the unique situation in
which he found himself. His prayer itself is unique, since it belongs
to this distinctive moment of his life and experience. When we examine it closely, however, we find that what it brings to light are the
enduring, universal truths which this very particular experience had
uncovered. Its theme is hope, and the way in which a truly durable

and effective hope can only be grounded in God; all other grounds of hope either derive from this or they are false.

> "After I had given the deed of purchase to Baruch the son of Neriah, I prayed to the LORD, saying: 'Ah Lord GOD! It is thou who hast made the heavens and the earth by thy great power and by thy outstretched arm! Nothing is too hard for thee, who showest steadfast love to thousands, but dost requite the guilt of fathers to their children after them, O great and mighty God whose name is the LORD of hosts, great in counsel and mighty in deed; whose eyes are open to all the ways of men, rewarding every man according to his ways and according to the fruit of his doings; who hast shown signs and wonders in the land of Egypt, and to this day in Israel and among all mankind, and hast made thee a name, as at this day. Thou didst bring thy people Israel out of the land of Egypt with signs and wonders, with a strong hand and outstretched arm, and with great terror; and thou gavest them this land, which thou didst swear to their fathers to give them, a land flowing with milk and honey; and they entered and took possession of it. But they did not obey thy voice or walk in thy law; they did nothing of all thou didst command them to do. Therefore thou hast made all this evil come upon them. Behold, the siege mounds have come up to the city to take it, and because of sword and famine and pestilence the city is given into the hands of the Chaldeans who are fighting against it. What thou didst speak has come to pass, and behold, thou seest it. Yet thou, O Lord GOD, hast said to me, "Buy the field for money and get witnesses"—though the city is given into the hands of the Chaldeans.'"
>
> (Jeremiah 32:16–25)

The prayer is very beautifully and skillfully constructed, built around a number of set phrases and familiar themes which are well known from the book of Jeremiah and other literature from this period. It is in this fashion that it achieves its effect, by drawing upon the resources of established themes and ideas and focusing them upon the particular situation which had just transpired. In a sense it appears a rather inconclusive prayer, since it is neither a confession, a petition, nor yet an intercession in the familiar sense. It is rather the deepest form of prayer which instead of seeking "answers to prayer" in the accustomed way, is concerned to discover "the Answering One." Thereby it proffers assurance knowing that in submission to God lies an infinity of answer.

We can separate the prayer into four sections which provide us with a way of understanding the contribution that each of its major themes makes to the overall work:

1. Verses 1–19: General Descriptive Praise of God
2. Verses 20–23a: Thanksgiving for God's Particular Goodness to Israel
3. Verses 23b–24: Confession of Guilt and Cry of Distress
4. Verse 25: Divine Assurance and Submission to God

The opening section, with its broad descriptions of who God is, draws our attention back to some well known themes: God is omnipotent, "nothing is too hard for thee"; God is merciful, yet with a mercy that is never unjust nor indifferent to human wrong and injustice; God is universal and omniscient, since God's "eyes are open to all the ways of men"; and God is impartial and just, "rewarding every man according to his ways and according to the fruit of his doings."

From this broad general understanding of who God is the prayer reflects on the particular features of the divine goodness towards Israel—delivering them out of the slavery of Egypt and giving them a land that was rich and plentiful. It was precisely this freedom and life as a nation that were now threatened with disaster by the armies of Babylon. The prophet, however, can offer no defense for his own fate, nor for that of his people—"they did nothing of all thou didst command them to do." It is from this awareness that the prayer makes its starkest and most painful assertion: "Thou hast made all this evil come upon them." No doubt the discerning historian could see and uncover a whole range of contributory factors which had brought Israel to its current predicament, with resistance virtually at an end and the Babylonian forces about to enter the city taking terrible vengeance. The prophet's prayer sees instead only one simple cause— the wrath of God—justifiably aroused against Israel for their willful refusal to obey God's commands. If it is in one sense an over simple way of explaining the human tragedy, it is nevertheless a very profound one. It is the ultimate confession and realization that the cause of ruin and disaster lies in the sinfulness of the human heart and not in some transcendent divinely appointed "fate" from which men and women can never escape. Jeremiah's accusatory laying of responsibility for its ruin at Israel's door retains the deepest possible conviction of the dignity afforded by human choice. The Israelites must not see themselves as the actors in a tragic drama, for which they neither wrote the script nor chose the several parts which each must play. On the contrary the disaster that now faced them was one for which they must bear the full weight of responsibility. The prayer moves towards its climax with a pointed reference to the violence and disease which was already tearing out the heart of Jerusalem, and to the Babylonian armies poised to deliver the final blows. Then, in a sharply contrasting conclusion it reflects on the injunction from God through Hanamel: "Buy the field for money and get witnesses." This is where the hope engendered by God turns on its head the awfulness of the tragedy about to take place.

It is especially important to note that this hope Jeremiah had discovered was not an easy optimism which trusted that in the final outcome the catastrophe would be averted and a way of escape would be found for all who remained alive in Jerusalem. On the contrary Jeremiah saw this disaster as inevitable and imminent. There could not now be any evasion of the consequences of all that had transpired between Judah and Babylon in the preceding years. In the darkest hours of judgment and suffering, however, God would not be absent and God's purpose would not be ultimately thwarted. The light would shine in the darkness and the darkness would not extinguish it, for this light was the light of hope given by God.

The divine response which follows in verses 26–44 is capable of being taken as, in a very real measure, simply the second part of Jeremiah's prayer, since it is a reflective elaboration of it. It reaffirms, with renewed certainty all that is contained so briefly and cryptically in the message of God relating to Hanamel's visit:

> "For thus says the LORD: Just as I have brought all this great evil upon this people, so I will bring upon them all the good that I promise them. Fields shall be bought in this land of which you are saying, It is a desolation, without man or beast; it is given into the hands of the Chaldeans. Fields shall be bought for money, and deeds shall be signed and sealed and witnessed, in the land of Benjamin, in the places about Jerusalem, and in the cities of Judah, in the cities of the hill country, in the cities of the Shephelah, and in the cities of the Negeb; for I will restore their fortunes, says the LORD."

> (Jeremiah 32:42–44)

It is not difficult for us to imagine how, in the long years of waiting for a restoration of normal life and reasonable prosperity after the Babylonians tore Jerusalem apart, this simple message from Jeremiah became a beacon of hope.

The Significance of the Prayer

So far as its character as a prayer is concerned we have already touched upon the most remarkable feature of this utterance of Jeremiah's. It is not a prayer looking for an answer in the traditional sense. Had it been set in some other time and circumstance we might almost have treated it as a thanksgiving for hope. The sense of imminent tragedy precludes this being so, however, and there is a strong confessional interest in affirming the justness of the punishment Israel had to face. Poised between a plea for mercy and thankfulness for the assurance of it, the prayer focuses all its concern on the contrast afforded by the knowledge: "Yet thou, O Lord GOD, hast said to me, . . . there is hope!" It is the certainty of hope, enshrined in the command to buy the field in Anathoth, which gives to the prayer its lasting meaning and significance. God means hope, and wherever we encounter God we encounter this reality of hope that sees no frontier which can separate us from it. It is a vivid anticipation in the Old Testament of the assurance St. Paul gives in the New: "Who shall separate us from the love of Christ? Shall tribulation, or distress, or persecution, or famine, or nakedness, or peril, or sword?" (Rom. 8:35). Similarly, in the darkest hour that the Old Testament story of Israel's history records, Jeremiah had learned that no disaster or suffering could raise a barrier that would ultimately cut off God's people. In a manner that the prophet never fully works out he had received an assurance that God was "in" the suffering. This in no way exonerated the people for their own guilt, a point which is very emphatically stressed in Jeremiah's prayer. It did mean that punishment, however just in the eyes of the world and in the eyes of God, would never be the final verdict upon Israel. Jeremiah had come to the realization of what modern religious writers would describe as the dimension of "depth" in our human make-up and in the nature of God. This depth establishes a common ground in which our human existence touches the ultimate reality and foundation of all existence, which we know as God. It is the fact of this "common ground" which generates the experience of hope. Hope represents the carrying over into our particular circumstances of the entire range of possibilities that God's creative power establishes.

The memory of the destruction of Jerusalem by the armies of Babylon in 587 B.C., combined with the recollection of the later destruction by the Romans in A.D. 70, is still retained in the Jewish celebration of 9th Ab, a celebration of confession and mourning. However, the retention of so tragic and gloomy a recollection is, in a paradoxical fashion, a symbol of hope. In a similar way the cross, token of human injustice and perversity, has become a symbol of hope for all Christians. The reason for this combining of tragedy with spiritual triumph and hope is closely bound up with the character of Jeremiah's prayer. It is only when the depths of human misery and disaster are uncovered that the reality of God and the hope that God brings are shown to be the ground that lies beneath them. It would certainly be wrong to try to turn Jeremiah's prayer into an apology for suffering, as though the ultimate discovery of the divine nature of hope somehow justified the agony and pain of death and ruination. This is certainly not its claim nor its intention. It does recognize, however, that even the depths of misery and disaster are not in themselves an end to the purposes of God. God is hope, God brings hope, and God can even turn a seemingly futile and meaningless business transaction into a sacrament of hope. Those who hope in things or plans or even in the durability of certain human institutions will in the end find that such hopes can disappoint and prove futile. Yet those who are forced to this realization will discover that they have not exhausted the power and possibility of hope but have simply uncovered that the final ground for hope lies in God.

14
A *Prayer of* EZRA

Ezra 9:6–15

Ezra the Man

According to Ezra 7:7 the scribe Ezra went from Babylon at the head of a mission to Jerusalem in the seventh year of the Persian king Artaxerxes. Assuming this refers to Artaxerxes I Longimanus this would have been the year 458 B.C., more than a century after the destruction of Jerusalem and its temple which forms so central a background to the preaching of the prophet Jeremiah. Ezra, however, was not a prophet but a "scribe, learned in matters of the commandments of the LORD and his statutes for Israel" (Ezra 7:11). In order to appreciate the significance of this role, and the fact that Ezra came, not from Judah but from Babylon, which was now under the imperial control of Persia, it is necessary to reflect upon what had happened to the survivors of Judah in the intervening years.

We know that two major deportations of citizens from Jerusalem and Judah took place at the hands of the Babylonians, and Jeremiah 52:30 also makes reference to a third deportation during the twenty-third year of Nebuchadnezzar's reign. These deportations resulted in the setting up in Babylon of a substantial community of exiled Judeans, who were forced to work out for themselves ways of surviving and of upholding their religious loyalty in an environment sharply hostile to them and their faith. Jeremiah had almost found himself among these deportees but had been allowed by the Babylonian officers to remain in Judah. Nevertheless there were prophets among the Babylonian exiles, most notably Ezekiel and the unknown prophet to whom we owe the remarkable prophecies of Isaiah 40—55. The exiles were not without leadership and certainly not without the guidance of priests who could serve as the custodians of the age-old traditions of Israelite worship. What they lacked was a sanctuary in which they could carry out their customary acts of worship and also no doubt much of the freedom that was necessary if they were truly to live their lives in accordance with the traditions of Moses. Here however a striking feature shows itself, for not only was there a richly endowed leadership of priests and prophets among the Babylonian exiles, but the circumstances compelling them to live in camps served to deepen their sense of "belonging" to Judah and to Jerusalem. They developed the mind and heart of men and women who knew themselves to be living a make-do, temporary form of existence. Their very worship must have emerged as a kind of temporary, makeshift arrangement, circumscribed by the inevitable limitations of their situation. It is, in retrospect, one of the most remarkable spiritual achievements of the entire Old Testament, comparable with the miracle of the exodus from Egypt itself, that these people did not lose faith and direction, but in a real sense increased and intensified their conviction that the God who had punished them by sending them into exile had also promised to bring them home again.

It is true that in 538 B.C., when the Babylonian empire finally collapsed before the armies of Persia, a small number of these exiles were able to return to their homeland. They were only a small part of those who had survived the miseries of exile in Babylon, however. Most remained settled and scattered in the country of their exile, and soon, under the new freedom which Persian control brought with it, began to spread more distantly throughout Persian-controlled lands. In this fashion there began, out of the experience of exile, the phenomenon that has been the most characteristic feature of Judaism ever since—the Dispersion. The wandering Jew arose, to travel and often settle in various foreign lands, while retaining a sense of belonging elsewhere—to Jerusalem, to Zion, and to Israel. It is from just such a changed and changing world that Ezra came, and in a very direct way he appears as a leader and protagonist for this new freer, international expression of the faith of Moses.

If we pause to reflect what had been happening to Jerusalem and Judah in the meantime, we find surprising contrasts. It is evident from the book of Jeremiah and from that of Lamentations that the initial shock of Babylonian capture and destruction had been fearful. There were survivors who must clearly have nurtured hopes that they would, given time, be able to restore their land and city and live to fulfill the hope of restoration which had been assured through the prophet Jeremiah. The situation deteriorated rather than improved, however, and even Jeremiah himself ended his life in Egypt, carried there against his will by frightened fellow Judeans after the Babylonian appointed governor Gedaliah had been assassinated. Perhaps with this event Babylonian patience was at an end, and entirely unwelcome conditions of administration and control were imposed upon what remained of Judah and Jerusalem. In any event we learn very little indeed of the situation in Judah after these setbacks for more than a generation. The editors of the books of Jeremiah and Ezekiel clearly came to focus all their hope for the future upon a return of the exiles from Babylon. The very notion of "return" took on a striking double sense—on the one hand as a spiritual returning to God in heart and mind, and on the other as a return to the homeland of those who had been deported.

The contingent that returned to Jerusalem from Babylon in 538 B.C., after the collapse of Babylonian power, followed in 520 B.C. by others under the leadership of a royal Davidic prince Zerubbabel, formed only a part of the now increasingly scattered Jewish community. In a real sense the years of Israel as a national state were ended and the years of Judaism as a religion of scattered heirs of Abraham and Moses living among the nations were just beginning. Even the rebuilding of the temple of Jerusalem in 515 B.C. marked only a step towards the fulfillment of the hope of restoration. Jerusalem was not rebuilt in any meaningful fashion, the Davidic kingship was not restored, and there was no return to full independent nationhood, such as people had hoped for. The population in what had been the kingdom of Judah became intermingled with incoming immigrants from the neighboring peoples and further to the north, in what had been at one time the capital of the Northern Kingdom, Samaria, the population became increasingly detached from, and hostile to, the leaders in Jerusalem. It becomes a fine point of comparison, and one which is incapable of being resolved, whether the population in Judea and Samaria was more mixed than was the case for devout Jewish communities living much further afield in exile. Judaism had in fact turned a corner, and having done so, it could not return to the days before the coming of the Babylonians.

It is in this situation that we can understand the significance of Ezra and of the title accorded to him as a "scribe, learned in matters of the LORD and his statutes for Israel." Tradition has pictured Ezra as a "Second Moses," fully furnished with the books of the laws of God, just as Moses had delivered them. This is unrealistic, unlikely, and unconvincing, however, to the majority of scholars who have studied his work. Rather we can see Ezra as the guide and administrator who had developed ways of remaining loyal to the essential spirit and tradition of the old constitution which was traced back to Moses, while at the same time adapting it to the new situation of those who had to live among Gentiles in a predominantly Gentile environment. Ezra was, understood in this light, the guide and administrator of the new Judaism of the Dispersion. He had adapted to the new environment and used his judgment and experience in showing how life in a Gentile world did not mean the abandoning of the ancestral faith of Moses. He was no doubt in the eyes of many an archconservative, urging people to retain a way of life that had its roots in a past that no longer fully applied. In the eyes of others he was undoubtedly seen as an archradical—a dangerous progressive who was developing ways by which Jews could come to some kind of *modus vivendi* in a Gentile world. To them he appeared to be sacrificing too much and conceding that there was to be no immediate return of all exiled Jews to their homeland so that everything could return to the situation before Jerusalem had been destroyed. No doubt too Ezra was seen by some as a dangerous collaborator, and it has been suggested that his very title as "scribe" may point to his having been a "Secretary for Jewish Affairs" in the Persian administration. Undoubtedly he was willing to work with the Persian authorities, to accept support from them, and he clearly believed that all the essentials of Jewish life could be preserved under the overall control of a Persian government which saw Judaism as merely one among a number of religions practiced by its subject peoples. Ezra was a very central figure of the later (postexilic) Old Testament period, therefore, and one who was almost certainly controversial. His was the task of establishing and maintaining a difficult and dangerous balance between traditional loyalties and present realities.

The Prayer

The prayer which we are now to examine belongs essentially to the situation of Ezra which we have described; yet precisely because this situation was one that was to become increasingly typical of the life of Jews in the postexilic period, it expresses so much of the atmosphere, tension, and concern that has colored Jewish life so extensively ever since. It is in the form of a lament to God, voiced very poignantly by Ezra in the first person, with a strong note of confession, and culminating in one very passionately felt plea:

"O my God, I am ashamed and blush to lift my face to thee, my God, for our iniquities have risen higher than our heads, and our guilt has mounted up to the heavens. From the days of our fathers to this day we have been in great guilt; and for our iniquities we, our kings, and our priests have been given into the hand of the kings of the lands, to the sword, to captivity, to plundering, and to utter shame, as at this day. But now for a brief moment favor has been shown by the LORD our God, to leave us a remnant, and to give us a secure hold within his holy place, that our God may brighten our eyes and grant us a little reviving in our bondage. For we are bondmen; yet our God has not forsaken us in our bondage, but has extended to us his steadfast love before the kings of Persia, to grant us some reviving to set up the house of our God, to repair its ruins, and to give us protection in Judea and Jerusalem.

"And now, O our God, what shall we say after this? For we have forsaken thy commandments, which thou didst command by thy servants the prophets, saying, 'The land which you are entering, to take possession of it, is a land unclean with the pollutions of the peoples of the lands, with their abominations which have filled it from end to end with their uncleanness. Therefore give not your daughters to their sons, neither take their daughters for your sons, and never seek their peace or prosperity, that you may be strong, and eat the good of the land, and leave it for an inheritance to your children for ever.' And after all that has come upon us for our evil deeds and for our great guilt, seeing that thou, our God, hast punished us less than our iniquities deserved and hast given us such a remnant as this, shall we break thy commandments again and intermarry with the peoples who practice these abominations? Wouldst thou not be angry with us till thou wouldst consume us,

so that there should be no remnant, nor any to escape? O LORD the God
of Israel, thou art just, for we are left a remnant that has escaped, as at
this day. Behold, we are before thee in our guilt, for none can stand
before thee because of this."

(Ezra 9:6–15)

The prayer is a confession of sin, and in part in takes the form of
a general confession of the sinfulness of Israel through its history
which had led to its heirs being scattered among the nations. This
remnant had not been rejected and abandoned by God, however, but
rather had been granted a remarkable "reviving" (Ezra 9:9). Whether
this "reviving" could continue and lead to a strong and purposeful
remnant of Jews among the nations focused sharply on one issue:
that of intermarriage with the sons and daughters of the nations from
which God had chosen their ancestors to be separate. We can discern
the following structure in the prayer, which is confessional in its
form, but firmly theological and ethical in its purpose. The prayer
begins with a general historical retrospect of the sins of Israel from
the days of its ancestors to the present: "our guilt has mounted up to
the heavens" (Ezra 9:6–7). Then, in spite of deserving the judgment
that had befallen her, Israel had by the great mercy of God received
the blessing of a certain reviving and restoration: "to set up the house
of our God, to repair its ruins, and to give us protection in Judea and
Jerusalem" (Ezra 9:9). Next we find an affirmation of the righteousness of God: "we have forsaken thy commandments" (Ezra 9:1–12),
followed by contrite reflection: "shall we break thy commandments again?" (Ezra 9:13–14). The prayer concludes with an affirmation: "we are left a remnant . . . we are before thee in our guilt"
(Ezra 9:15).

The prayer is, for the most part self-explanatory, but one feature
cannot be emphasized too strongly: confession of sin and the acceptance of forgiveness is never a path to excusing sin and saying that it
does not really matter. It is in reality quite the opposite—a recognition that sin does matter, but that it need never be our last response
to God; nor will God's indignation against our sin ever be the last
word to us. Confession is a path to forgiveness, and the acceptance
of forgiveness is the most creative and restoring experience that we
can have. By focusing upon one particular issue that had so pro-

foundly affected Israel's past—Israel's election to be separate from the ways of the nations—the prayer secures for itself maximum attention in the present. This narrowed down to the issue of intermarriage with Gentiles and the concomitant threat of assimilation. From all that we know of the life and circumstances of Ezra it is not difficult to see why this had become a major issue. Israel was now living in intimate proximity to Gentile peoples as a consequence of the Dispersion and, even in Judah and Jerusalem, the population had become very intermixed and multinational. As the result of the upheavals brought about by the periods of Assyrian, Babylonian, and Persian rule and conquests, so many of the older ethnic, social, and political groupings in the lands of the eastern Mediterranean had been broken up. For many this was a matter of indifference, whereas for others, conscious of a rich and distinctive religious heritage, it was a matter of deep concern. Should such a process be allowed to continue to its inevitable conclusion, with the complete leveling and intermingling of cultures? Ezra clearly felt passionately that it should not and that, while there were reasonable areas of flexibility over many issues of a political and social nature, some concessions could not be tolerated. Mixed marriage was clearly one such issue and, evidently, one that was most keenly felt by several important spiritual leaders. The rightness of such a verdict in the circumstances of the time and some of the wider issues that it raises will be considered in a moment, but for the character of Ezra's prayer it marks a central feature. Confession is a way of breaking free of sin, not a wallowing in it. Even though the language about sin in Ezra's prayer is very forthrightly worded—"our iniquities have risen higher than our heads, and our guilt has mounted up to the heavens"—this is in no way a merely verbal exaggeration. It is against such a background of sin that God's acts of reviving appear so remarkable and so completely undeserved. In the face of such a gracious and merciful God almost anything is possible, but all this would certainly have been lost if there had been a yielding to the inevitable pressures imposed by mixed marriages. Instead of a remnant, Israel simply would have been assimilated, and its unique spiritual heritage would have lain buried in that assimilation.

The Significance of the Prayer

How we view Ezra's prayer, richly worded and carefully constructed in its form, must inevitably rest on our judgment towards his policy of resisting marriages with non-Jewish (Gentile) men and women. Some have certainly seen here the erection of a barrier which, when combined with the closely contemporary work of Nehemiah, served to set Jews and Judaism apart. It was not entirely unconnected with the later medieval emergence of ghettoes and with a corresponding Gentile reaction against Judaism in the form of anti-Semitism. Later Christians saw in the work and freedom brought by Jesus of Nazareth a breaking down of the old barriers which separated Jew from Gentile. It was also true that the early Christians found the unique bonds of marriage set under considerable strains when Christian and non-Christian were joined together (cf. 1 Cor. 7:12–16). Mixed marriages have been as readily seen as a danger to spiritual health and vitality among Christians as they have among Jews.

We may look at the issue which Ezra faced in a constructive and positive light, however, and the insights of modern social anthropology would certainly support our doing so. Ezra faced a remarkably changed world from that in which the older Mosaic legislation had been drawn up. When Israel had been a nation, not only families, but whole towns and villages naturally shared a common religious life and heritage. The enormous social dislocations brought about by the imperialist ambitions of Assyria, Babylon, and Persia had changed all of this to an extent that it is hard for us to realize in the modern world. Two centuries had passed which had witnessed for Israel and Judah the loss of the relative social stability and cohesion that the formation of the kingdom under Saul and David had brought about. There was no longer an Israelite nor even a Judahite nation as such but rather a diverse number of Jewish communities living in different territories, mostly but not exclusively under Persian administrative control. We should not suppose that even these formed wholly homogeneous village and town communities in all cases, however, although this must often have been sought after. What the earlier traditions and legislation of Israel had provided for in a relatively few and manageable number of cases—learning to live with aliens and foreigners who had become neighbors to Israel—had now become an everyday necessity. We have already noted that the work of Ezra, when we look carefully at what it presupposes, reveals a very bold and progressive attitude on his part. He had, so far as we can tell, conceded that Jews would have to learn to live under the restraints of an imperialistic Persian government and to accept that for the present at least there would be no return to an independent Jewish kingdom with its capital in Jerusalem. The life of exile had already begun to be translated into the life of a Judaism of the Dispersion. Within the adaptations and "openness" that was now required of Jews, if they were to survive among the nations, there were obvious dangers. Judaism too might disappear, and its entire spiritual heritage cease to exist, if Jews of this new pattern of life allowed themselves to become assimilated. Against this Ezra set himself and saw in the strength and wholeness of the family the necessary bulwark against such a happening. The bonds of kinship were to be respected through marriage and the interlocking of cultural, religious, and family ties was to be maintained. So far as Ezra's prayer is concerned it proclaims one deep and passionate plea: let there be no mixed marriages, or else Israel, and all that it stands for, will be swallowed up among the nations! In this we see a very shrewdly observed, and no doubt also painfully experienced, realism. The family lay at the very foundation of society and formed its most basic and indispensable unit. If the religious heritage of Moses was not to be maintained and observed at this level, then it would no longer be maintained at all. Certainly all the insights of modern social anthropologists would strongly agree with Ezra in recognizing the primary role of the family in society.

It is important for the Christian to recognize the reasons which underlie Ezra's deep concern with the question of mixed marriages, since both he and his close contemporary Nehemiah have frequently appeared unattractive to the Christian mind and, in varying degrees, have been seen as architects of that spirit of separatism which colored so much the life of Judaism in the New Testament period and also thereafter. Seen in the circumstances which they were facing neither man can be judged in so negative a light. Certainly for the Christian faith the barriers of distinction between Jew and Gentile were broken down by Jesus Christ and a new path of shared access to God and openness to the spiritual heritage of Abraham and Moses became possible. To a considerable extent the period of Hellenistic and Roman rule had brought a new social leveling into being by the time of Jesus. A new reality had come about which made possible a church which could accommodate both Jew and Gentile. Such was not the case in Ezra's time, and we can fully appreciate the remarkable boldness of so many of the steps which Ezra was advocating. Judaism was coming to terms with the fact that what had appeared to be merely a temporary phase of "exile" was in fact becoming a more enduring state of affairs in "Dispersion." It is not entirely false to see the work of Ezra as a progressive step towards the freeing of the laws and traditions of Moses from their particularist and national limitations (which their original form had enshrined) and their application and extension to provide a pattern and lifestyle for a new generation. The world and religion of "the Israelite" had been destroyed when Nebuchadnezzar had captured and destroyed the central institutions of the kingdom of Judah in 587 B.C. Now the world of "the Jew" had to become a reality. In contributing to this transition, Ezra had a most important role to play in the origins of Judaism.

As a prayer, one last reflection on this particular spiritual legacy of Ezra may be permitted. This passionate plea regarding the issue of mixed marriages is set out in the form of a forcefully worded lament and confession. Israel had denied its unique spiritual heritage in the past and was now in danger of doing so again, perhaps conclusively. The strong language about the extent and fearful nature of Israel's sin, which might otherwise appear exaggerated and extreme, is therefore properly justified. Ezra viewed his concern as a matter of spiritual survival. It is as well that we should keep this fact in mind since it is all too easy for such a deep sense of contrition to become misplaced and overdone. Not only may an act of prayerful confession give voice to regrets and remorse we do not really feel, but it may also lend a note of severity and exaggeration to issues which are, when rightly seen, relatively trivial. This is not to belittle any form or instance of sin, but simply to note the necessity for maintaining a sense of realism and proportion in the pursuit of a spiritual ideal.

Nothing can more quickly undermine a worthy spiritual ideal than to give it an unjustified importance or to magnify minor faults in an extreme fashion. In the end such attitudes merely become artificial and may even show a pathological side. All too often we find that the epithets "spiritual" and "virtuous," when applied to individual persons, take on a mildly critical sense. They are taken to indicate an attitude of self-conscious striving after goodness which is unrealistic, or even to point to a rather detached and unbalanced temperament. Prayers of confession therefore must be handled with care and not made into an excuse for magnifying the trivial and unimportant. This is certainly not the case with Ezra's prayer which, on the contrary, highlights an issue that had become of central importance to the world of Judaism as it was adapting itself to a changed political and social situation. Whatever verdict we take regarding the particular advocacy adopted by Ezra over this issue, we cannot deny that it was a matter of the greatest importance. Should not then all our prayers serve in just such a fashion towards clarifying in our minds the issues with which we are faced and enabling us to face them more honestly?

15
A Prayer of
NEHEMIAH

Nehemiah 1:4–11

Nehemiah the Man

Nehemiah appears to us in the old Testament as the leader of a mission to Jerusalem in the twentieth year of Artaxerxes (Neh. 1:1), which would be the year 445 B.C., and would thus date his initial activity thirteen years later than that of Ezra. Undoubtedly we have to view his life and work in close conjunction with that of Ezra, although the precise sequence in which their separate achievements were made has occasioned a great deal of scholarly debate. Many have felt that the respective actions and concerns of the two men, both of whom acquired their authority from the Persian administration, can more easily be understood if Nehemiah's work was completed first. Yet no decisive evidence that this was the case exists, and it is better to adhere to the order and dating which the Old Testament books of Ezra and Nehemiah present. Where Ezra's task had a distinctly religious character, Nehemiah's bore a much more obviously practical and political nature. This note of practicality pervades the entire story of Nehemiah's activity, and it is noteworthy that the memoirs, preserved for us in the first person as though they derive from a diary or report contain the prayerful petition: "Remember for my good, O my God, all that I have done for this people" (Neh. 5:19). Essentially Nehemiah was a man of action, and it is attractive to see this as a matter of temperament, as well as a feature of the circumstances in which his life was set. In fact the particular details which we learn about Nehemiah suggest that it was this strongly activist side to his nature which led him to embark so successfully on a mission which was not, in the first instance, one that very directly concerned him.

He was the cup-bearer to the Persian ruler Artaxerxes I Longimanus (Neh. 1:11), and it is not wholly clear what the duties of this royal office entailed since, although it suggests a rather menial palace servant, we know that such officials were often men who enjoyed considerable status. As a trusted person at the Persian court in Susa, the capital city, Nehemiah was no doubt able to use his influence for the benefit of his fellow Jews. As in the case of Ezra we find that Nehemiah was the representative of a new generation of Jewish people who had established themselves in the Dispersion. No longer was he even in Babylon, where the exiled citizens of Judah had first had their main center, but in the Persian city of Susa. He had risen to a position of eminence, so that we can reckon upon his settlement as a Jew of the Diaspora as a relatively fixed and considered condition. All of this is of the utmost significance when we look in detail at his achievements concerning affairs in Jerusalem and the immediately surrounding areas of Judah.

Nehemiah's prayer was offered to God when news had come to him by the hand of his brother Hanani of the pitiable state of affairs in Jerusalem: "The survivors there in the province who escaped exile are in great trouble and shame; the wall of Jerusalem is broken down, and its gates are destroyed by fire" (Neh. 1:3). At first glance the fact that this information was brought does not appear surprising, since we have knowledge from other parts of the Old Testament that Jerusalem had been destroyed by the armies of the king of Babylon. Yet it is precisely this awareness that makes this news so interesting. The attack by the Babylonians had taken place more than 140 years previously, and so this in itself cannot have constituted news for Nehemiah. Either Nehemiah had supposed that recent years had witnessed a great improvement in Jerusalem's situation, which proved not to be the case, or more probably, recent events in the city had brought about further destruction and turmoil. Either way it is evident that the mission of Ezra had either been of only very limited success or had even provoked a dangerous backlash upon the citizens living in Jerusalem. Whatever the precise cause of Jerusalem's misfortunes, Nehemiah was a man who would take such a situation deeply to heart. It was this fact which brought him to God in prayer, a prayer burdened with the convictions that something needed to be done.

What Nehemiah did was to seek an interview with the Persian king—undoubtedly a very bold and potentially dangerous action from a foreigner who had a servant's role at the court. From this interview Nehemiah acquired leave from the king to go to Jerusalem to sort out affairs there (Neh. 2:7–8), and this eventually led to his being appointed governor in Jerusalem for a period of twelve years (Neh. 5:14). Nehemiah was able to implement interesting and constructive changes in Jerusalem during this period, acting with commendable courage and selfless dedication (cf. Neh. 5:15). All of this adds up to a picture of a man of decisive determination and genuine concern for his people and for the city which he felt was still in a real sense "his" city. The one measure which is reported most fully in respect of Nehemiah's period of governorship and for which he is most fully and justly remembered, however, is the rebuilding of the wall of the city of Jerusalem. This was clearly a very controversial issue, since even with the backing of the Persian court, Nehemiah felt it wise to survey the need for the work under cover of darkness (Neh. 2:13). Then, once a clear plan of action had been drawn up, a full muster was taken of the people who would be responsible for the work (Neh. 3). The work was then undertaken with a singleness of mind and heart that has gained for the participants an everlasting memorial in the Bible for their determination (Neh. 4:6). Yet the willingness to work was not all that was necessary, since Nehemiah had powerful and influential enemies who threatened the progress of the rebuilding by planning to attack the workers (Neh. 4:15–23). Only a rigorous system of guards and the policy of arming half the workmen with spears enabled the plan for the rebuilding of the city wall to be carried through successfully. Jerusalem and its citizens were thereby in a position to defend themselves from attack and to organize their affairs, including their religious affairs, without undue interference. It is entirely clear therefore that this one very basic task of organizing the rebuilding of the city wall of Jerusalem was the essential presupposition of everything else that Nehemiah was able to achieve during his term of office. But what lay behind the need for this wall? The very fact that it was so important renders extraordinary the failure of the inhabitants of the city to undertake the work earlier.

Unfortunately no complete picture of what lay behind the work of Nehemiah is possible, in view of the paucity of our information for the years which preceded it. We have also to bear in mind that Ezra's mission had taken place not long previously, if the chronological order which the Old Testament presents is to be adhered to. Clearly Ezra had not achieved all that he set out to do, and perhaps more importantly, the attempts to bring about some kind of religious consensus and common policy in both Samaria and Jerusalem had proved unworkable. It is this that most probably provides the key to understanding the significance of Nehemiah's wall. Ezra had endeavored to bring about some reconciliation between Jerusalem and Samaria, whereas Nehemiah's wall was the public recognition that this was not possible, and that Jerusalem must, in consequence, be free to administer its own affairs, free from the meddling interference of the powerful in Samaria. To all intents and purposes therefore Nehemiah was establishing a *de facto* partition of the land which would leave Jerusalem and its immediate environs in Judah in control of its own destiny, within the general framework which the Persian administration in Susa would tolerate. Nor is it hard to see that such would have been a formidable decision to make, as it was undoubtedly difficult to implement. It was, in some measure, giving up any immediate hope of reestablishing a harmonious community across the old lands of Israel and Judah. It was instead looking to making the city of Jerusalem the focus and pivotal center of the religious inheritance of Abraham and Moses. Henceforth "the city," rather than "the land" was to enjoy the forefront of spiritual and political attention. Once again, under the leadership of Nehemiah, Judaism had turned another important corner in its history and a remarkable man of prayer and decisiveness had enabled it to do so.

The Prayer

We have already noted the situation in which Nehemiah's prayer was offered to God, at the very beginning of the work that is recorded of him and at the time when he was set to embark on a seemingly difficult and uncertain venture. That Jerusalem proffered a task needing attention was already clear to him as a result of the news brought by his brother Hanani; that he would be able to provide the leadership to carry it through to a successful conclusion was still very far from certain. His is a prayer of a man about to embark upon a difficult and dangerous assignment:

> When I heard these words I sat down and wept, and mourned for days; and I continued fasting and praying before the God of heaven. And I said, "O LORD God of heaven, the great and terrible God who keeps covenant and steadfast love with those who love him and keep his commandments; let thy ear be attentive, and thy eyes open, to hear the prayer of thy servant which I now pray before thee day and night for the people of Israel thy servants, confessing the sins of the people of Israel, which we have sinned against thee. Yea, I and my father's house have sinned. We have acted very corruptly against thee, and have not kept the commandments, the statutes, and the ordinances which thou didst command thy servant Moses. Remember the word which thou didst command thy servant Moses, saying, 'If you are unfaithful, I will scatter you among the peoples; but if you return to me and keep my commandments and do them, though your dispersed be under the farthest skies, I will gather them thence and bring them to the place which I have chosen, to make my name dwell there.' They are thy servants and thy people, whom thou hast redeemed by thy great power and by thy strong hand. O LORD, let thy ear be attentive to the prayer of thy servant, and to the prayer of thy servants who delight to fear thy name; and give success to thy servant today, and grant him mercy in the sight of this man."
>
> (Nehemiah 1:4–11)

The prayer is essentially a petition, and the request that forms the subject of this petition is contained in the very last clauses: "give success to thy servant today, and grant him mercy in the sight of this man." Anyone who has encountered a fit of nervous apprehension before a major interview or some important public ordeal will immediately feel kin to Nehemiah in his plea. This was to be the most significant undertaking of his life and would require the most careful preparation. He had to win the favor and support of the Persian king for a venture which could at best have been a matter of indifference to him, and might, at worst, have aroused deep suspicion. It is understandable therefore that Nehemiah should have sought the assurance that God would be with him in making his request, and would bring it through to a successful outcome.

For all the simplicity and directness of the petition, "give success to thy servant today," we cannot fail to notice that it is given a long and discursive introduction, couched in very formal language. Evidently Nehemiah's prayer was felt to require the same kind of thoughtful preparation as the larger venture on which he had already set his heart. So far as its character as a prayer is concerned, it is this fact that should engage our attention. As we have already seen in the case of Ezra's prayer, and as we shall see further in other prayers from this postexilic period, a deep sense of sin in which Nehemiah knows he has a personal share hangs heavily over all the people of Israel—"Yea, I and my father's house have sinned." This is certainly not to be dismissed as an ornate theological flourish but rather taken as a necessary perspective on the entire historical context. Israel lay in deep trouble and no longer was there any nation as such but only a diverse and scattered series of communities who had their eyes and hearts set on Jerusalem and Judah. For them the temple and what took place in the city of Jerusalem were matters of deepest concern, even though most of these people lived in other lands and had not even visited the place. This was nevertheless the city to which they hoped one day to return and on which they pinned so many of their hopes for the future—"though your dispersed be under the farthest skies, I will gather them thence and bring them to the place which I have chosen, to make my name dwell there." We can readily imagine how, to Nehemiah, the Persian city of Susa appeared to be set under the farthest skies and how strange it was that he should be concerning himself with affairs in Jerusalem. To a significant extent therefore we can understand why a sense of the sinfulness of all his fellow Jews lay heavily upon Nehemiah. This sin explained not only the distance from God, but also the distance from Jerusalem. The confession of sin which forms the formal opening part of Nehemiah's prayer must therefore be seen as an essential ingredient of it. We have already had many opportunities to note the paradoxes and many-sided nature of biblical prayer. At times it can be simple and direct, and yet it repeatedly and necessarily combines with this a surprising degree of formality and stereotyped language. It is presented as though it is the easiest of all the actions of religion which a person can perform, and yet it is also the hardest! It requires a mere handful of words directed to God, and yet these words can be the hardest to find and are required to be the most carefully chosen of all words. Such words have to fit the facts of the situation and, therefore, have to be based upon a right and proper understanding of it. They also have to fit the requirements and needs of the worshiper who must look into his or her heart as never before to see what it is that he or she really wants. We can understand why it is that here Nehemiah's prayer makes impressive use of a developing theological and liturgical tradition, relevant to the situation in which Jews found themselves scattered in different parts of the Persian empire, in order to make his own very direct and personal petition. All too often we fall into the mistaken assumption that a world of difference lies between the formality of public prayer and the informal simplicity of private prayer. Does Nehemiah's prayer not show this to be a false contrast, and instead impress upon us the fact that, at the moment when it came to making the most intensely personal plea to God, Nehemiah found guidance and direction for his prayer through the considered formality of Jewish liturgy? We shall find other prayers from this period which display the same features. The language of liturgy can become a school of private prayer!

One further facet of the prayer exists which we have already touched upon. The very wording of Nehemiah's petition shows that he had already made up his mind what he wanted to do and how he proposed to set about doing it. His request was therefore certainly not of the "What should I do now?" variety! Here too is surely something of complete centrality to the biblical understanding of prayer. It is not and should never be allowed to become a reason or excuse for failing to think in a practical and responsible way. Perhaps "prayers for guidance" are apt to become one of the most abused and mishandled types of prayer. God has endowed us with powers of thought and furnished us with a rich tradition by which we can learn of God and of the divine purpose. It would be weak self-indulgence to pay no attention to either our own rational faculties or the guidance afforded by Christian experience and understanding, in order to seek some other "sign" of what we should do for God. No doubt Nehemiah's practical temperament gave him a degree of boldness and decisiveness in making his request. We should not suppose, however, that he was in any way preempting God's guidance. Certainly much would have to await further decision if, and only if, he arrived in Jerusalem. It was clear to him already however that, until he could get there honestly and with the full backing of the Persian governmental authorities, such further steps would have to wait. For him at least, embarking on a venture in a genuine spirit of prayer was not an excuse for avoiding difficult decisions.

The Significance of the Prayer

Already in the case of the prayer of Ezra we have encountered a feature that colors this period of Jewish life and development to a remarkable extent. Both men acted under the full authority of the imperial Persian government. So far as we can unearth the facts of the situation both men held positions of importance in the Persian administration. Yet the Persian king and certainly the entire Persian governmental machine remained committed throughout to the religion of Zoroaster. It is clear that this proved to be a relatively enlightened and tolerant administration so far as the treatment of the religious traditions of minority groups was concerned, but there was certainly no assumption that the Persian king had become converted to the faith of the Jews. Nor did either Ezra or Nehemiah suppose that this would happen. In their eyes they were looking for God to act through a pagan ruler, who did not openly acknowledge the Lord's sovereign power. In this we come face to face with the boldness and complexity of the biblical understanding of God's providence. Through these men we have an acceptance in a very personal fashion of a principle that had been voiced earlier by the prophets (cf. Isa. 45:1–7): that the gracious purposes of the Creator are worked through those who acknowledge more than one divine name. This might appear to point to a kind of bland leveling in which everything that occurs in our world is assumed to be, in the end, "the will of God." That is certainly not the biblical teaching, which fully and frankly recognizes the reality of evil and of human freedom. Nevertheless, it views actions according to their character and purpose, and points us to see that, through what later generations of thinkers have come to term "natural grace," God is at work through our entire world and not simply through a handful of chosen ones.

In reflecting upon the important changes that took place for Judaism in the Persian period of imperial domination, we should not leave out of the reckoning some of its longer term repercussions. On the one hand this awareness that God is at work throughout the whole life of women and men, irrespective of their color, race, or religious faith was to become one of the cornerstones of Jewish existence in the Diaspora. That generations of Jewish men and women, intent on remaining loyal to God, should have continued to live in different countries and among Gentile neighbors was due to the conviction that God could "maintain their cause" in their various domiciles. The basic necessities of stable life in the form of security, freedom to trade, and opportunity to express their own way of life could be assured by pagan Gentile rulers. In this respect both Ezra and Nehemiah had established important social and theological precedents. Inevitable dangers were found in such a policy which trusted heavily in the beneficence of Gentile rulers, however, and which proved at times to be seriously misplaced. Later in Old Testament times the religious revolt of the Maccabees in the second century B.C. presents a classic illustration of a situation in which the ruling political authority turned savagely against the loyal community of Jews, threatening their very survival.

In another respect also Nehemiah's prayer draws our attention to a feature of religion which has perennially reappeared. The clothing of Nehemiah's work in an atmosphere of prayer lends to it a certain seal of divine approval. In any case the very fact of recording an account of it in the Old Testament implies a very positive evaluation of it for later Jewish life. Yet Christians have not always found Nehemiah to be a very congenial figure and have looked upon his wall-building achievements as questionable. In the epistle to the Ephesians the breaking down of the "wall" that divided Jew from Gentile was seen as one of the most central consequences of the life and ministry of Jesus of Nazareth (Eph. 2:14). Religion, in its noblest manifestations, has been an agency of reconciliation and peace, breaking through the barriers which have divided communities and which have generated suspicion and fear. Should we then not look upon Nehemiah's achievement as a very dangerous and unwelcome precedent? More than ever in the present world situation are we not forced to see religion as a divisive force, setting Jew against Muslim, Protestant against Catholic, and one which has, in the past made the relationships between Jews and Christians an often bitter and bloody affair? Clearly to these questions there can be no easy answers, and we must frankly recognize those dangerous, as well as beneficent, features which are inherent in all passionately felt religious loyalties.

It becomes very dangerous for us to try to generalize and universalize Nehemiah's action. What may be good and ultimately sensible in one situation may become disruptive and irrational if it is made into a generally applicable policy. From the perspective of the New Testament this was undoubtedly how Nehemiah's action in isolating and separating the Jewish community in Jerusalem had come to be viewed. In the circumstances of the time, however, when Ezra had already earlier attempted a more broadly based attempt to bring peace, Nehemiah's action may be seen as constructive. Better to agree to differ than to remain in constant and open hostility. Furthermore, we are not left in any doubt over the vicious and hostile attitude displayed by the powerful of Samaria towards the Jews living in Jerusalem. Clearly the Samarians were not people who could be easily persuaded to adopt a more conciliatory and constructive line. There is therefore a note of realism about Nehemiah and his work which was of the greatest importance for the way that Jewish life developed during the difficult years of Persian rule. We can sense that men and women were having to come to terms with their own disappointed hopes and unrealized expectations which they had so zealously nurtured during the years of exile. Nehemiah represented an antidote for despair, and also an antidote to those extreme expectations which continued to mesmerize Jewish life for centuries to come of a final cataclysmic intervention of God to put right all the wrongs the Jewish people had suffered. He was content to take one small, but very necessary, step to protect his fellow Jews in Jerusalem and to secure for them and their children a faithful city.

Before leaving our reflection on Nehemiah's prayer we should not let pass its great importance for all that it implies about biblical prayer. All too often prayer is allowed to become a mechanism of passivity in which we ask God to do those things which we feel unable or unwilling to do. False contrasts are thus drawn between

God's work and our own. Prayer is not and cannot be a mechanism of this kind. What is so striking and invigorating in this prayer is that it is a petition which seeks God's help to achieve something through Nehemiah. That he would have to act is already fully accepted, so that the prayer becomes a way of seeking the right direction and the right manner of this action, not of sparing Nehemiah the pain of undertaking it! In this area, too, much clearly can be learned from Nehemiah's prayer about the nature and working of divine grace, which is all the more important because it lies in the very assumptions of the form of the prayer and not in its actual words.

16
A Prayer of
THE LEVITES
Nehemiah 9:5–38

The Levites

It is perhaps unfortunate for the Levites that in the parable of the Good Samaritan (Luke 10:29–37) a Levite is mentioned alongside a priest as one of those who failed to go to the assistance of the man who fell among robbers (Luke 10:32). Certainly their long history of ministry and service in Israel in biblical times calls for a much nobler memorial than this. If then we are to look elsewhere for an indication of the rich contribution made by the Levites to Israel's spirituality, we cannot find a more exciting pointer than in the prayer ascribed to them in Nehemiah 9. As a footnote in the text of the RSV notes, it is the ancient Greek (Septuagint) text which ascribes the prayer that follows to Ezra, whereas the original Hebrew text accords it to the Levites, several of whom are mentioned in the preceding lists of names. It is in any case a truly magnificent prayer, and one which, for all its length, conveys a warm piety and a sense of perspective. It is in its essence a prayer of praise and confession based upon a historical survey of the history of God's people from the days of Abraham. However, before we consider the prayer in detail we should look further at who the Levites were and the role they played in ancient Israel's worship.

In the time after the exile when the books of Ezra and Nehemiah came to be compiled, the Levites were entering upon a new period of ministry. This then remained essentially constant up to the New Testament period, when the Jerusalem temple was destroyed by the Roman armies in A.D. 70. They became a class of "middle rank" clergy, ordained and set apart for a special ministry to, and on behalf of, Israel, and yet debarred from exercising a full priestly role in the offering of sacrifice. This restriction goes back to the ruling set out in Ezekiel 44:10–14 that Levites should not be direct servants of the altar since their ancestors had "gone astray" after idols. Such a limitation had not always applied to the Levites, since we know that Moses was descended from Levites (Exod. 2:1) and they had at one time formed the main class of persons from whom priests were drawn (cf. Judg. 17:7–13, especially vs. 13). It is this priestly role fulfilled by the Levites that acquired for them their reputation as those who were uniquely loyal to and zealous for the Lord God of Israel. This unflinching zeal for God forms the basis for the story in Exodus 32:25–29 of the slaughter by the Levites of those who had succumbed to idolatry by worshiping the golden calf which Aaron had made. As we read it today it is hard not to feel horror and alarm at the violence of the event and the disregard for human life which it displays. Yet we cannot and are not meant to endorse the story in all its features. It derives from an age more brutal than ours in which the putting to death of idolators was certainly countenanced. It is not the bloodthirstiness of the Levites which is praised but rather their loyalty to God at a time when others had easily allowed themselves to be carried astray.

A further word of praise for the zeal of the Levites is to be found in the blessing of Moses in Deuteronomy 33:8–11. Here again it is the willingness of the Levites to set their love of God above their love for parents and brothers which is the central point. During the years when kings reigned in Jerusalem the Levites had undoubtedly exercised a full priestly role. With the great reforms instituted by Josiah (2 Kings 22–23) and the subsequent destruction of the temple in Jerusalem by the Babylonians, the Levites had entered a very changed world. The lists of those who returned to Jerusalem after the exile to serve in the restored temple show that the various Levite families had been heavily affected by the deportations. Nor is it difficult for us to see that both their training and the attitude of uncompromising loyalty to God in which they had been brought up became qualities that mattered greatly during the pressures of life in exile. That the religious life of those who were taken to Babylon remained as strong and influential as it did must have been due in no small measure to the leadership and instruction afforded by those Levites among their number. Thus we may see the functions fulfilled by the Levites undergoing significant changes in the altered circumstances in which they found themselves. From being a priestly group of temple servants they became teachers and guides and developed their skills in a ministry of song and liturgical prayer. When therefore we find in the books of 1 and 2 Chronicles a number of richly liturgical prayers, the new generation of Levites should be looked to as their authors. Also the new richness of prayer that we have noted in the books of Ezra and Nehemiah should be viewed as an extension of this expanded role played by the Levites. Far from their debarring from priestly service acting as a frustration of their hopes, it appears to have spurred them to fulfill their work in new directions. These new directions were to prove of inestimable value to the Israel that was emerging in the Dispersion, in which so many found themselves cut off from the actual temple worship in Jerusalem. The Levites therefore formed an important bridge between the older situation in which the religious life of Israel had found its natural focus in the sacrificial rites of the temple and the newer one in which the focus was a simplified form of worship, based on the singing of Psalms, the offering of prayer, and the reading of Scripture. Eventually much of the worship life of Israel was to lie in the hands of Levites and lay persons. Certainly we should not suppose that all Levites lived up to the fullest ideals of their calling, and the prophet Malachi presents us with a sharp attack upon some Levites who had clearly betrayed the trust that was vested in them (Mal. 2:1–9). It is in the prayer of the Levites preserved in Nehemiah 9, however, that we encounter the richest fruits of the levitical tradition.

The Prayer

Since the prayer is a very long one and is, by its very character, suitable for any age and situation, it is as well that we should examine it straightaway:

> Then the Levites, Jeshua, Kadmiel, Bani, Hashabneiah, Sherebiah, Hodiah, Shebaniah, and Pethahiah, said, "Stand up and bless the LORD your God from everlasting to everlasting. Blessed be thy glorious name which is exalted above all blessing and praise."

And Ezra said: "Thou art the LORD, thou alone; thou hast made heaven, the heaven of heavens, with all their host, the earth and all that is on it, the seas and all that is in them; and thou preservest all of them; and the host of heaven worships thee. Thou art the LORD, the God who didst choose Abram and bring him forth out of Ur of the Chaldeans and give him the name Abraham; and thou didst find his heart faithful before thee, and didst make with him the covenant to give to his descendants the land of the Canaanite, the Hittite, the Amorite, the Perizzite, the Jebusite, and the Girgashite; and thou hast fulfilled thy promise, for thou art righteous.

"And thou didst see the affliction of our fathers in Egypt and hear their cry at the Red Sea, and didst perform signs and wonders against Pharaoh and all his servants and all the people of his land, for thou knewest that they acted insolently against our fathers; and thou didst get thee a name, as it is to this day. And thou didst divide the sea before them, so that they went through the midst of the sea on dry land; and thou didst cast their pursuers into the depths, as a stone into mighty waters. By a pillar of cloud thou didst lead them in the day, and by a pillar of fire in the night to light for them the way in which they should go. Thou didst come down upon Mount Sinai, and speak with them from heaven and give them right ordinances and true laws, good statutes and commandments, and thou didst make known to them thy holy sabbath and command them commandments and statutes and a law by Moses thy servant. Thou didst give them bread from heaven for their hunger and bring forth water for them from the rock for their thirst, and thou didst tell them to go in to possess the land which thou hadst sworn to give them.

"But they and our fathers acted presumptuously and stiffened their neck and did not obey thy commandments; they refused to obey, and were not mindful of the wonders which thou didst perform among them; but they stiffened their neck and appointed a leader to return to their bondage in Egypt. But thou art a God ready to forgive, gracious and merciful, slow to anger and abounding in steadfast love, and didst not forsake them. Even when they had made for themselves a molten calf and said, 'This is your God who brought you up out of Egypt,' and had committed great blasphemies, thou in thy great mercies didst not forsake them in the wilderness; the pillar of cloud which led them in the way did not depart from them by day, nor the pillar of fire by night which lighted for them the way by which they should go. Thou gavest thy good Spirit to instruct them, and didst not withhold thy manna from their mouth, and gavest them water for their thirst. Forty years didst thou sustain them in the wilderness, and they lacked nothing; their clothes did not wear out and their feet did not swell. And thou didst give them kingdoms and peoples, and didst allot to them every corner;

so they took possession of the land of Sihon king of Heshbon and the land of Og king of Bashan. Thou didst multiply their descendants as the stars of heaven, and thou didst bring them into the land which thou hadst told their fathers to enter and possess. So the descendants went in and possessed the land, and thou didst subdue before them the inhabitants of the land, the Canaanites, and didst give them into their hands, with their kings and the peoples of the land, that they might do with them as they would. And they captured fortified cities and a rich land, and took possession of houses full of all good things, cisterns hewn out, vineyards, olive orchards and fruit trees in abundance; so they ate, and were filled and became fat, and delighted themselves in thy great goodness.

"Nevertheless they were disobedient and rebelled against thee and cast thy law behind their back and killed thy prophets, who had warned them in order to turn them back to thee, and they committed great blasphemies. Therefore thou didst give them into the hand of their enemies, who made them suffer; and in the time of their suffering they cried to thee and thou didst hear them from heaven; and according to thy great mercies thou didst give them saviors who saved them from the hand of their enemies. But after they had rest they did evil again before thee, and thou didst abandon them to the hand of their enemies, so that they had dominion over them; yet when they turned and cried to thee thou didst hear from heaven, and many times thou didst deliver them according to thy mercies. And thou didst warn them in order to turn them back to thy law. Yet they acted presumptuously and did not obey thy commandments, but sinned against thy ordinances, by the observance of which a man shall live, and turned a stubborn shoulder and stiffened their neck and would not obey. Many years thou didst bear with them, and didst warn them by thy Spirit through thy prophets; yet they would not give ear. Therefore thou didst give them into the hand of the peoples of the lands. Nevertheless in thy great mercies thou didst not make an end of them or forsake them; for thou art a gracious and merciful God.

"Now therefore, our God, the great and mighty and terrible God, who keepest covenant and steadfast love, let not all the hardship seem little to thee that has come upon us, upon our kings, our princes, our priests, our prophets, our fathers, and all thy people, since the time of the kings of Assyria until this day. Yet thou hast been just in all that has come upon us, for thou hast dealt faithfully and we have acted wickedly; our kings, our princes, our priests, and our fathers have not kept thy law or heeded thy commandments and thy warnings which thou didst give them. They did not serve thee in their kingdom, and in thy great goodness which thou gavest them, and in the large and rich land which thou didst set before them; and they did not turn from their wicked works. Behold, we are slaves this day; in the land that thou gavest to our fathers to enjoy its fruit and its good gifts, behold, we are slaves. And its rich yield goes to the kings whom thou hast set over us because of our sins; they have power also over our bodies and over our cattle at their pleasure, and we are in great distress."

Because of all this we make a firm covenant and write it, and our princes, our Levites, and our priests set their seal to it.

(Nehemiah 9:5–38)

The prayer reads more like a history lesson than any of the prayers that we are more familiar with, although we have already noted in the case of the prayer of Ezra (Ezra 9:6–15) the importance of a long historical retrospect as a part of a plea to God. In character this historical meditation is both an act of thanksgiving for God's providential purpose (cf. Ps. 105) and also an act of contrition and confession of sin (cf. Ps. 106). No doubt we should see within the prayer a combination of the double role that the Levites had come to play in the life of Israel; they were the teachers and instructors of the Jewish community, reminding people of their identity as Jews, of their past with all its triumphs and tragedies, and most of all of their God whose providential care had watched over them and their ancestors. At the same time, the prayer is an act of worship—a liturgical offering—confessing the temptation to waywardness, disillusion, and despair, and finding reassurance through God of deliverance. In its concluding complaint—that foreign rulers control the land and its produce and thereby much of the fruit of its inhabitants' lives—it directs a plea to God for the freedom and justice which could only come through the removal of foreign oppression and a just measure of self-determination in government. To this extent its implied understanding of God's looked-for salvation has a strikingly political overtone. For all this it is a simple prayer, however, in the form of a meditative reflection, which has much to teach us about the right use and understanding of history and about the importance of retaining a proper sense of proportion in relation to the past. Only by understanding the past can we find adequate sense and meaning in the present, and by achieving both of these things we can derive a reasoned and balanced hope for the future.

The Significance of the Prayer

From a perspective of unthinking pragmatism this prayer of the Levites appears to be reminding the all-knowing God of facts already known. Moreover it proceeds to reiterate these facts at very considerable length, even when there appears to be a certain repetitiveness in the recollection of the recent past. Yet to view it in such a manner would be to miss altogether one of the most central and positive contributions that prayer can make. This is in giving us a sense of identity. Prayer can be a way of discovering who we really are and of learning who the people are to whom we belong and what our past is that gives us dignity, purpose, and significance. Clearly the Levites never supposed that God was in need of constant reminders of the history of divine interactions with the people of Israel. However, their work in the community of Jewish people who were coming to terms with the fact of living under the government of Persian authorities, of living in a land amidst others who they recognized only as foreigners, and of knowing that many of their kith and kin were living abroad in scattered and isolated Jewish communities impressed on them the need to retain a sense of identity. Ultimately this was not a question of location nor even of retaining a particular name or address, but rather a matter of spiritual ancestry and heritage. The question "Who am I?" could be answered in practical terms, relating only to name, age, location, and work. In order to satisfy the deeper levels of the human psyche, it needed to answer such a question in spiritual terms as an issue concerning personal and moral values, intellectual and artistic resources, and of personal meaning and destiny. In other words such a question of identity needs a response in religious terms. It is not at all difficult for us to imagine how deep and widespread was this felt need to retain a sense of belonging and spiritual identity in the new situation in which Judaism now found itself. Already the achievements of both Ezra and Nehemiah have highlighted for us that the Judaism which we know—a religion of a people scattered among the lands and nations of the world—was slowly coming into existence as a result of the collapse of the older national states of Israel and Judah. What was achieved through such leaders as Ezra and Nehemiah in regard to the central institutions of

Jewish life in Jerusalem needed to be carried through afresh in the
lives of every individual Jew who sought to remain loyal to the spiritual heritage of the people. We can see how superbly well the prayer
of the Levites addresses itself to such a need. It is a kind of creed—
a confession of faith and an affirmation of hope. God is the same
yesterday, today, and forever, and it is in the knowledge of this unchanging goodness and mercy that those who put their trust in the
Lord discover their spiritual heritage. Far from the lengthy recounting of the highlights of the past amounting to an empty repetition of
events that were finished, it represented instead an endless treasure
and resource for rediscovering the meaning and possibilities of the
present.

In another way also we may reflect upon the meaning of this
"historical" prayer. The past is always with us, not only in the material sense that its buildings and artifacts lie all around us, but in the
deeper psychological sense that each of us carries a vast storehouse
of remembered and half-forgotten experiences that mold our thinking
and attitudes. We even speak metaphorically of those who carry with
them "a chip on the shoulder," by which we refer to some deep hurt
or resentment that people find it difficult or even impossible to forget.
In order to come to terms with our present we must come to terms
with our own individual pasts. So often it is that, in making the effort
to deal with the present, we fail to see that it is not really the present
that poses the problem but rather the past from which we cannot
break free. It is certainly not difficult to find instances of people who
have suffered hurts, injustices, and loss of such magnitude in their
lives that one can only stand in awe of their cheerfulness and ability
to accept it without letting it disfigure their lives. Certainly too we
discover that apparently well balanced and cheerful people carry
with them an inner spiritual room of private feeling and sorrow which
they know could never be shared with anyone except God. In this
very personal and private side of life, we come face to face with a
deepened sense of the importance of such historical meditations as
the prayer of the Levites. Perhaps all of the most essential and vital
aspects of our own personal past experiences need ultimately to be
faced by us in prayer. Only then can they take on the right and proper
perspective that God would give to them. In this way every single

person, whether he or she does so willingly or otherwise, has to come to terms with the past in the private world of prayer. The sober balance which the prayer of the Levites displays between pride and shame—regret and thankfulness—offers us a good example.

We may also pause to consider the valuable insight that this prayer gives into the changed role fulfilled by the Levites in the Jewish community after the exile. It is indicated in the Old Testament that the years which followed the restoration of worship in the temple in Jerusalem were marked by a considerable number of controversies about the privileges and duties of the temple ministry. It was in these disputes and arguments that the Levites eventually found themselves debarred from a priestly office which they believed had rightly belonged to their ancestors. Their years of loyal service to the worship of God in Israel appeared to have left them in an inferior position to those priests—the sons of Aaron—who were entrusted with the full privileges of the priesthood. As we have already mentioned, however, the Levites appear to have developed their arts and skills in the direction of becoming teachers and liturgical guides. The rich development of psalmody, the skilfully constructed prayers that we have noted already, and a general enlargement of the spoken offering to God in worship appear to be a product of their new role. In the longer term when the Jerusalem temple was finally destroyed by the armies of Rome in A.D. 70, it was this verbal praying, teaching, and singing that became the ongoing center of Jewish worship. All offering became the offering of the lips and mind, without any further recourse to the slaughter of animals or the physical presentation to God of creatures slain on an altar. Many of the most central aspects of the Jewish prayer book and liturgy that we know today were established on the foundations laid by the Levites. Something very important therefore had happened to the biblical tradition of worship with the contribution made by the Levites in the post-exilic age. Such a prayer as this, with its unique combination of instruction and liturgical relevance, marks a splendid memorial to them.

17
A Prayer of
JOB

Job 42:1–6

The Story of Job

Job is referred to in Ezekiel 14:20 as a righteous hero of Israel's past, alongside Noah and Daniel. He was evidently famed for his piety and goodness, since the point of Ezekiel's reference to these three men is that even their goodness would not prevail with God to deliver the people of Israel who had become immersed in their sins. Apart from the book which bears Job's name nothing else is known directly about him, not even whether he was a real figure or merely a figure of legend. It is possible that there was such a person whose reputation for piety and goodness had long outlived him in popular memory and storytelling. In any case these historical questions have little bearing on the book of Job and its place in the Bible. It is evident that Job was already a distant figure of the past whose reputation for piety and faith made him a suitable subject for the reflections and discussion which the book contains. These concern the experience of suffering in life, and the questions which such suffering may raise about God's providential care and justice. It is, in essence, the perennial question "Why do people suffer?" It is not difficult to see that often people suffer as a result of their own wrongdoing so that they can be properly held to be responsible for their own miseries. Moreover, when we can sometimes discern a kind of "balancing out" of a willful disregard for the safety and welfare of others with a subsequent experience of misfortune, we can feel that it is as a consequence of God's just government. The book of Proverbs expresses such a viewpoint with vivid poetic realism:

He who digs a pit will fall into it,
  and a stone will come back upon him who starts it rolling.
                                        (Proverbs 26:27)

A kind of "poetic justice" is found then in much of our experience
of misfortune in life which, far from casting doubt on our sense of
God's just government of the world, rather points us to it.

The point at issue in regard to human suffering therefore is not
whether this can sometimes be regarded either directly or indirectly
as a consequence of human sinfulness, but whether this can always
be assumed to be the case. A central feature of the book of Job is the
demonstration that this is certainly not so and that sometimes innocent and righteous people suffer through no fault of their own. More
than this, however, the story shows that through such suffering of the
righteous a higher and more mysterious side of God's purposes may
be served which men and women, because of the inevitable limitations of their understanding, cannot possibly hope to discern. The
book is both a story, which accounts for only a quite small part of its
forty-two chapters, and a long sequence of disquisitions and reflections between Job and his friends. In these disquisitions, set out in
some of the most beautiful poetry of all that has come down to us
from the ancient world, various aspects of the problem of suffering
are aired and discussed.

The story concerning Job is contained in what we may best describe as the prologue and epilogue of the book, covering chapters
1—2 and 42:7–17. Very probably the tale told in these chapters was
already current when it came to be used as the basis for the present
book. The scene is set by showing the reader the exemplary righteousness of Job and the wealth and prestige which had accrued to
him. The scene quickly shifts, however, from Job to heaven where
Satan suggests to God that Job's blameless life is not based on genuine piety but rather on self-interest (Job 1:6–12):

> Then Satan answered the LORD, "Does Job fear God for nought? Hast
> thou not put a hedge about him and his house and all that he has, on
> every side? Thou hast blessed the work of his hands, and his posses-
> sions have increased in the land. But put forth thy hand now, and touch
> all that he has, and he will curse thee to thy face."
>
>   (Job 1:9–11)

The story then unfolds with a series of disasters befalling Job's family and property so that he is quickly deprived of his dearest possessions. Job refuses to be shaken from his trust in God and God's goodness by succumbing to the temptation to curse God for what had happened to him: "Then Job arose, and rent his robe, and shaved his head, and fell upon the ground, and worshiped. And he said, 'Naked I came from my mother's womb, and naked shall I return; the LORD gave, and the LORD has taken away; blessed be the name of the LORD.' In all this Job did not sin or charge God with wrong" (Job 1:20–22).

This is not the end of the matter, however, with Job's piety vindicated, since Satan then proceeds to intensify his accusations that Job's piety is merely a form of self-interest by suggesting that he had not yet suffered enough:

> Then Satan answered the LORD, "Skin for skin! All that a man has he will give for his life. But put forth thy hand now, and touch his bone and his flesh, and he will curse thee to thy face." And the LORD said to Satan, "Behold, he is in your power; only spare his life."
> So Satan went forth from the presence of the LORD, and afflicted Job with loathsome sores from the sole of his foot to the crown of his head. And he took a potsherd with which to scrape himself, and sat among the ashes.
> Then his wife said to him, "Do you still hold fast your integrity? Curse God, and die." But he said to her, "You speak as one of the foolish women would speak. Shall we receive good at the hand of God, and shall we not receive evil?" In all this Job did not sin with his lips.
> (Job 2:4–10)

With this the scene for all that follows in the book is then set, since this is the point at which Job's three friends, or "comforters" as they have become popularly described, arrive to speak with him. Their names are Eliphaz, Bildad, and Zophar, and in spite of some rather distinctive emphases displayed by each of them, their messages are essentially one and the same: God is just, and this justice can never be impugned by people, so that Job must be guilty of some very serious offense against God. It could be that Job honestly does not know what he has done to affront God or that God's goodness is so infinitely wonderful that, by comparison, even the goodness of men and women is tarnished and faulty. They insist that the traditional assumptions that all human suffering is the result of having offended God holds true. By contrast Job insists that this cannot be so in his case since he has done nothing to offend God. Later on a further friend, Elihu, appears and makes further speeches in chapters 32—37 in keeping with the assertions of the other friends. To these speeches Job replies that he has committed no sin commensurate with the sufferings that he is forced to endure, holding equally fast to his conviction that all God's dealings remain totally just. During the course of the debate between Job and his friends the possibility of a life after death in which God might put right and even compensate for the injustices of this life is discussed, but this idea is dismissed as no true answer to the problem which Job had encountered. God's justice must be a real justice that is applicable to life in this world.

We can discern as the various arguments are rehearsed by Job and his friends that several important questions about the nature of human existence are raised. The most prominent is, of course, that of suffering itself, which, because Job has no knowledge whatsoever of the conversations which have taken place between God and Satan, appears mysterious and inexplicable to him. The very notion that his reactions to this could be serving as a hidden witness to the purposes of God and to the truly disinterested and unselfish nature of true piety is completely hidden from him. The story of the opening chapters supplies the reader with suggested answers of which none of the actors in the drama are aware. The reader therefore is in a position like that of viewers of a TV quiz game where they know the solution while the participants do not.

Beyond the question of human suffering and its significance, further issues are raised by the arguments of Job and his friends. Not the least of these is the nature of God's righteousness and of humanity's piety, in view of the unfathomed depths of divine power and wisdom. The question raised by Eliphaz in his first speech is one that constantly recurs in different forms:

> "Can mortal man be righteous before God?
> Can a man be pure before his Maker?"
>   (Job 4:17)

We know that, in the strictest sense, the answer to this must always be "No he cannot!" By insisting on this point so heavily, however, it is possible to rob the idea of God's righteousness and justice of any worthwhile meaning. If all our good works are 'like a polluted garment" (cf. Isa. 64:6), then they are quickly stripped of any worthwhile significance. Job, in countering such an argument, insists that not only is God's justice done in this world, but it can be seen to be done. While admitting that human beings know so very little, he nevertheless insists that what men and women know they really know. In this way Job is able to hold fast to his conviction that God's justice is real and relevant. All along therefore he is able to cling to his basic point that his sufferings must have some other point and purpose than to serve as the punishment for some offense. No hidden sin nor inadvertent folly nor even some unknown infringement of an ancient taboo can be the explanation for his miseries. God's righteousness is a real righteousness, not an arbitrary standard which can leave people without hope of effective compliance with its demands.

By the way in which the opening scenes are presented the reader of the book of Job can make a reasonably informed guess as to the outcome of the story. In truth the story is little more than a framework for the speeches which make up the substance of the book. In a long speech contained in chapters 38—41 God answers Job "out of the whirlwind" pointing to all the infinite variety of life on earth and to the unimaginable skill and craftsmanship that is everywhere displayed. Since these speeches affirm that men and women know so little of the power and purposes of God, how can they presume to have an answer to all their questions? Nevertheless, in a final disclosure, God deals with Job's three friends insisting that they have not spoken the truth in the way that Job has: "the LORD said to Eliphaz the Temanite: 'My wrath is kindled against you and against your two friends; for you have not spoken of me what is right, as my servant Job has'" (Job 42:7). Job is then bidden to pray for his friends and this prayer is accepted by God. It is, however, before this final episode takes place in which Job is vindicated, and his wealth, family, and riches restored, that Job's prayer is offered to God. This is quite unique in its character in the entire Bible and comes as Job's response to the speech of God "out of the whirlwind." In it Job humbly submits himself, his thoughts, and his entire life to God in reverent awe, confessing that he knows so little of anything at all in comparison with the limitless wisdom and majesty of God.

The Prayer

Job's prayer represents the spiritual climax of the whole book, since it is a contrite act of submission and acceptance in response to God's speech. Seen in such a light it offers a kind of goal for all prayer, with its twofold emphases. On one side it is an acknowledgment of human ignorance and frailty, recognizing that even our deepest thoughts cannot penetrate to the ultimate range of God's majesty. What we know is as nothing when compared with what there is to be known. On another side Job's prayer marks an end to striving and a release from all frustration and resentment against life and its demands. Simply to know that God is there is a sufficient ground of assurance and faith. By such submission the pained sufferer will not be able to answer the question of why he or she is called upon to endure such pain, but will be able to live with it without letting it distort all of life.

The simplicity of Job's prayer enables it to speak for itself, yet it would be a mistake to try to understand it or to find some repeatable pattern in it without recognizing that it is a response to God's speech and to the intense arguments that have preceded this:

> Then Job answered the LORD:
> "I know that thou canst do all things,
>   and that no purpose of thine can be thwarted.
> 'Who is this that hides counsel without knowledge?'
> Therefore I have uttered what I did not understand,
>   things too wonderful for me, which I did not know.
> 'Hear, and I will speak;
>   I will question you, and you declare to me.'
> I had heard of thee by the hearing of the ear,
>   but now my eye sees thee;
> therefore I despise myself,
>   and repent in dust and ashes."
>
>   (Job 42:1–6)

Virtually everything that can be said about prayer is contained in the short confession 'I had heard of thee by the hearing of the ear, but now my eye sees thee." Prayer is essentially seeking—seeking help from God to cope with the demands of life, seeking guidance to make wise choices and avoid unwelcome pitfalls, seeking understanding in order to obtain a sense of meaning and purpose. Seeking is not an attitude with which we wish to persevere, however, if it does not also result in finding. What form this ultimate finding may take has been variously described as the vision of God, blessedness, peace, or even ultimate reality. Also, as Job's prayer reminds us very vividly, a consistent pattern displays itself in all the greatest religious quests. Thus a sense of frustration, despair, and helpless ignorance occurs. This is followed by a recognition that what one has striven so hard to find is then given by God with the utmost simplicity and directness. It is so simple that a little child can grasp and understand it. God's kingdom is not a kingdom that can come with human building and ingenuity, it is a gift from God. The truth that we searched the wisdom of all ages to uncover is in fact a truth that we have known since childhood. The nature of the Infinite Being, who is the ground of all existence, can be enshrined in the most familiar and conventional of terms—Thee! Seeking thus becomes finding, and the search for God comes to an end with the realization that it need never have begun, since God has in fact been present and responsive all the time. God's face has never been hidden from us; it is we who have a hand raised to shield ourselves from the brilliance of the light which God beams upon us. We had heard of God through what others had told us, but suddenly and directly the words are transformed into reality and we discover, as if for the first time, what the words about God really mean. So it is that the language of faith is the language of revelation—the self-disclosure of God to us—rather than of a never-ending quest. The pathway to God is a pathway that can only be trodden through prayer.

We may pause to reflect that Job's prayer offers what we can only properly describe as a mystical sense of God. Whether or not the religion of the Bible contains any very dominant strand of mysticism has been much discussed. In many respects the extraordinary down-to-earthness of biblical religion has been viewed as too reasoned and earth-bound for it to be reckoned among the more characteristically "mystical" religions. However, a conviction central to any genuine religious understanding of life is expressed in Job's prayer. This is that God cannot properly be grasped simply as an "idea" or a "concept." God is not a great abstraction which we must postulate in order to understand the nature of things. God is too personal and practically involved in our own striving to live satisfactory and worthy lives to be relegated in this fashion to the realm of abstract ideas. Religion is about being and existing, so that encountering God must be related to our fulfilling the demands of existence, and not simply to speculations that we may make about the difference between existence and nonexistence. Of course it must be frankly acknowledged that when we first learned to "say prayers" or when we discovered that there were things in life that we wanted so dearly that we were prepared to ask God for them, we did not anticipate that our praying would start us off on so deeply serious a quest to discover the ultimate Author and Giver of our lives. Yet this is, through a process of spiritual education and asking of questions, the goal to which even the asking of the simplest of prayers will ultimately lead. How is it that any mere creature can presume to ask the Infinite Creator for "just one thing more" to make life a little easier or a little better? In the end such asking leads to the discovery of truths about the nature and being of God.

The Significance of the Prayer

The book of Job is, first and foremost, a book about human suffering, and scholars continue to debate whether the author did intend to present a firm conclusion regarding the meaning and purpose of human suffering. It is true that the opening episodes in the prologue suggest that Job is to be a living witness to the truth that genuine piety is free of self-interest. Job does in fact "serve God for nothing," since any genuine love can only be offered unconditionally. If men and women loved God solely because they had come to realize that it paid them well to do so, since God rewarded them for their piety, this would represent a very poor kind of love. The author of the book of Job therefore highlights the nature of true piety and shows how the bearing of pain and suffering can become an opportunity for showing genuine love of God. This is certainly not to claim that suffering should in some rather contrived way be welcomed but rather to show that suffering does not and need not dislodge those deeper foundations upon which the spiritual life is built. On the contrary, it can even make those foundations more firm and secure.

Even the reader of the book who knows and understands the significance of the dialogue between God and Satan with which the book begins is offered only a very partial solution to the problem of suffering. It is hinted that some higher purpose of God is being served by it, but nothing more than this. Job's prayer, however, draws our attention to another facet of the situation altogether. In his long "out of the whirlwind" speech to Job God never discloses to Job that he has been made the subject of a special test and ordeal. In fact God never so much as mentions to Job all that lies behind the time of trial through which he has passed. It was a mystery to Job from the beginning, and it is left to remain a mystery. What God has disclosed is the vast and unimaginable array of wonders and mysteries that the Creator has created. How then can Job hope to understand more than a tiny fragment of all this? Even though it is impossible for Job to understand the reasons and purposes that underlie human suffering, he may however discover a way by which he can learn to live with it. It is this practical aspect of the problem that is resolved through Job's prayer: "I had heard of thee . . . but now my eye sees thee." Job had found in God a light and a sense of reality which made suffering bearable.

In another direction Job's prayer highlights a further feature of biblical faith which reappears constantly. On one side Job has all along maintained that he knows very little and the world in which he has been set is full of mystery. How then should he, or any one, expect to ask questions and receive answers regarding the Almighty? Is not the very idea of doing so a foolish act of human presumption? The perennial question is thus raised of whether finite beings can have knowledge of the Infinite. This in turn has so often promoted a strand of anti-intellectualism in Christian life which turns its back on philosophy and the powers of human reason. This certainly finds expression to a limited extent in the Bible, most especially in the book of Ecclesiastes, with which that of Job is often compared:

For in much wisdom is much vexation,
and he who increases knowledge increases sorrow.
(Ecclesiastes 1:18)

This insistence belongs more appropriately to Job's friends than to Job, however. It is they who tell him not to ask too many questions and to be content with the traditional and conventional answers. It is Job who insists that in the end this would be dishonest, and that it could not possibly honor God to admit to truths which in his heart he did not believe. It is this intellectual stubbornness on the part of Job which is so highly praised by God, and the refusal of Job's friends to face unpalatable facts and admit the possibility of being wrong which is so roundly condemned by God: "you have not spoken of me what is right, as my servant Job has" (Job 42:8). The author of the book of Job, therefore, draws our attention to a most fundamental feature of true spirituality. Simply because we cannot know everything does not mean that we cannot really know anything! When we discover that we do not know the answer to a particular problem, it certainly does not imply that there is in fact no answer and that human reason and questioning should be despised. It is, when faced with a difficult problem, all too easy to seek a way out of it by claiming that the problem belongs to "the wisdom of the world" and that the conventional truths that appear to come into conflict with it represent "the wisdom of God." In the end such a division in our thinking becomes a recipe for dishonesty and disaster.

Seen in this light the book of Job is both a very bold and a very speculative book. The very extent to which the opening scenes of dialogue between God and Satan present only a vague and incomplete explanation of Job's ordeal points us all the more surely to the element of mystery that surrounds all our lives. Equally Job's prayer and the final rejoinder from God regarding the wrongness of the attitude of Job's friends provide one of the most powerful affirmations that the Bible has to offer us of the right and duty to think honestly about God. Reasoning and questioning may often be inadequate and imperfect instruments by which to understand our world and the place of our lives within it, yet they are the best instruments we have. Far from faith being a kind of antidote or alternative to reason it is in reality the greatest stimulus to use it rightly and constructively. Job represents the spirit of enterprise in human thinking, and his prayer marks a kind of frontier which he had reached in his questioning. To go forward remained difficult and unknown, yet to go back upon his convictions would have been to sacrifice honesty and integrity for the sake of God. Such a sacrifice is one that God insists that we should not make.

It is also worth remarking that Job's prayer draws our attention to the relationship between praying and thinking. All too often prayer is an exercise undertaken in a spirit of conformity and in deference to a habit which we learn in childhood. For some people even the very prayers they use may change little over the years, so that a sense of familiarity and swift recognition add to their attachment to them. Certainly some prayers are so rich in their language and imagery and so deep in their understanding of the human condition that they can bear such continued and exclusive use. But such prayers are few! Even where such prayers can provide a foundation for an active spiritual life, their exclusive use is likely to result in intellectual stagnation. True prayer calls for a spirit of adventure and for a willingness to allow our growing intellectual questions to intrude themselves into our spiritual ambitions. To this extent the dramatic finality and assurance with which Job's confession comes offers an incentive of spiritual reward: "I had heard of thee . . . but now my eye sees thee."

18
A Prayer of
DANIEL
Daniel 9:3–19

Daniel: The Man and the Book

The figure of Daniel is introduced in Daniel 1:6 and he thereafter appears as one who received visions and dreams in which God's intentions were disclosed. Earlier he appears, alongside Noah and Job, in Ezekiel 14:20 as a traditional hero and pious figure of Israel's more distant past. Yet nothing specific is reported about him, unlike the flood hero Noah. All that can properly be inferred in regard to him is that he was a devout and loyal servant of God.

So far as the book of Daniel is concerned it is noteworthy that, although it is included among the Old Testament books of prophecy in modern translations of the Bible, it is quite unlike prophecy in a great many of its features. In fact its closest biblical counterpart is to be found in the book of Revelation in the New Testament, although a number of comparable Jewish writings are in existence, deriving from the period close to the time of the birth of Christ. Their distinctiveness and the particular way in which they present God's intentions and purposes toward the people Israel have led modern scholars to describe them as "apocalyptic" writings, in order to show their special character. Essentially such a title refers to the way in which such documents present a message concerning God's purposes in the form of "revelations" contained in dreams and visions. In a formal sense such a belief in divine revelation through dreams and visions goes back centuries earlier, since it is a fundamental characteristic of prophecy that God's will can be discovered in this way. The Jewish and Christian "apocalyptic" writings differ considerably, however, from this much older feature of prophetic experience in the highly

complex and detailed form of the dream-visions that they contain.
Where the older type of vision or dream was generally short and
straightforward in its significance, the apocalyptic visions are highly
intricate and mysterious. They are, in reality, a most skillful and
elaborate development of religious imagery and figurative language,
and this language itself needs careful interpretation. The relationship
to prophecy is in many ways more evident in the special interpretations given to the visions and dreams.

When we ask how Jewish visionaries and scribes developed this
special kind of writing, which they then passed on to the early Christian church, we can answer in two directions. In the first place it is
noticeable that a book like Daniel marks a drawing together of various strands of Old Testament tradition. Foremost here is the tradition
of prophecy itself, so that it is noteworthy that quotations of earlier
prophetic sayings are made and fresh interpretations given (e.g., that
from Jer. 29:10 in Dan. 9:2,24). It is also evident that a book such
as that of Daniel is a distinctly "literary" work, displaying a strong
interest in traditional folk themes and a mysterious fascination with
names, key-words, and numbers. All of this suggests that some influence has been felt from a kind of popular folk wisdom, which may
also help to explain why heavenly beings (angels) are given names.
Yet a further line of influence can be traced from a very ancient
tradition of religious symbolism and figurative language, which is
usually described as ancient Near Eastern "mythology." However,
this is probably too undefined and negative a term by which to understand the importance that such symbolism and imagery played in
enabling men and women to picture the reality of the unseen divine
world which they thought of as underlying the everyday world.

Such traditional "ingredients" of the Jewish apocalyptic writings
explain only a small part of their character. More directly pertinent
to understanding them is the troubled and confused world in which
devout Jews found themselves. We have already noted how such
leading men as Ezra and Nehemiah had been compelled to come to
terms with a greatly changed political and religious situation when
Judah and Jerusalem came to be set under Persian imperial rule. In
spite of tensions and difficulties a workable way of living had
emerged in which Jews realized that they could still remain true to

their ancestral faith without constant confrontation with their political masters. The book of Esther reminds us that from time to time serious and bloody conflicts could arise. By the time the major apocalyptic writings appeared, however, the rule of Persia had given way to that of the Greeks. So far as Judah was concerned this meant that, for rather more than a century, most of Judah and Jerusalem came under the imperial control of the Greek Ptolemaic rulers of Egypt. Thereafter, for a brief period the Greek Seleucid rulers from Syria gained the upper hand and controlled Judah. For almost the entire period from 331 B.C., when Alexander the Great gained control of the Eastern Mediterranean coastlands, until 167 B.C., when a fierce guerrilla uprising took place in Judah against such foreign rule, conflicts and wars between the Ptolemies and the Seleucids marred the life of Jews. Inevitably different factions in Judah and Jerusalem found themselves drawn to support either one side or the other.

It is salutary to recognize that in spite of bold and enlightened efforts to spread the cultural and intellectual heritage of Greece among these smaller Mediterranean states, political tyranny and brutality on a large scale intermeshed with the arts, science, and philosophy of Greece. No wonder pious Jews felt their own loyalties deeply divided over the benefits that "Hellenism" had to offer. In many respects it appeared to offer so much that was liberal and liberating in its ideology, yet on the other hand it appeared often as an instrument of repression and hostility towards local religious traditions. This intellectual ferment too and the political repercussions that went with it are also essential ingredients of the rise of Jewish apocalyptic writings, especially the book of Daniel. A new kind of political absolutism is apparent, therefore, with the kingdom of God threatened and challenged by the kingdoms of the world becoming a central theme. Similarly the appeal for loyalty to traditional values emerges exemplified in a timeless and classical way in Daniel's refusal to defile himself by eating the rich food and wine offered to him by the king of Babylon (Dan. 1:8). Daniel's resolve not to forsake his ancestral faith, and even to risk the consequences of imprisonment in a den of lions (Dan. 6:1–28) in order to practice it, indicates the sharpness of the conflicts which the new cultural and political tensions presented to devout Jews.

The book of Daniel can be seen, in the light of such a background, to present a twofold message. In the first part (chapters 1—6) it contains a series of traditional stories focused upon Daniel, encouraging loyalty to God at whatever cost. In the second part (chapters 7—12) it contains a series of dream-visions in which the history of the Jewish people from the time of the Babylonian exile down to the time of the Maccabean uprising is surveyed. The imagery is strange and at times clumsy, with pictures of numerous horns growing up out of fabulous beasts, etc. For all its mysterious and "other-worldly" symbolism, this system of vision-revelations is an attempt to portray the inner meaning of the events that had befallen the Jewish people since the days of the dispersion into exile had first begun. The imagery is an attempt to grasp the nature of history in a broad and world-encompassing manner. It is pictorialized history, but it is not fiction, and its intention is to highlight the tensions and conflicts which such history will bring. Perhaps most surprising for the reader of the book of 1 Maccabees (in the Old Testament Apocrypha) is the fact that even the piously motivated rebellion of Mattathias and his sons is viewed in the book of Daniel only as "a little help" (Dan. 11:34) towards the final establishing of the kingdom of God.

It is understandable that the book of Daniel, like that of Revelation in the New Testament, has often been misinterpreted and misapplied by well-intentioned people. Yet it undoubtedly does have an important message, even in the manner in which it presents, through the starkness of its imagery, a sense of the absolute values which the kingdom of God represents. In a world which had become accustomed to continued compromises and to the painful choices of tarnished political loyalties, the kingdom of God came to offer a new ideal and a new beginning. No doubt it is true that where politics had become circumscribed as "the art of the possible," so faith and religion had come to embrace "the art of the impossible." Such is the nature of visions, however, and such visions have renewed for men and women a new sense of ideals and a new goal to strive for the kingdom of God that will last forever.

Daniel's prayer, which is a long one and is essentially taken up with a deeply-felt confession of sin and intercession on behalf of all

Israel marks an interval between Daniel's visions. It is much more than a pause between more exciting disclosures of God's plans. It is rather a necessary ground and foundation for all the visions, for it voices the anguish, disillusionment, and despair which provide a backdrop for them. As a devout and loyal Jew, Daniel represents a tradition of faith and spiritual concern which had come to feel increasingly submerged and overwhelmed in the turmoil and violence which had swept across Judah for more than a century. The very location given to the heroic figure of Daniel in the court of the king of Babylon, experiencing for the first time all the rigors and bitterness of exile, portrays the way in which loyal Jews saw their own lives. For them exile had never ended, even though they lived within the walls of Jerusalem and could stand within the courtyards of the temple there. Foreign emissaries, foreign soldiers, and foreign customs were everywhere to be seen, so that even living in Jerusalem was like living in a foreign land. The prayer of Daniel therefore is a great outpouring of grief and yearning for a better world, a prayer which could do no more than survey the miserable and disordered society in which the people passed their days and cry out: "O LORD, forgive!"

The Prayer of Daniel

The closest biblical parallels to the prayer of Daniel are to be found in the prayers of Ezra and of the Levites which we have already examined. They all represent deeply felt confessions of sin, followed by passionate pleas that God forgive the chosen people and act in mercy to right the misfortunes that had befallen them. The sense of sin is therefore very prominent, and yet it should not be construed as "sin" in any very narrow or overly pious sense. It is a sense of "sin" that describes a whole human condition, embracing the sickness of society and the disillusionment and despair which invade the human heart when it senses that there can be no easy remedies and no swift injection of a spiritual pain-killer. The political order had become corrupt and ineffective; justice was up for sale, and even the guardians of religion had become carried away with self-gratification instead of spiritual ministry. The book of 2 Maccabees tells of priests in Jerusalem who neglected the temple services in order to get to the

athletic competitions (2 Macc. 4:14). It is therefore a sense of sin on
a personal, civic, and ultimately national scale that lies beneath the
surface of Daniel's prayer. Nor can we suppose that the divine forgiveness for which it pleads so desperately was understood merely
as God's willingness to "close the books" and regard the account as
settled. It was rather a radical change in the whole way of life of
God's people that it looked for. We must recognize that its repetition
of certain basic themes, and its broad and abstract language of a sin
that has infected every part of society, is no merely formal acknowl-
edgement that "there is no man who does not sin" (1 Kings 8:46). It
is instead a reaching out to understand the root causes of human
misery and despair in men's and women's radical alienation from
God and their loss of any clear vision of the spiritual foundations of
society:

> Then I turned my face to the Lord God, seeking him by prayer and
> supplications with fasting and sackcloth and ashes. I prayed to the LORD
> my God and made confession, saying, "O Lord, the great and terrible
> God, who keepest covenant and steadfast love with those who love him
> and keep his commandments, we have sinned and done wrong and
> acted wickedly and rebelled, turning aside from thy commandments
> and ordinances; we have not listened to thy servants the prophets, who
> spoke in thy name to our kings, our princes, and our fathers, and to all
> the people of the land. To thee, O Lord, belongs righteousness, but to
> us confusion of face, as at this day, to the men of Judah, to the inhabi-
> tants of Jerusalem, and to all Israel, those that are near and those that
> are far away, in all the lands to which thou hast driven them, because
> of the treachery which they have committed against thee. To us, O
> Lord, belongs confusion of face, to our kings, to our princes, and to
> our fathers, because we have sinned against thee. To the Lord our God
> belong mercy and forgiveness; because we have rebelled against him,
> and have not obeyed the voice of the LORD our God by following his
> laws, which he set before us by his servants the prophets. All Israel has
> transgressed thy law and turned aside, refusing to obey thy voice. And
> the curse and oath which are written in the law of Moses the servant of
> God have been poured out upon us, because we have sinned against
> him. He has confirmed his words, which he spoke against us and
> against our rulers who ruled us, by bringing upon us a great calamity;
> for under the whole heaven there has not been done the like of what has
> been done against Jerusalem. As it is written in the law of Moses, all
> this calamity has come upon us, yet we have not entreated the favor of
> the LORD our God, turning from our iniquities and giving heed to thy

truth. Therefore the LORD has kept ready the calamity and has brought it upon us; for the LORD our God is righteous in all the works which he has done, and we have not obeyed his voice. And now, O Lord our God, who didst bring thy people out of the land of Egypt with a mighty hand, and hast made thee a name, as at this day, we have sinned, we have done wickedly. O Lord, according to all thy righteous acts, let thy anger and thy wrath turn away from thy city Jerusalem, thy holy hill; because for our sins, and for the iniquities of our fathers, Jerusalem and thy people have become a byword among all who are round about us. Now therefore, O our God, hearken to the prayer of thy servant and to his supplications, and for thy own sake, O Lord, cause thy face to shine upon thy sanctuary, which is desolate. O my God, incline thy ear and hear; open thy eyes and behold our desolations, and the city which is called by thy name; for we do not present our supplications before thee on the ground of our righteousness, but on the ground of thy great mercy. O LORD, hear; O LORD, forgive; O LORD, give heed and act; delay not, for thy own sake, O my God, because thy city and thy people are called by thy name."

(Daniel 9:3–19)

The prayer is both a confession of sin and a pleading for God's forgiveness. It achieves its effect in a striking spiraling movement, affirming the fact of Israel's sin in broad and general terms as a transgression of the laws given through Moses and pleading for God to act in forgiveness of this. The cycle of confession and plea is then repeated with even greater intensity and a stronger plea for God to act in mercy. The climax is then reached in a dramatic staccato repetition of the plea; "O LORD, hear; O LORD, forgive; O LORD, give heed and act; delay not." The ideas contained in the prayer are for the most part very broad and familiar ones, and no specific request is added to define how God's mercy is to take effect in changing the fortunes of Jerusalem and Israel. All such details are left to the open future which God's mercy will make possible. The overall character of the prayer is one of striking freshness and vigor achieved by its clever spiral pattern and sharply focused ending. The reader's (and worshiper's) attention is brought to an unmistakable concluding focus upon God and God's power and willingness to act.

In one detail, however, the prayer does introduce us to an important original feature in the thought which underlies it. In its confession of the weakness and humiliation ("confusion of face") which has come upon God's people it defines this people in a significant

way: "the men of Judah . . . the inhabitants of Jerusalem . . . all
Israel," and it then goes on to define who it is that constitutes Israel
as "those that are near and those that are far away, in all the lands to
which thou hast driven them" (Dan. 9:7). This is, in fact, the fullest
and clearest definition which the Old Testament contains of an Israel
which comprised both the community in Judah and the Diaspora of
Jews settled in various lands. Such a point could easily be overlooked, but it is a most important affirmation that those who had
gone into exile and who had over a period of four centuries settled in
other lands, nevertheless, remained part of "Israel" and "sons of
Abraham." A vital step had been taken towards the recognition that
Israel was no longer a nation in the proper sense but a scattered
community spread across many lands. Ultimately, as we now know,
such a community of Judaism was to become worldwide. No doubt
it is true that such an understanding was already implicit in what we
have learned of the work and activities of Ezra and Nehemiah.
Nevertheless it is here in the prayer of Daniel that the international
meaning of "Israel" is given its fullest range in the Old Testament.
Christians must undoubtedly see here a most important step towards
the recognition that ultimately the biblical perspective of the people
of God is that of a world-wide community, drawn from all nations,
which constitutes God's "church." In the letters of Paul this extension
in the understanding of the people of God comes to light.

The Significance of the Prayer

We may begin our reflection upon Daniel's prayer by noting how
frequently it has been overlooked by those who have, in other respects, been most zealous in their interpretation of the book of Daniel. The intricate visions, with their mysterious symbols and stark
contrasts between the kingdoms of the world and the kingdom of
God, have made this book a dangerous hunting ground for those who
would understand God's plans for the world's political future. In
times of political tension and uncertainty and in near despair at the
tarnished and compromised bargaining of the human political scene,
Christian interpreters have sought, through a reinterpretation of
Daniel's visions, to discover a new message. From the frustrated
ambitions of the Jewish community at Qumran at the time of the

Roman-Jewish War (A.D. 66–70) through the pious aims of the "Fifth Monarchy" men in the seventeenth-century English Civil War to the more recent responses to threats of a worldwide nuclear conflict in the twentieth century, the book of Daniel has appeared to take on a new meaning and significance. All too frequently it has led to disastrous misinterpretations and false expectations, built round dangerous political identifications of Daniel's symbolic beasts and horns. All such expectations might have taken on a different character if they had begun with Daniel's prayer as a basis for understanding God's intentions. This has a truly evangelical emphasis, with its stress upon the righteousness of God, the centrality of the need for forgiveness, and the awareness that such forgiveness must be an expression of God's gracious mercy rather than of people's deserved destiny. Hope begins with God, and individuals can only find God and truly reasoned grounds for hope when they set forgiveness at the center of spiritual understanding. Political vision without a spirit of prayer to give it perspective can become a most dangerous and disturbing goal. Perhaps the difference between spiritual fervor and fanaticism lies in the element of prayer which belongs to the one and is absent in the other. It is also worth remarking that, in the visions which succeed Daniel's prayer, a new theme emerges which is both personal to Daniel and yet also indicative of the paths of spiritual renewal, which finds expression in the angelic address to Daniel: "O Daniel, man greatly beloved." In this a fresh awareness of the role of the individual in times of social distress surfaces and also a reassuring and consoling discovery of God's commitment to the cause of righteousness, even when merely a handful of godly men and women remain loyal. Daniel did not stand alone, but remained an object of God's love and the vanguard of those through whom God's love could reach out to restore, heal, and transform society.

We have already made mention of the interesting fact that in Daniel's vision the event of the Maccabean uprising, which began with the protest of Mattathias and thereafter came under the leadership of Judas Maccabeus, is referred to in Dan. 11:33–34 as "a little help." From the picture given in the book of 1 Maccabees of the course of that revolt, which was largely instrumental in checking the brutal excesses of the Seleucid ruler of Judah, Antiochus V, Epiphanes, we might have expected that Daniel would have appeared more wholeheartedly enthusiastic about such events. It was certainly the uprising led by Judas which brought an end to the persecutions ordered by Antiochus and the desecration of the Jerusalem temple which had been imposed. With all these developments the visions of Daniel are wholly in agreement. Nevertheless, an unexpected element of reserve and caution in the visions certainly looked for the coming of God's kingdom as something greater and fuller than anything that Judas could achieve. No doubt this was wisely and rightly so, since, in spite of all that it did achieve, the Maccabean uprising left many tasks unfinished and led to the re-establishing of a short-lived line of native Jewish kings in Judah whose conduct left much to be desired.

We are currently very much aware of the broader implications of the concept of "revolution" in the historical and political realms. The impact of the French Revolution in the eighteenth century and the Russian Revolution in the twentieth have made us very conscious of the painful intermingling of noble ideals and ignoble human brutality which all such revolutions display. Nor was it very significantly different in the time of Judas Maccabeus, or two centuries later in the Jewish uprising against Rome. Idealism and terror became uncomfortably linked together. An awareness remains evident, then, in Daniel's prayer, with its passionate cry to God: "O LORD forgive," that the righteousness of God cannot easily be identified with any one political movement or party or social order. God constantly calls upon us, not only as individuals to transcend our own less worthy and sinstained lives, but also as a society to transcend our tarnished and imperfect organizations and institutions. Even as a church we are called to recognize that hallowed forms and familiar practices can all too easily be continued after the love and vision that once gave them life and meaning have ebbed away.

Daniel's prayer reminds us that faith, politics, and spirituality have not easily gone hand in hand. No age has found a secure formula for achieving complete harmony between them, and no set of rules or guidelines has come to light which has proved applicable to all societies and all situations. At times politics, faith, and spirituality have contributed greatly to each other, and each has shown itself to be very much in need of the other two. Politics without faith has so easily slipped to the level of a cynical pragmatism. Yet, when people have sought to pursue their spiritual paths in indifference to politics, they have quickly learned, as pious Jews had to learn in a time of resistance to persecution during the Maccabean revolt, that there can be no security for spirituality without genuine political expression. Nor can the righteousness of God be striven for unless it is embodied in the way in which society is organized and governed. Thus Daniel's prayer and the visions of God's coming kingdom which followed from it remind us of the necessity of keeping spiritual vision and political realism in a fruitful bond.

19
A Prayer of
MARY

Luke 1:46–55

Mary the Woman

It must already be very striking to any reader who is sensitive to issues relating to modern feminist thinking, or to any campaigner for "equal rights for women," that, so far, only one of the prayers of the Bible that we have examined belongs to a woman. This is that of Hannah, the mother of Samuel, and it is noteworthy that it is very markedly similar in many of its features to the prayer that we are now to consider. This is the prayer of Mary, the mother of Jesus, which, under its title "The Magnificat" has become one of the best-known and mostly widely used prayers. It is evident too that both this prayer and that of Hannah show a special sensitivity to the spiritual needs and the divine grace towards the weaker and underprivileged members of society. It cannot be a matter of any surprise to the modern Christian reader to learn that, in the ancient world, women occupied a very restricted and frequently unjustly constrained position in society. The story of Ruth and of her widowed mother-in-law Naomi in the Old Testament highlights very poignantly the restraints under which women could find themselves and the difficulties that they faced when they were no longer protected by the economic and social strength of a husband and his family. In so many ways society in biblical times was very much a "man's world," and this can be readily compared with a broad societal pattern which shows itself throughout antiquity. Such patterns, which are only now beginning to change to any very marked extent, have not been so negatively reflected in Christian ideals of piety, courage, and unselfish service which have found in the persons of particular women unique examples of the divine ideal. Among such women, none stands in a position of greater prominence nor occupies a station of greater exaltation than Mary, the mother of Jesus.

To a western European Protestant the degree of exaltation of Mary in Christian tradition during the early centuries of the church's growth has often appeared puzzling. It has often been branded, not entirely without some justification, as an attempt to transform a human being whose role in the biblical tradition is actually a relatively modest one into a goddess. Even the honorific titles which have been heaped upon Mary in Christian liturgy—Mother of God, Queen of Heaven—may sound strange and sometimes even offensive to Protestant ears. Contrastingly, anyone attuned to the inner feelings of warmth and devotion, which bring liturgy to life and convert the brittle logic of doctrines into the fluent emotions and longings of spiritual vitality, will recognize how it is that a large area of Christendom, especially in its Catholic and Latin forms, has found in the figure of Mary a never-failing symbol of the caring and understanding nature of God. Where ritual and dogma have at times appeared locked in a rigid institutional Christian edifice, through the unconscious reasonings of the heart, Mary has remained as the symbolic embodiment of the caring and consoling features of divine love. Nor should we set aside the importance that has emerged of setting "Motherhood" alongside the more familiar biblical images of "Fatherhood" and "Sonship" in understanding the nature of Deity.

When we turn from these larger considerations of Mary as a unique figure of Christian tradition and the embodiment of a divine ideal to consider the human being to whom it applies, we discover a person of immense interest. All the more is this interest aroused when we compare the very limited and quite minimal information which the Gospels give to us concerning Joseph, the carpenter of Nazareth, Mary's husband and the human father of Jesus. In the events of Jesus' later life, especially those concerning his sufferings and crucifixion, it is Mary who appears prominently, whereas Joseph is never mentioned. This has suggested to many the very real probability that Joseph had already died and left Mary a widow before the time of Jesus' own death. At any rate it is certainly Mary who becomes the most notable and important figure within the immediate family of Jesus.

According to Luke 1:26, which tells of the visit of the angel Gabriel to Mary, she was a native of the city of Nazareth in the region of Galilee. Hitherto this had been a town of no great importance in biblical tradition, and probably at the time of our Lord's birth, it remained only a relatively small town. Nazareth was set in the region of Galilee, quite low lying because the Sea of Galilee itself lies well below sea level and therefore susceptible to a hot and rather oppressive climate during the summer months. However, in biblical tradition another aspect of the situation of Galilee comes most prominently to our attention. The region of Galilee is referred to in Isaiah 9:1, which forms the introduction to an important "messianic" prophecy, as "Galilee of the nations." Why precisely it had acquired this title is not wholly known. Probably from a period of considerable antiquity the ethnic groups which made up the population of Galilee were very much more mixed and varied than was the case in other parts of Israel. In any event, as a consequence of its location, it suffered a good deal more than many other parts of Israel from the political upheavals and turmoil that affected the entire region of the Levant throughout the millennium before the birth of Christ. Even aside from such frequent changes of political control, a feature which has certainly provided the occasion of Isaiah's mention in his prophecy, Galilee was inevitably destined to see a very varied range of racial, national, and cultural crosscurrents affecting its life. To the northwest the famous Phoenician seaports of Tyre and Sidon were not far away, while to the northeast routes led across to the ancient city of Damascus and further across to the Mesopotamian world of Nineveh and Babylon. Southwards, passing through Galilee and down the Jordan valley the way was open to Egypt and Arabia. Geography and history had combined therefore to ensure that Galilee truly deserved its epithet as being "of the nations." It is almost certainly this reputation for its mixed population, its varied religious and cultural associations, and the fact that so many features of the worlds of Greece, Rome, and the East appeared to meet in Galilee that prompted Nathaniel's rather self-assured question: "Can any good thing come out of Nazareth?" (John 1:46). In contrast to the great history and reputation that belonged to Jerusalem and Samaria, and even to such foreign cities as Tyre, Sidon, and Damascus, Nazareth appeared to represent nothing in particular.

In the time of Mary, Nazareth was almost certainly witnessing many important changes which undoubtedly have a bearing upon the life of Jesus generally and the gospel story. It was situated not too far from the coast, in hilly country which enjoyed a rather more pleasant atmosphere in the summer than lower down by the lakeside in Galilee, so that it must have attracted many Roman settlers, and also traders and travelers from other parts of the Levant. Unlike the recently founded city of Tiberias, which was set further down by the side of the Sea of Galilee, Nazareth was certainly a traditionally "Jewish" town in its retention of a religious character and customs. Such new foundations as Tiberias were more self-consciously set up in the Graeco-Roman style, with well designed and attractive buildings, a solidly Greek-speaking element of population, and ambitions to pursue the arts and learning of the Hellenistic world. Probably to the citizens of such a town those who came from Nazareth appeared rather backward and uncultured. Mary would almost certainly have been thought of as a rough "country girl," easily exploited if there were no protective family group to look after her interests and secure her welfare.

Perhaps rather paradoxically in view of its traditionally "Jewish" character, Nazareth, and the region of Galilee generally, were not thought of with much respect by the Jewish authorities in Jerusalem. The traditional "Gentile" reputation of the Galilee region as a whole set a stigma upon it, and the learned teachers of the Rabbinic schools of Jerusalem saw themselves, rather self-importantly, as the educated elite of the Jewish people. In their eyes neither the people of Galilee nor any of their popular religious teachers were worth more than a passing mention. The area was not sufficiently "Greek" to make it interesting and reputable on that account nor was it sufficiently associated with Jewish learning and tradition to elicit attention on that score.

What kind of teaching and education might have been afforded to Mary in her youth can only be inferred generally from comparable societies throughout the world. So often the protective social pressures which confined girls to their home towns, and sometimes even to the area around their own homes, brought restrictions and some degree of deprivation. By way of compensation, the women in such a relatively small town would have formed a very close-knit and mutually supportive group, whose loving concern would allow little in the life of the town to escape their attention. Frequently they would prove more knowledgeable regarding local tradition and the latest "gossip" than their menfolk, even though none would ever have admitted this to be so. Schooled for marriage, almost certainly at a surprisingly early age by our conventions, Mary would have learned the values of the home, the skills and wisdom of a very practical way of life, and the piety and liturgy of the synagogue. She was undoubtedly brought up in a very well defined tradition, with an almost rigidly defined role to play in it. Economically the homes of Nazareth were mostly poor, depending on a pattern of farming and trading that had scarcely changed in a thousand years; yet in its spiritual and intellectual traditions it was rich, and Mary would certainly have been able to share extensively in this, even though in a rather different manner from the town's menfolk.

Mary's Prayer

Mary's prayer comes as a response, in the first place to the angelic announcement to her (the Annunciation) that she is to bear a son who will be called "the Son of the Most High" and who will establish a kingdom of which there will be no end (Luke 1:32–33). This is further confirmed by the assurance that such a child will be conceived by the Holy Spirit (Luke 1:35). It is not until Mary has visited her relative Elizabeth in the hill country of Judah, however, that the full impact of these promises comes home to her. Once she had spoken to Elizabeth who was also pregnant, she was able fully to put into prayer her feelings and reactions to the angelic assurances that had been given to her. In putting her feelings into words it is clear that Mary was deeply affected by the much earlier prayer of Hannah at her rejoicing over the birth of Samuel:

And Mary said,
"My soul magnifies the Lord,
and my spirit rejoices in God my Savior,

for he has regarded the low estate of his handmaiden.
For behold, henceforth all generations will call me blessed;
for he who is mighty has done great things for me,
and holy is his name.
And his mercy is on those who fear him
from generation to generation.
He has shown strength with his arm,
he has scattered the proud in the imagination of their hearts,
he has put down the mighty from their thrones,
and exalted those of low degree;
he has filled the hungry with good things,
and the rich he has sent empty away.
He has helped his servant Israel,
in remembrance of his mercy,
as he spoke to our fathers,
to Abraham and to his posterity for ever."

(Luke 1:46–55)

Mary's prayer is in the form of an "Individual Song of Thanksgiving," and as such it conforms to a well-established type of prayer which is to be found in the psalter. Its close similarity to the Song of Hannah in 1 Samuel 2:1–10 has already been remarked upon. It falls readily into three parts, evidencing a clearly planned structure: Luke 1:47–49, individual thanksgiving for God's grace to his "lowly handmaiden"; Luke 1:50–53, general thanksgiving for God's grace towards the poor and underprivileged; and Luke 1:54–56, thanksgiving for God's grace towards Israel.

We may comment briefly on some instructive and rather unexpected aspects of the prayer. In Mary's direct offering of thanks to God two features stand out. Mary's description of herself as God's "handmaiden," literally a "servant girl" or even "slave girl," is both a deferential reflection of her weakness, as compared to God's majesty, but also a hidden reference to the very constrained position of women. Secondly, although the context in which the prayer is set makes the meaning clear, nothing is said directly regarding Mary's pregnancy and the expected birth of a child. The centrality of this theme, though, comes right to the fore with the exuberant affirmation: "henceforth all generations will call me blessed." Through childbearing, and the role of motherhood, Mary's womanhood will leave its legacy of blessing for all the future generations. Thereby she will achieve, in a unique measure and in an unparalleled fashion, an importance and a reputation which belongs to her sex. The role of motherhood, indispensable to the continuance of the human race, will find in Mary an incomparable religious expression. Thus, during the history of Christian faith with its unique emphasis upon the theme of holy nativity and the doctrine of the incarnation, it has so often been the figure of Mary which has "humanized" the concept of God. By involving the notion of the divine taking of human form in the images and experiences of motherhood and family life, Mary has stood for the "humanizing" of the understanding of God. In a remarkable way too, Mary's prayer, "The Magnificat," has captured the sense of joy, confidence, and unselfishness which comes with the bringing of new life into the world. In this way it takes nothing from the uniqueness of Mary as "The Holy Mother of God," that her prayer lifts into the realm of the holy and the transcendent an experience which belongs to the very heart of all human family life.

The second part of Mary's prayer, the general thanksgiving for God's unparalleled power to change the face of human society, follows closely the theme of Hannah's earlier prayer. Its poetic contrasts do not altogether avoid a measure of mischievous delight in noting that those who think they have everything may find that they have nothing from God. God is One who can "put down the mighty," "scatter the proud," and even "send empty away" those who are rich. These contrasting negative images are not the essence of the prayer, however, but are rather present in order to provide counterpoise for the more striking manifestations of God's mercy. God fills the hungry with good things and lifts up those who, like Mary, are regarded in the eyes of the world as "of low degree." Such vivid and vigorous imagery presents a most powerful reminder of the imperfections of human society. It is well that we should be reminded, in every repetition of Mary's prayer, that the social and economic patterns of our human world do not correspond, save in a rather imperfect fashion, to those of the ideal divine society. Increasingly in the modern world the shortcomings of human social order and the evident injustices which this so often contains have drawn attention to ambitions of reform and even revolution. Certainly, as the emergence of a radical Liberation Theology has endeavored to show, there are times when

The Prayers of the Bible

dramatic change may be called for if God's mercy and justice are to reach out to the lives of all men and women. This prayer reminds us that, in Christian perspective, the task of righting wrongs, redressing grievances, and alleviating poverty and disease, is one that never ends and must be constantly pursued if God is rightly to be served. Such is God's work, and it is a work that is and must forever be seen as such. For this we need constant reminding that thanksgiving is due to God.

After such a broad and world-encompassing theme of thanksgiving in the second part of Mary's prayer it comes as rather a surprise that the third and concluding part is concerned with God's mercy and help towards Israel. God has spoken to the ancestors of Israel, and it is on this account that the Bible comes to us as a revelation of the divine will and purpose. Here too the balance and contrasting emphases of the prayer reflect certain fundamental aspects of humankind's spiritual tradition. Where we are concerned to implement the insights of faith in a broad and universal fashion, we need constant reminding of the historical and particular features through which this tradition has come down to us. The individuality of the religious personalities of the Old Testament—Abraham, Moses, David—and the particularity of their lives present a note of realism, concreteness, and firm definition, which prevent faith from dissipating itself in woolly abstractions. The epistle to the Hebrews tells us that through the promises which they mediated, these ancestors of our faith saw but did not fully experience the fullness of God's purpose: "Since God had foreseen something better for us, that apart from us they should not be made perfect" (Heb. 11:40). In its conclusion, however, Mary's prayer serves to keep before our attention the corresponding truth that, without them, we too could not have come to enjoy the hope of God's perfection. It is a commonplace observation, yet one that should not be left unremarked, that Christianity, Judaism, and most of the great religions take their origins in a very remote antiquity. They concern themselves with figures and events that are strikingly remote from us in terms of our historical knowledge. An essential element of depth and human relevance which true faith requires lies in this. All too easily the myth of modernity leads to a mistaken and misjudged despising of events and experiences which relate to a time more than a few decades back. The biblical perspective is very different from this, though, seeing in the notion of "origins" and "beginnings" those aspects of life coming to the fore which belong most fundamentally to the "depths" of human society and human experience. It is on this account that Mary's prayer, in accordance with a true biblical perspective, reminds us to give thanks for "our fathers," for Israel, and for Abraham. Hidden as it is in an imperfectly known and distant antiquity, their world is still essentially our world, and their humanity is still essentially at one with our own. As the epistle to the Hebrews draws to our attention, a succession of faith binds the faithful of today to the men and women of faith of the past.

The Significance of the Prayer

In further reflection upon such a well-known prayer as Mary's exuberant "Magnificat" we may single out a number of valuable themes. Since this is the first of the prayers of the New Testament for our consideration, it is worth reflecting that so far as the understanding of prayer is concerned and its forms and conventions are developed, there is no great difference between the prayers of the Old Testament and those of the New. We shall see that some important new spiritual themes begin to be incorporated in the New Testament, but in general there is complete continuity of character and form between the prayers of the two Testaments. Mary's prayer is so very like that of Hannah in the Old Testament. Not least therefore we should note that the Gospel of Luke, in its account of the birth of Jesus of Nazareth, is concerned to show the spirit of prayerful piety in which Jesus was born, and also, through these prayers, the continuity that binds the events of Jesus' birth to the great divine acts of salvation recounted in the Old Testament. In this fashion the prayers are themselves the foremost links that connect the gospel events with Israel's past. God's actions and saving work are viewed as part of an extended historical movement that began with the call of Abraham and came to a climactic fulfillment with the birth of Jesus. The human and worldly side to this divine work is then viewed, not through the continuity of some great institution such as the temple of Jerusalem, nor yet through some unbroken chain of priesthood, even though both of these were clearly seen as important. Rather it is the spirit of prayer, and even the prayerful love of a relatively impoverished girl in the obscure country town of Nazareth, which provide the setting for God's work. With a remarkable and colorful setting and an enchantingly simple "plot," Luke reaffirms the ancient truth from the Old Testament: "for the LORD sees not as a man sees; man looks on the outward appearance, but the LORD looks on the heart" (1 Sam. 16:7). Once such a simple basic truth is conceded, then, in the spiritual world, a whole new range of possibilities emerge.

We may note also a further feature of Mary's "Magnificat," which has a considerable bearing upon the portrayal of Mary in the New Testament, and upon the way in which Christian devotion and spirituality have remembered her. This prayer is one of complete and unqualified joy in God. The sheer delight in using and repeating the "Magnificat" in Christian worship reawakens constantly this note of joy. It recalls vividly to our attention that it is through such moments of joy when we feel "lifted out" of ourselves into another spiritual realm that we discover that we are encountering God. Joy is one of those experiences of "depth" in our human lives which point us to God and the spiritual realm. Life is not, however, one constant and undimmed experience of joy, which we encounter rather as brief and temporary "high points" of a world that has many shadows. Mary has so often been remembered as "Our Lady of Sorrows," and a forewarning of this shadowed aspect of life is given early to her (Luke 2:35), when the time came to present Jesus in the temple in accordance with the law of purification. In recalling Mary's prayer, therefore, and in thinking our way through it, we are made very much aware that its note of joy and happiness in looking forward to the birth of her child was not one that could last indefinitely. Somewhat earlier the Old Testament preacher in the book of Ecclesiastes affirms that life brings many experiences and "seasons of the soul." Among these are included: "a time to weep, and a time to laugh; a time to mourn, and a time to dance" (Eccles. 3:4). It is all too easy in life to lose a proper sense of perspective in a time of pain and sorrow and to forget that there has been in each of our lives, as for Mary, "a time to dance." Perhaps also, however, from a theological point of view, it is possible to become so caught up in thought and discussion about the "problem of pain" and the question marks that this sets against the power and purpose of God, that we forget altogether about the experience of joy. For us there is no "problem of joy," since this represents a side to life that we welcome and will actively seek. Joy and sorrow, however, are two edges of a spectrum which has many colors, and we cannot properly and fairly consider one without paying attention to the other. They both belong to the world of human relationships and of human experience. It is a very fitting and memorable tribute to Mary, therefore, that through her prayer of overwhelming joy and delight in God, she should constantly bring our attention back to a recollection of the spiritual dimension of human happiness. Her prayer conveys to us a picture of her as "Our Lady of Joy," lifting up to God the sheer thrill of one of life's most exuberant and exciting moments—the coming into the world of new life!

A further feature of the figure that Mary has presented for Christian spirituality is important in its theological implications. We have already pointed out the immense popularity of the person of Mary in early Christian tradition and the way in which this appears to have lost none of this vitality in the modern world throughout large areas of Catholic Christendom. In pointing out the dangers of this and the extremes to which it has sometimes been taken, Protestant Christendom has failed to note the deep human and psychological factors which have contributed to it. So often it has been the person of Mary who has conveyed a sense of human warmth and understanding in our practical response to the doctrine of the love of God. Without Mary such a doctrine could so often have been construed as a formal abstraction, and at times even as a rather Spartan and joyless determination to "do the right thing." Mary has sounded a family note in the understanding of divine love, and her role in the "Holy Family" of Nazareth has warned us of the constant necessity to transform abstractions into concrete practicalities. Love itself is just a word, until it is given life and content through examples and experiences which serve to clarify and define its true significance. More than this, however, it is evident from Christian history that, in a well-meant endeavor to stress the transcendent quality of divine love, Protestantism has at times allowed it to become divorced from the realities of human love. Surely Mary's prayer reminds us that when and if we allow this to happen, we have lost touch with one of the most fundamental biblical aspects of faith in God. Human joy can never be a merely profane and secular experience when it is interpreted in the light of Mary's "Magnificat."

20
A Prayer of
ZECHARIAH

Luke 1:67–79

Zechariah the Man

The visit of Mary, the mother of Jesus, to her relative Elizabeth
has introduced us to the parents of John the Baptist. This was to be
the name of the child born to Elizabeth and a certain priest, by the
name of Zechariah. His prayer, which Luke's Gospel records under
its title "The Benedictus," has become one of the most familiar of
those which are regularly used in the Christian liturgy. In fact Luke
records it not as a simple prayer but rather as a prophecy for which
Zechariah was inspired by the Holy Spirit. It is essentially a prayer
of thanksgiving of a very distinctive kind, however, and one which
introduces us to several of the most central and profound theological
themes of the New Testament. Certainly the Bible presents no un-
bridgeable gulf between prayer and prophecy. Instead, not only is
the prophet seen as essentially a person of prayer, but prayer itself,
when truly inspired of God and seeking insight into the divine ways,
becomes "prophetic" in that it is able to attain to a new and deeper
level of understanding of the divine purpose. This is how it is with
the prayer of Zechariah, which offers a further revelation of the spirituality of the Judaism into which Jesus was born. More than this,
however, it foresees the role of John the Baptist as "the last of the
prophets" and the forerunner of Jesus the Christ.

Zechariah is described as a priest "of the division of Abijah"
(Luke 1:5), and we learn that it fell to him to burn incense "when his
division was on duty" (Luke 1:8). This reflects the very changed
circumstances in which Israel's priesthood was placed in Jerusalem
at the time of the birth of Jesus, when they were required to serve for

only one month in the year, since there were far more priests than the actual duties of the temple required for more permanent service. However, Zechariah was fully representative of the tradition of priesthood of the Old Testament which was traced back, through Aaron, to the time of Moses. We can readily define the task of the priest as one of mediation, representing the people before God in prayer and ritual service, yet also representing God to the people through the tasks of teaching and instruction. The priesthood of ancient Israel has not attracted to itself anything like the same level of interest and attention as has prophecy, where a more directly revelatory function in mediating the will of God to men and women is evident. Priesthood and prophecy were in no sense mutually exclusive religious vocations in biblical times, however, as the figure of Zechariah makes clear. Already much earlier prophets such as Jeremiah and Ezekiel were drawn from priestly families, and it is highly probable that a prophetic role was at one time common among those varied religious duties which came ultimately to be described under the general title of priestly ministry.

In general we may see that the Jewish tradition of priesthood represented continuity, stability, and carefully defined order in religious life. This work therefore was performed centrally in Jerusalem, in the temple, which provided the sole place of recognized sacrificial worship and the natural center of Jewish religious life. Prophecy, on the other hand, was a more colorful, undisciplined, and intermittent feature of religion. Our knowledge of this is drawn largely from the great named figures who have left us a legacy of their spiritual insights in the prophetic books of the Old Testament. The last of these, the book of Malachi, already antedates the time of Zechariah by several centuries. Therefore a tradition of a "silent period" of prophecy has grown up in which no really significant figures emerged between Malachi and the time of John the Baptist. This is only a partial truth, since prophecy continued its role in Jewish life in two ways. On the one hand there certainly were a number of men and women who maintained the tradition of prophesying, even though they achieved none of the eminence which was accorded to their more illustrious forbears. On the other hand we need to keep in mind the fact that there was now in existence in Judaism a considerable body of written prophetic literature, and the continued study and exposition of this occupied the minds and attention of many scribes. From these arose a considerable "secondary" literature of fresh interpretations and commentaries upon earlier prophecies, which constituted in themselves a genuinely prophetic element to Jewish religious life.

Zechariah is important to an understanding of the birth and background of Jesus, not so much for Zechariah himself, even though his prayer is a very remarkable one, but because he was the father of John the Baptist. John performed the role of the "herald" of Jesus, since his ministry summoning the Jewish people to repentance and to expression of repentance through baptism in the River Jordan, prepared the way for the subsequent ministry of Jesus. Where John the Baptist was a powerful prophetic voice declaring that the promised reign of God was to come "very soon," the early church recognized that this "very soon" had been turned to "is now here" through the ministry, death, and resurrection of Jesus.

It is very fitting therefore that Zechariah and the son John that was born to him in the relatively late years of his life should together provide a combined priestly and prophetic witness to the fact that, with the birth of Jesus of Nazareth, the age of Israel's "fulfillment" had dawned. Furthermore, it becomes clear on close examination of the New Testament that, in spite of the brutal manner of his early death (Matt. 14:1–12), John the Baptist had been a most influential figure and had acquired such a following that years later Paul encountered a group of disciples of John the Baptist in Ephesus (Acts 19:1–7). All the more important therefore was it to make clear that John the Baptist was the "forerunner" and herald of the long-awaited Messiah, but that with Jesus the Messianic age was no longer a future hope but a present reality. This is already the central feature of the angelic message to Zechariah when the news of the forthcoming birth of John (the Baptist) was announced:

"And you will have joy and gladness,
and many will rejoice at his birth;
for he will be great before the Lord,
and he shall drink no wine nor strong drink,
and he will be filled with the Holy Spirit,

even from his mother's womb.
And he will turn many of the sons of Israel to the Lord their God,
and he will go before him in the spirit and power of Elijah,
to turn the hearts of the fathers to the children,
and the disobedient to the wisdom of the just,
to make ready for the Lord a people prepared."

(Luke 1:14–17)

A special sign of the divine meaning of the birth of Zechariah's child is found in the fact of the priest's dumbness until the child was actually named after his birth (Luke 1:20–22,62–64).

All of this direct concern with the person of John the Baptist and the relationship of his ministry and message to that of Jesus is of the utmost importance when we come to consider Zechariah's prayer. This is a most highly theological composition since, although it is in the form of a general thanksgiving, it is a thanksgiving for the kingdom of God. What this kingdom means for the world and for the lives of individual men and women, as well as a reflection upon the form and manner of its expectation in Israel, are all contained within it. It is therefore a thanksgiving for hope, but this is no longer a vague and undefined hope that somehow things will "get better." Rather it is a sharply focused hope, for although it does not name him, this hope is centered upon the Messiah of the house of David, for whom John the Baptist was the last prophetic herald.

The Prayer of Zechariah

The writer S.T. Coleridge describes how he encountered a deep spiritual experience after he first read the poem by William Wordsworth entitled *The Prelude*, and he describes it simply as "I found myself in prayer." Since praying is usually an exercise which we consciously aim for and prepare for, it is helpful to note that on occasion instead of our seeking prayer, prayer overtakes us. It becomes something spontaneous and irrepressible so that we cannot deny its claim upon us. It is just such a setting which Luke's Gospel presents as the occasion for Zechariah's prayer. With this son born to him late in life, and the child's name now determined as John, Zechariah recovered the power of speech and was filled with an overwhelming joy through the power of the Holy Spirit. It is all of a piece with this therefore that his prayer should be about God, the coming kingdom, and the role that his child was to fulfill as a herald of this kingdom:

"Blessed be the Lord God of Israel,
for he has visited and redeemed his people,
and has raised up a horn of salvation for us
in the house of his servant David,
as he spoke by the mouth of his holy prophets from of old,
that we should be saved from our enemies,
and from the hand of all who hate us;
to perform the mercy promised to our fathers,
and to remember his holy covenant,
the oath which he swore to our father Abraham, to grant us
that we, being delivered from the hand of our enemies,
might serve him without fear,
in holiness and righteousness before him all the days of our life.
And you, child, will be called the prophet of the Most High;
for you will go before the Lord to prepare his ways,
to give knowledge of salvation to his people
in the forgiveness of their sins,
through the tender mercy of our God,
when the day shall dawn upon us from on high
to give light to those who sit in darkness and in the shadow of death,
to guide our feet into the way of peace."

(Luke 1:68–79)

As a prayer of thanksgiving it puts into words a feeling of joy in all that God has made possible, and especially for the coming kingdom of God, for which John the Baptist will serve as herald. It is therefore a song of thanksgiving for the kingdom of God. It interprets this kingdom in unique and distinctive ways, however, and in doing so, it draws together the most central themes of the Old Testament, showing that they are about to find their fulfillment in the new age that is just dawning. We may set out these themes in a simple list:

First, God has raised up a "horn" of salvation for us in the house of his servant David. This is a reference to the promise made by God through the prophet Nathan to David in respect of his son (descendants): "I will establish the throne of his kingdom for ever" (2 Sam. 7:13). Generations of scribes and prophetic interpreters, to say nothing of less specialized men and women of Israel, had seen in this promise a key to understanding the way in which an era of salvation would one day bring a new order of life to Israel.

Second, God is about to deliver the chosen people from the hand of their enemies. This had for centuries been linked with the promise regarding David's descendants (cf. Isa. 9:4–5), yet what precisely it signified remained indeterminate because it left open who precisely the enemies were. Originally it had been understood in almost exclusively political terms as promising freedom from political aggression, such as had occurred in Isaiah's time from the Assyrians. The passage of time and a deeper experience of human life had shown, however, that "enemies" exist within each human heart in the form of evil desires and tendencies. Moreover the antispiritual forces which reside in the heart are matched by larger cosmic powers and pressures for evil and injustice in the world. Since Zechariah's prayer stands at the very threshold of the gospel story, the promise of deliverance from the hand (power) of one's enemies is set, therefore, in the forefront of what the work of God in Jesus will mean. To a generation increasingly obsessed with its political enemies in the presence of the Roman occupying power the message and work of Jesus was to mark the overthrow of the enemies that fought against spiritual health and freedom.

Third, God was about to fulfill the promise made to the patriarch Abraham. This is mentioned in Genesis 12:1–3 and represents one of the most formative of the narrative and theological themes which bind the Bible together into a unified whole. The promise is threefold in its form: that Abraham's descendants would inherit the land promised to them, that they would become a great nation, and that they would become a blessing among the nations of the world. In Zechariah's prayer the introduction of this theme is so important because it establishes the continuity of God's purpose and work through John the Baptist and Jesus with all that had already transpired. In this fashion Zechariah's prayer cements the connection between God's work with Israel in the Old Testament and through Jesus among all the nations of the world declared in the New Testament.

Fourth, John the Baptist is to be called "the prophet of the Most High." This makes clear that Zechariah's child will not himself be the long awaited Messiah, but he will be a very special prophet because he will bring the age of prophetic expectation to a close. He will in fact become the "greatest" of the prophets, identified even as an effective return of the prophet Elijah (cf. Matt. 11:7–15). John the Baptist will mark the high point of prophetic waiting, for with the coming of Jesus of Nazareth the age of waiting will have passed and the age of fulfillment will have dawned.

Fifth, the meaning of the kingdom of God is set out in a number of vivid and evocative key themes: the knowledge of salvation, the forgiveness of sins, light to those who sit in darkness, and guidance in the way of peace. Together these provide a basic compendium and guide to the spiritual riches which the kingdom of God will offer. In many respects we may see them to be broad and open-ended, yet it is essentially this feature of openness and freedom which the gospel presentation of the kingdom of God now discloses.

All in all therefore, Zechariah's prayer is a most important guide towards understanding the most central theological themes of the Bible. It is a very "theological" prayer, since it conveys and demands reflection upon important religious ideas and themes which cover the entire Bible. All of this is done in a spirit of thanksgiving that "God has visited and redeemed his people."

The Significance of the Prayer

The most striking and memorable feature of Zechariah's prayer is the way in which it presents in a simple but most dramatic way a theological guide to the Bible. Its widespread use in the liturgy of Christian worship therefore would appear to be a most inspired and valuable pointer to the binding together of theological understanding and insight into the ways of God with prayer and the cultivation of the spiritual life. Too often the two aspects of Christian grace and development are kept apart from each other and left to follow their own separate paths. Certainly it is always right for the Christian to express joy in and thanksgiving to God. Yet it ultimately matters very greatly what it is about God and the divine work that causes us to rejoice in the Lord, and express thanks to God. Zechariah's prayer supplies these necessary ingredients of prayer by focusing on the vast range of God's work spread across the whole span of biblical history and the manner in which this divine work, which the Bible interprets in the language of the coming of God's kingdom, has reached a special high-point with the birth of John the Baptist. He is the "link" figure who reawakened all the hopes and promises encapsulated in the Old Testament from the days of Abraham, through those of David, to the close of the age of prophecy. He is therefore an "Old Testament" person since he brings to a climax and an end the period we grasp and interpret theologically as the age of the "Old Covenant" of Abraham, Moses, and the prophets. John the Baptist is a "New Covenant" figure since in his days the New Covenant through Jesus of Nazareth would begin to be disclosed. It is important to see and understand the purpose of God which we have learned to recognize in terms of two covenants as essentially one work wholly unified in its riches and meaning. Zechariah's prayer presents us with a foundation for understanding and reading the Bible as a unified whole and for seeing that, because God is one, the manner and goal of God's working among men and women is part of a single unified whole. It is this whole work of God that we understand under the form and language of "the kingdom of God."

Prayer and understanding belong inseparably together therefore in the spiritual life, and ideally, they should react upon and stimulate each other. That this is often not the case simply signifies the prevalence of the temptation to think of prayer, in its biblical setting, as very unformed and undeveloped. Zechariah's prayer warns us against thinking that this is so. Prayer requires a proper understanding of the nature and purpose of God, yet in turn it makes possible the further development of such an understanding by establishing certain patterns or themes by which the wider relevance of our experience can be grasped. It is very appropriate therefore that Zechariah's prophetic prayer should stand at the very beginning of the new age—the age of salvation.

A further practical consideration comes into view with this prayer—"The Benedictus" of the Christian liturgy—as it has already done in the case of "The Magnificat" of Mary. The use of such prayers in the daily office of worship ensures their widespread use and popular familiarity as expressions of thanksgiving. At the same time it also ensures such a level of repetition as to dull the freshness and sparkle that properly belongs to them. Understandably therefore many Christians have turned away from the practice of constant use of the same prayer out of fear that overuse will ultimately lead to a sense of meaninglessness attaching to the words. Perhaps all that is necessary is that the dangers should be recognized. It is in any case very hard to avoid a measure of constant repetition, if prayer is to be a formative and constructive habit. What Zechariah's prayer brings most vividly to our attention is the need for the liturgical and intellectual uses of the Bible to be inseparable. Moreover the manner in which we learn to pray in a formal and public way will inevitably mold and characterize the way in which we learn to pray in private. All the more value attaches therefore to ensuring that those prayers which are central to our public praying should also be most formative and basic to our private awareness of and response to God. Zechariah's prayer is undoubtedly a very fitting model of a biblical prayer, maintaining a timeless relevance for every Christian. It celebrates the coming of the kingdom of God by tracing the various stages in its appearing and by rejoicing in the experiences of forgiveness, light, and hope which this brings into individual lives.

A further aspect of Zechariah's prayer inevitably invites closer investigation. In a penetrating affirmation of the blessing that the coming of God's kingdom brings to us it includes: "that we should be saved from our enemies, and from the hand of all who hate us." No doubt many in Zechariah's time could respond immediately to such an assurance by concluding that this meant the overthrow of the imperial power of Rome. If we trace back the way in which the enemies of God's people would have been identified in David's time we should be brought face to face with such ancient peoples as the Edomites, Ammonites, and Moabites, to say nothing of the more familiar Philistines. Later a long succession of foreign imperial powers enforced their will upon Israel and the Jewish people who derived from it. First the Assyrians, then the Babylonians and Persians, and subsequently the Greeks and Romans became each in turn the foreign ruling power over God's people. Always therefore throughout the biblical period a prominent foreign power filled the role of the primary "enemy" of the kingdom of God. We could very easily modernize and adapt the biblical perspective by arguing that it was not this or that particular imperialist power that constituted the "enemy" but rather the very notion of imperialism itself, with its inevitable legacy of exploitation and oppression which constituted the real "enemy." Certainly this represents a proper and reasonable inference from the biblical experience. Even this would fail to comprehend adequately the whole perspective which the Bible accords to the portrayal of the "enemies" of the people of God, however. During the long historical experience of Israel with a succession of changes in the international political scene, a deeper and more spiritual awareness emerged of the enmity which threatened God's kingdom. Already we have noted in other prayers the way in which the idea of God's kingdom as a spiritual kingdom is necessarily matched by an awareness that its enemies are spiritual enemies. They are no longer recognizable therefore purely in national, economic, or social categories. The enemies emerge in a more private manner as those forces and impulses, both within our lives and within our society, which impede and hinder the full realization of the justice and welfare which we associate with the kingdom of God. It would be too easy to conclude from such a biblical insight that we should therefore abandon any attempt to identify particular "enemies." This would not be truly in accord with the biblical understanding, however, which certainly recognized that particular individuals and particular social and political systems may embody the principle of hostility towards God and God's kingdom. What the biblical perspective has achieved for us is a discovery of depth and scale in the understanding of evil. No longer does evil simply exist outside of our own selves nor in specific ethnic or political groups but constantly manifests itself in a host of ways which challenge and threaten God's kingdom. It is in this deeper, spiritual sense that the biblical language regarding those who are our enemies has maintained a continued relevance in Christian spirituality.

21
A Prayer of SIMEON
Luke 2:29–32

Simeon the Priest

The elderly priest Simeon is mentioned in Luke's Gospel in connection with the presentation of the baby Jesus in the temple in Jerusalem, although he is otherwise unknown outside the gospel story. His prayer, perhaps better known as "The Nunc Dimittis," has become one of the most familiar and valued prayers of the daily office in the Christian liturgy. It is both short and straightforward and expresses a splendid note of confidence, hope, and trust in God which has made it a widely adaptable prayer for general use. It is also a very personal and individual prayer, intimately bound up with the particular situation in which Simeon found himself, and also with the unique moment in Jewish history when the infant Jesus was presented in Jerusalem in accordance with Mosaic law, as a child of Abraham's lineage.

It is significant that the event of the infant Jesus being brought to the temple as an act of dedication to the service of God marks the first of the visits made by him to Jerusalem. Luke records that Mary and Joseph went annually to Jerusalem for the Feast of Passover (Luke 2:41), and ultimately the death of Jesus was to take place just outside the city. As a native of Galilee he lived and grew up in a region where life was simpler, people were poorer, but where also religion was much less discussed and argued about than was the case in Jerusalem. This city was the intellectual, as well as political center of Jewish life. It was there that the rabbis formed their schools and learned to interpret the ancient law of Moses. It was there also that the priests officiated in the temple. It was to the temple that devout

Jews came from every land in order to celebrate the great religious festivals. Sooner or later therefore every significant Jewish religious figure was bound to find his way to Jerusalem in order to learn, to teach, or even perhaps simply to observe the intensity of religious devotion and intellectual ferment which characterized the city. In this Jesus was to be no exception, even though the major part of his work and ministry was to be lived out in Galilee. Even so the fact of Jerusalem and the traditions and activities which the city represented were to hover like a cloud over the head of Jesus throughout his life.

The priest Simeon appears suddenly, with no prior introduction, when Joseph and Mary brought Jesus to the temple "when the time came for their purification" (Luke 2:22). Strictly speaking this act of purification applied to Mary after she had given birth to a son. Leviticus 12:1–8 requires that a woman be regarded as ceremonially unclean for seven days after the birth of a son, and that she then remain at home for a further thirty-three days. Thereafter she was to offer a sacrifice at the temple gate on the east of the Court of Women. Combined with this was an act of offering the child to God, since he was a first-born child and the law required that a price be paid for his redemption. The presentation of the infant in the temple is also viewed in the Gospel record as an act of dedication of the child to the special service of God, much in the manner of the dedication of the child Samuel by his mother Hannah (1 Sam. 1:28). It is at this point that the otherwise unknown priest Simeon appears in the temple and discerns the unique significance of what is happening through the inspiration of the Holy Spirit. Like Zechariah therefore Simeon is a priest with the gift of prophetic understanding, and it is through this prophetic inspiration that he discerns the unique meaning for Israel of what the presentation of Jesus, in accordance with the Mosaic law, really foretells. The era of salvation has begun and a whole new order of religious observance and experience is about to begin. It is important therefore to see the priestly-prophetic prayer of Simeon and the entire priestly order of Israel which he represented, as conveying a consciously double meaning. Simeon was aged, and had not long to live. The Gospel narrative intends us to understand that the priestly order of Israel and the covenants and election promises related to this order were on the brink of passing away. Jesus, in his presentation in the temple of Jerusalem, was being dedicated to the service of God and would thereby become a "light for revelation to the Gentiles" (cf. Isa. 49:6). With him the old order which restricted the election promises to the heirs of Abraham would "depart" and a new order which embraced the Gentiles also would begin.

Since nothing is known of Simeon outside of what is stated in Luke's Gospel it is all the more essential that particular attention be given to the description set out there. This description is fourfold in its comments, although the last of these—the affirmation that "the Holy Spirit was upon him"—refers essentially to the gift of prophecy which his prayer revealed. He was "righteous," "devout," and "looking for the consolation of Israel." That he was "righteous" describes his own concern for the well-being of his fellow Jews and his broad commitment to keeping the requirements of the Mosaic law. A more specific interest attaches to the description of him as "devout," since this uses a Greek term which did not subsequently retain a widespread use as a description of Christian piety. In the strictest sense it describes Simeon as a person who was "cautious," or "guarded" in his attachment to the demands of the Mosaic law. Almost certainly this indicates the care with which he kept the specific priestly duties and obligations as a priest of the ancient line which traced its origin back to Aaron, the brother of Moses. In this, therefore, Simeon represents the very best in the tradition of the Jewish religion of his day. It is, however, the third element in the description which elicits most attention, for Simeon is described as a person who was "looking for the consolation of Israel." It is perhaps a little unfortunate that the modern sense of "consolation," or "comfort," indicates a very much weaker focus of hope than the original Greek would have conveyed. For this reason Today's English Version describes him as one who "was waiting for Israel to be saved." The reference in fact is to the expectation of the dawning of the Messianic Age which was a most deeply rooted and passionately longed for fulfillment of all that the prophets had foretold in the Old Testament. Such an expectation was undoubtedly widespread in the time of Simeon, although it was not universally adopted throughout Judaism, since some saw in it a threat to their position and political stability, especially in relation to the

Roman occupation. Simeon's life was marked by devout and careful
attention to the requirements of the Mosaic law (especially in its
ceremonial details) and concern for the general well-being of his
fellow Jews. He eagerly looked forward to the coming of the Messianic Age. He was a representative of the contemporary Jewish
thought and practice at its best, and as such he was able to recognize
the moment when the old era would pass and the new age of universal salvation would dawn.

The Prayer of Simeon

The words of Simeon's prayer have become widely familiar to a
great many Christians through their adoption in the liturgy of worship. How early such a practice began is not known, but it is highly
probable that it started very early in the life of the church and that all
three of the great prayers with which Luke's Gospel recounts the
story of the birth of Jesus—"The Magnificat," "The Benedictus," and
"The Nunc Dimittis"—were already being regularly used in worship
by the end of the first Christian century. Part of the reason for this
obviously lies in the valued way in which these prayers related the
forms of worship to the text of Scripture and especially to the central
events of the Gospel story. In a further direction, however, as we
shall see when we investigate the importance of the great prayer of
Jesus himself, these prayers were able to convey a message of the
utmost centrality concerning what it means to be a Christian. Some
truths are so important and the experience that they embody so penetrating in their effect on the human personality that they take a long
time to "sink in." We may even go so far as to claim that they never
do "sink in" fully in this life and that they require both constant
repetition and ever widening exploration if their contents are to be
fully brought home to us. So it is with the joy expressed in "The
Magnificat," the sense of a world-embracing purpose described in
"The Benedictus," and now with the declaration of fulfillment which
is the essence of Simeon's prayer:

"Lord, now lettest thou thy servant depart in peace,
according to thy word;
for mine eyes have seen thy salvation
which thou hast prepared in the presence of all peoples,

a light for revelation to the Gentiles,
and for glory to thy people Israel."

(Luke 2:29–32)

The prayer is a very short one, suggesting possibly that it is no longer in its complete form. This is worthy of further consideration in the light of another significant fact. In form it is of a rather unusual kind, since we can best describe it as "a prayer of confidence." When we look in the Psalter for other comparable expressions of confidence and trust in God, we discover that even there they are not at all numerous. The best known of such, in fact, is Psalm 23, the Shepherd Psalm. This has also occasioned comment in view of its highly distinctive form, being neither a straightforward hymn of praise nor a prayer of thanksgiving in the usual sense. What we do discover in the Psalms is that a short expression of trust and confidence frequently appears at the close of Psalms which are evidently expressions of lament and which begin in another mood altogether. A very marked example of this is to be seen in Psalm 54, which begins with a passionate request: "Save me, O God, . . . and vindicate me . . . Hear my prayer." It is easily recognizable as a prayer for utterance by a person in acute distress. However it finishes in a surprisingly calm note of confidence and assurance, without indicating what it is that had enabled the worshiper to see the situation so differently: "For thou hast delivered me from every trouble, and my eye has looked in triumph on my enemies" (Ps. 54:7). Either the worshiper has already experienced some great deliverance, or is looking forward to the time when he or she will have done so. Such is the worshiper's confidence in God that anxieties and fears have been allayed and faith in God's power to deliver fully restored. As a Psalm of confidence, Psalm 23 appears to have developed and extended this note of assurance from forming a part of prayers that were essentially expressive of lament to independent psalms of confidence. In the case of Simeon's prayer we have this same note of confidence expressed towards God in his prophetic utterance.

What had been revealed to Simeon by the prophetic inspiration of the Holy Spirit is a unique and momentous interpretation of what the dedication of the infant Jesus to the service of God meant. He would be "a light for revelation to the Gentiles" and "for glory to thy people Israel." The language here echoes very deliberately the ancient prophetic promises expressed centuries before in Isaiah 42:1–4; 49:1–6. Reference to these passages provides a most illuminating comentary upon what the dedication of Jesus to his life's work was to mean for the contemporary Jews who made up "Israel" and for the nations of the world. Jesus was to be the one in whom all the promises to Israel recorded in the Old Testament would find their fulfillment. Simeon therefore saw himself as a man most remarkably and singularly blessed by God to have lived to see the day when all that had been promised to and through Israel would reach its destined fullness. It is true that for the most part all this lay in the future, since Jesus was still a tiny child. Nevertheless, the act of purification and dedication by his parents marked the anticipated fullness of Jesus' ministry. Simeon's presence in the temple on that particular day and his seeing the parents of Jesus fulfilling the requirements of the Mosaic law had enabled him to see the beginning of the era of salvation both for Israel and the nations of the world. It must undoubtedly have occasioned the most immense surprise for the parents of Jesus to discover that there was one honored and discerning priest who saw, even more fully than they did themselves, the momentous significance of the life that Jesus would lead.

Simeon's insight was carried beyond his prayer in words which he then addressed to Mary. Why Mary alone is mentioned when Joseph also was present is not clear, but it may well indicate that by the time Jesus was crucified, at which Simeon's prophecy hints, Joseph had died. His words are heavy with meaning:

"Behold, this child is set for the fall and rising of many in Israel,
and for a sign that is spoken against
(and a sword will pierce through your own soul also),
that thoughts out of many hearts may be revealed."

(Luke 2:34–35)

The prophecy is of great significance for the further unfolding of the gospel story and ominous in what it foretells about the manner of the life that Jesus will lead. It marks the first warning that not all in Israel will show themselves to be as righteous and devout as Simeon had been throughout his life and that many among the Jewish people would not be as eager as he had been to "see the consolation of

Israel." Jesus would provide a challenge which would test and try the hearts of every single Jew. As he would arouse an enthusiastic following, so also some would become his enemies and would oppose everything that he did and taught. Like so many of the prophets of old, Jesus would find himself a prophet "without honor in his own country," and ultimately his triumph and exaltation would be upon a brigand's cross, unjust and undeserved as that would be. Mary was to learn that the joy and delight of motherhood establishes a love and a self-giving that is always vulnerable.

The Significance of the Prayer

Language is a remarkable, if sometimes clumsy, human instrument. It can convey the deepest feelings and secrets of the human heart, establish relationships where none existed before, and make possible a rich expansion of life inconceivable without it. Without it we should find ourselves severely curtailed and limited in the range and quality of our human activities. Language is also a mysterious vehicle of communication, however, binding together people who share the same tongue and holding apart those who do not. It can, when highly developed and made precise, be a most valuable instrument for clarifying thought and polishing and developing ideas. It may also provide a series of links and connections bringing together images and insights through its similes and metaphors. Prayer too, makes use of language, even when no words are actually spoken or written down. More frequently, we find it most constructive and helpful in praying to focus our concern to communicate with God in a series of spoken or written words. The language of prayer therefore may also become a many-sided means of communication, commencing at one simple and straightforward level and then developing its images and ideas in new directions. Nowhere is such a phenomenon of a multi-layered sequence of meanings in prayer more fully to be seen than in "The Nunc Dimittis." Simeon is presented as an old man, convinced of God's promise that his life will not come to an end until he has seen God's salvation. When he caught sight of the infant Jesus being presented in the temple in Jerusalem he saw, in that inspired moment, his expectations fulfilled. The Gospel quite clearly intends us to discern a further and deeper level of meaning.

It is not just for Simeon and his own private world of hope and ambition that fulfillment has come, but for Judaism as a whole, and even for the nations of the world. That Simeon can then "depart in peace" is not simply an assurance that his own life will have achieved a richly fulfilling high-point but so also will the entire order which he represents have done so. Mosaic law, priestly ordinances, and prophetic promises will all have come to a "fulfillment" with the presentation of Jesus in the temple so that they too can "depart in peace." In this therefore the Gospel brings to the fore a very important aspect of what "fulfillment" means, since it is more than just a "best" and "richest" moment in a story but a whole new order which renders any further continuance of the old order unnecessary. This is a point which the writer of the epistle to the Hebrews was subsequently to develop more fully (Heb. 7:23–28). As Simeon prays joyfully to God that his life has found a fulfillment in the discovery of Jesus, so is there a hidden meaning in his words that the old order of priesthood and waiting for the era of salvation can also now slip quietly away. The age of salvation has dawned with Jesus, and in him the Jewish people, as well as the nations of the world, can experience a new quality of life.

Surprising as it may be, a further layer of meaning lies latent in Simeon's prayer which relates to its use as an act of submission to God at the end of each day. In this manner an individual Christian can find in Simeon's words a means of refocusing the cares and concerns of each day and of setting them in the light of God's salvation. By using the prayer in this fashion, each day can have its own "fulfillment" which, although it will not be the whole of that which Simeon was so pleased to have seen, will nevertheless be a part of it. The words of Simeon confidently submitting his own life to God have become through the centuries a way by which each Christian life can experience a refocusing upon God and a reawakening of the knowledge that it is only by finding fulfillment in God that the fullest meaning of existence can be explored. Much of the beauty and import of Simeon's prayer is to be found in the manner in which it affirms this sense of life finding fulfillment in God.

In considering Simeon's prayer therefore it is valuable to see it not simply as expressive of what the age of fulfillment means for

Israel and its priesthood but what fulfillment means for each individual life. Here we are immediately brought face to face with the fact that the idea of fulfillment remains a very meaningful and treasured description of the goal of life. Where more common words such as "happiness" and "satisfaction" have too easily become devalued as descriptions of life's ultimate aim, this has not become the case with "fulfillment." Even when we may neglect to give the matter much attention, we remain aware that we do look for and strive for a genuine element of fulfillment. Whether we seek this through career, through family and friendships, or through other forms of private ambition, we are very much aware that life is an irreplaceable gift which should not be wasted. We seek some genuine measure of fulfillment, which indicates a much deeper level of personal satisfaction than can be offered by simply looking for easy paths. In fact, in a great many cases, it is the search for fulfillment that has led men and women to take on the most hazardous of enterprises and to undertake the most arduous of responsibilities and tasks. Their reward is that they feel "fulfilled" by having extended and tested their gifts and abilities. Fulfillment may then be seen as a socially enriching aspect of human life and ambition. The dangers and misfortunes lie not in seeking to find fulfillment in life but rather in neglecting to do so or in doing so in ways that are too limited and inadequate for such a goal.

In this regard Simeon's prayer is a constant reminder that the seeking of fulfillment is one of the ways in which life brings us face to face with God. God alone is totally adequate to offer such fulfillment, since God alone is the Lord and Giver of life. This does not mean that the only kind of fulfillment that the Christian should seek must be of a distinctively "religious" kind. Far from it, since that would be a denial of the divine origin of the whole Creation. Instead, by recognizing the immense range of possibilities that our existence as human beings brings to us, we are made to consider that dimension which the theological language of the age has come to describe as "ultimacy." What is the *ultimate* goal of life? Perhaps there can be no more telling interpretation of the biblical message about sin for the modern world than that it concerns the "wasting" of life. This concerns not only the awfulness of violence and warfare, and such threats to existence, but the tragedy of triviality, where life is spent in the pursuit of frivolous and ultimately unsatisfying goals. Simeon's prayer is a constant reminder that life challenges us to seek fulfillment and that such fulfillment must be big enough and enriching enough to absorb the immensity of the possibilities that human life brings.

22
A Prayer of
JESUS

Matthew 6:9–15

Jesus the Man

For Christian men and women throughout the world the Lord's Prayer, which we are now to consider, is not just *a* prayer, but *the* prayer which stands in importance above all others. It has become the great family prayer of the whole Christian church. It was, presumably, just one of many prayers that Jesus prayed and taught his disciples to use in their own communion with God. The Gospels present Jesus as a person who was very much given to prayer and who could be found spending long hours in prayer alone. Since he was himself so much a man of prayer, it is understandable that his disciples should have been eager that he should teach them both what and how to pray. It can be no accident therefore that this particular prayer has been singled out as being of unique importance in the teaching of Jesus and that its careful preservation was a matter of great significance for his disciples in the early church. This was clearly how Jesus wished to guide and inform his followers about prayer, and in a very special way, about the inner secret of his own prayer life. It is very brief, containing just six simple petitions to God which could be easily remembered. It has therefore a very special significance as a means by which Christians can share in something of the inner life and spirit of Jesus, and as such, it came to be regarded in the early church as a special privilege to offer this prayer on the part of new initiates into the Christian faith. They had come to the position where they could through Jesus see and know God as "Father."

Its very simplicity and brevity, however, should not blind us to its

extraordinary complexity and depth. If it is on the one hand the first
and simplest prayer that the Christian can offer, it is also, paradoxically, the hardest of all prayers to utter with that intensity of meaning
which would enable the Christian to say: "I know that with all my
heart I truly mean that prayer." Such is its depth and the demands
that it makes upon our own desires for God that we can easily be
tempted to say: "It is too high, I cannot attain to it!" In order to
understand it more fully it is useful to set it against the background
of life in which Jesus grew up. This sheds considerable light on the
reasons why this particular prayer was chosen to be "the Lord's"
prayer.

The society of Galilee was affected by a considerable mixture of
religions. We have already noted that Nazareth, where Jesus was
brought up, appears to have been a fairly traditional small Jewish
town but not too far away was the city of Tiberias, named in honor
of the Roman emperor, and a modern Graeco-Roman foundation
from the days of Jesus. Since the time of the conquests of Alexander
the Great 300 years before, the whole of the eastern Mediterranean
region which we know as the Levant had become a great "mixing
bowl" for the peoples of East and West. The philosophy, the art and
architecture, the love of games, as well as the language of Greece
had all been exported to the Orient. This had in no way lessened
since Pompey had replaced Greek rule with that of Rome. New political institutions, traditions of law and justice, together with the
mythology and religious traditions of Rome had been added to the
already rich inheritance of Greece in Galilee and Judea. Yet the traffic
was certainly not all in one direction, so that even in the time of Jesus
the sense of oriental "mystery," the reputation of the East for religion
and the magic arts, and not least a remarkably ancient tradition of
religious learning and spirituality, had been brought westwards. Galilee was a region where East met West, and this would certainly have
been very evident to Jesus from his earliest days.

From a religious, and specifically Jewish, point of view this in-
termixing of culture and religions between East and West was not a
development which could be looked upon with uniform favor. The
religion of Judaism, as we know from the pages of the Bible, was
strongly conservative in many of its features, and this had not made

the spread of Jews in the Dispersion a very easy experience to accept. It is true that there were some who openly welcomed the freeing of Judaism from many of its traditional restraints and restrictions, but for a great many others there was a deep feeling of unease and suspicion. Jewish men and women had come to think of "Gentiles" as dangerous and threatening to the purity and integrity of religious faith. They looked upon Gentile food as "unclean"; Gentile dress was often regarded as immodest, but above all Gentile religion was frowned upon as "paganism," and its altars and rituals were dismissed as "profane." Inevitably therefore there emerged from time to time feelings of distrust and encounters which generated friction. Gentiles sensed that their own achievements in architecture and learning were ignorantly rejected by Jews, while Jews felt that their own deep moral concerns and simple and austere religious faith were not properly respected by those who were not Jews. These suspicions were, no doubt, simply expressive of extremes, for certainly some Gentile "God-fearers" developed a strong and positive regard for Jewish religion, some even going so far as to become full "proselytes" to the faith. Similarly Jews such as Philo, the great first-century philosopher of Alexandria, showed a great love of and concern for Hellenistic learning and culture. Many others found themselves torn somewhere between the two. Most striking, perhaps, were those Jews who formed themselves into the party of the Pharisees, whose very name means "Separatists." On the one side they fully respected the need for Jews to live and work among Gentiles; yet on the other hand they insisted upon a clear and unfailing demarcation between the "holy" religious life and world of the Jews and the "profane—unclean" world of the Gentiles. This was an issue that was to have a most profound effect upon the teaching of Jesus and the further development of Judaism during the next two centuries.

If there was this deep sense of a religious divide between Jew and Gentile. which increasingly meant between one neighbor and another, it was certainly matched within Judaism itself by internal dissensions of a political kind. Ever since the Babylonian exile Jews had found themselves living under the foreign domination of one or other of the great imperial powers: Persia, Greece, and Rome. Some saw this as part of the divine will, so that it should be accepted and even used to their advantage. They became active collaborators with the Roman administration, serving it as tax-collectors and intermediaries. Others accepted this foreign rule but only as a sign of God's anger against the chosen people and so viewed it as a misfortune to be borne patiently rather than as something to be endorsed. Others became actively hostile to it, forming themselves into a party of "Zealots" who were dedicated to the active overthrow of Roman rule and all its concomitant features. Eventually it was this party that was to play so large a part in an uprising against the Roman administration during the years A.D. 66–70. Politically speaking, scarcely any other event until the Holocaust of the twentieth-century left so profound a mark upon Judaism as did this Roman-Jewish war. It brought to a head tensions and issues that had brought danger and unease to Jewish life for two centuries. Thus, it is noteworthy that a marked variety of attitudes over political questions had emerged in the Judaism in which Jesus grew up. So far as we can interpret the different positions it appears that the party of the Sadduccees had adopted an openly collaborationist position towards the Roman administration. The Zealots, however, were totally and irrevocably opposed to it. The position of the Pharisees is less clear-cut, since it was indifferent over some issues, but deeply concerned and committed over others. In general it adopted a kind of "open" or neutral position in which it did not actively campaign against the restraints and taxes imposed by the Roman administration but did little to support them. A more extreme position was adopted by those Jews who lived a monastic existence on the shores of the Dead Sea, since these had effectively cut themselves off from active involvement in political life. All these different political attitudes involved attitudes toward the coming of the expected Messiah and the coming of the kingdom of God. Some certainly took up a position which was largely negative towards the whole of the existing political order and looked for the coming of God's kingdom, much in the manner of a divine gift coming down from heaven. As a consequence such themes as those of "the Messiah," "the kingdom of God," and "The New Age" were very much talked about and discussed, but quite different conclusions were drawn as to what they would mean in terms of a new political and social order. Experts in the interpretation of the Scriptures could argue about these issues on the basis of the texts of which they regarded themselves as the masters. Others, impatient of seemingly endless theological argument, were anxious to take action in a very direct way in order to hasten the coming of the kingdom. Virtually all, however, were agreed upon one thing. This was that the kingdom of God would come "soon." Nevertheless, even this left unanswered how soon this was to be and what could be done to hasten the day.

The Prayer

The words of the great prayer of Jesus are so well known that it is often difficult to stand apart from it and to study it in such a way as to ensure that its form and contents strike freshly upon our minds:

> "Our Father who art in heaven,
> Hallowed be thy name.
> Thy kingdom come,
> Thy will be done,
>   On earth as it is in heaven.
> Give us this day our daily bread;
> And forgive us our debts,
>   As we also have forgiven our debtors;
> And lead us not into temptation,
>   But deliver us from evil."
>   (Matthew 6:9–13)

Matthew's Gospel adds a further elaboration of the importance of forgiveness, which is not included in Luke's account (Luke 11:2–4):

> "For if you forgive men their trespasses, your heavenly Father also will forgive you; but if you do not forgive men their trespasses, neither will your Father forgive your trespasses."

>   (Matthew 6:14–15)

The prayer opens with a brief invocation of God as "Father" and an ascription of praise, "hallowed be thy name." There then follow six petitions to God, seeking God's work and power among men and women:

> Thy kingdom come,
> Thy will be done, . . .
> Give us . . . daily bread . . .
> forgive us our debts, . . .

lead us not into temptation . . .
deliver us from evil.

As with all truly great prayers we should perhaps also note that
there is a certain added significance in what is left out, although we
should probably not make too much of this.

First and foremost in the prayer attention has been drawn to the
remarkable form of address in the invocation—"Our Father." This
translates into Greek a title that was so significant in its original
Aramaic form—Abba—that this form itself came to be retained in
use in the early church even in places and communities where the
Aramaic language would have sounded very strange. Certainly the
image of God as the Father of the people Israel appears in the Old
Testament, nowhere more poignantly and strikingly than in
Jeremiah 31:20:

Is Ephraim my dear son?
    Is he my darling child?
For as often as I speak against him,
    I do remember him still.
Therefore my heart yearns for him;
    I will surely have mercy on him,
                says the LORD.
            (Jeremiah 31:20)

What is so striking in the Lord's Prayer is that this title "Father"
has been chosen in preference to and above all others. Even more, it
has been argued, it uses not the solemn and formal language which
might have been expected, but the intimate family word, more akin
to our affectionate "Daddy!" Yet perhaps the most far-reaching element in the choice of such a term to invoke God lies in yet another
direction. By the time of Jesus we know that the Jewish people had
adopted the convention of substituting the honorific title "Lord"
where the more distinctive divine name appears in the Old Testament
(sometimes transcribed as "Jehovah"). Among the mixed population
of Judah and Galilee, however, it cannot have been all that uncommon to have heard other divine names being used: "Zeus" or "Jupi-
ter," for example, or even more strange sounding titles. In fact it
appears that a certain kind of "fashion" had emerged, trading in
divine names and actively striving after the more exotic and myste-

rious, as though they had some kind of special "pull" upon God. At the very least the name by which men and women called upon God readily separated Jew from Gentile, and became a simple indicator of the kind of religious allegiance which a person felt. The more exclusive religious groups actively tried to keep the name by which they were encouraged to call upon God a secret, reserved only for use by those who were fully initiated members. A kind of religious "one-upmanship" grew in the use of divine names. The response of Jesus to this bizarre world of name-trading in religion is startling in its simplicity. God is simply to be called "Father." In such a usage all people, no matter what their previous religious tradition, come equally before God. The very title by which God is known marks the breaking down of barriers rather than the setting up of them. Therefore the use of the invocation "Abba—Father" as central to the understanding of God in the prayer which Jesus gave to the church marks a gigantic leap forward for faith. It is simple; it is universally recognizable in its meaning; it puts an end to the false exclusiveness of the various religious traditions which focused their distinctiveness on the name by which they called upon God.

A similar step forward in the breaking down of barriers and the removal of false distinctions also appears in the ascription of praise to God: "Hallowed be thy name." The retention of the Old English "hallow" represents a concern for an established convention which is rather at variance with the simplicity of the text. It affirms "May your name be holy," and in this it upholds a prominent feature of Jewish life and religious practice which sought to protect the name of God from misuse through profane, magical, or dishonorable acts (cf. Exod. 20:7). The concern that God's name should be treated with honor therefore was in no way new to this prayer. Much importance evidently attaches itself to the nature of the emphasis that is given and what is omitted. In a world where religion impinged on the everyday lives of men and women to an extent and in a fashion that is scarcely conceivable today, the prayer of Jesus establishes a principle that is simple and basic. Where the mixed religious world of Galilee and Judea witnessed a bewildering complexity of objects, places, actions, and words believed to be "holy," the teaching of Jesus brought a transforming simplicity. Let God's name be seen as "holy," not an endless confusion of holy places, holy men, holy names, and holy signs. By such a simple recognition that holiness belongs to God and is to be found in the respect and honor in which God's name is held, men and women were set free from the superstitious tyranny of an almost limitless chain of scruples and traditions which colored and distorted everyday life. In his prayer, Jesus has established a truth which was to affect very deeply other aspects of his teaching (cf. Mark 7:14–23).

A similar breakthrough into simplicity is to be found in the first of the great petitions which follow; "Thy Kingdom come," to which the parallel "Thy will be done" serves as a fuller definition and amplification. We have already had occasion to mention the confused world of politics in the time of Jesus and the central role which the expectation of the coming of the kingdom of God played in such a confusion. Everywhere people talked about God's kingdom and its coming, but how, when, and what this would mean were interpreted differently. Jesus taught that with him the kingdom of God had drawn near (Mark 1:15), and in reflecting upon his ministry, death, and resurrection, the early church recognized that the kingdom of God had indeed come among people. What was so new and startling about this teaching of the kingdom was the radical way in which the expectation of it had been given a new depth and range. It was a spiritual, eternal, inward, and perfect kingdom, which was not to be straightforwardly identified with any simple change in the political order. Jesus resolutely refused to allow his teaching of the kingdom to be identified with a political movement to overthrow the Roman occupying power. It was certainly not indifferent to political issues, however. It was not to be thought of in terms of a "national" Jewish kingdom, yet it was in no way indifferent to Jewish teaching and expectation. In accepting the contemporary hopes and convictions concerning the imminent coming of God's kingdom, Jesus both fulfilled and transformed them. In the teaching which he gave and which he incorporated as a central petition in his prayer, Jesus extended the understanding of the kingdom of God to an extent that was more truly commensurate with the understanding of one single universal God, the Father of all people. It is a kingdom that has come with Jesus, and still comes, as men and women incorporate the power and message of Jesus into their own lives. It is wholly fitting therefore that the prayer for the coming of God's kingdom should be amplified by the further request: "Thy will be done, On earth as it is in heaven." As soon as such a petition is set before God, a whole new world of challenge and possibility lies open before us.

The petitions which follow this are startlingly modest in their range, but evidently are a result of deliberate design: "Give us our daily bread; forgive us . . . as we have forgiven." The singling out of a request for sufficient food "for the day," is almost breathtaking and deeply disconcerting in its restraint. How easy it is to think of God, and by inference of prayer, as a way to get those many things which we see as desirable and which we can persuade ourselves are for our greater benefit. Yet Jesus taught the utmost restraint and modesty in such requests, if we are to understand his teaching in this prayer. Our concern for ourselves should be a concern for what is needful, not for what is luxury. As Jesus taught restraint and self-discipline in our material requests, so also does the plea for forgiveness impose restraint upon our emotional and personal demands. Even the Psalter of the Old Testament contains a significant number of entreaties that God destroy enemies or avenge wrongs they have perpetrated. In the prayer which is so central to the teaching of Jesus, however, all such pleas for vengeance and triumph over enemies are transmuted by the centrality of the petition for forgiveness: "forgive us . . . as we have forgiven." The Christian life is one of reconciliation, both within the life of the church, and also in extending its reconciling power outward into society. In this way the message of forgiveness takes on the power to revitalize all human relationships, and in doing so, it recognizes that forgiveness may be one of the hardest of all gifts to offer to others. Had it been easy, it would not have needed so prominent a place in the prayer of Jesus.

The final two petitions: "Lead us not into temptation, but deliver us from evil," bring together a general portrayal of the right direction of life. They draw into one the awareness of God's sovereignty over our lives and of our own individual responsibility within it. If we choose to follow difficult and dangerous paths, we should not cry out in anguish at misfortunes that we have brought upon ourselves. Even within that area over which we have control, it is often tempting not

to exercise due responsibility, so that we must blame our own fool-
ishness for some ills and misfortunes. Beyond this, however, God is
sovereign over our lives and over our world, and we must learn to
trust in that perfect will which God has purposed for each of us. God
alone can ultimately deliver us from evil.

The Significance of the Prayer

In assessing the overall significance of this great prayer of Jesus
we may begin by summing up certain aspects of its content. Prominent here must certainly be the manner in which it expresses a complete rejection of any approach to prayer which regards it in a
magical or semimagical fashion. Most evident is the simplicity and
intelligibility which belongs to the invocation of God, the Source
and Guardian of all creation, as "Father." In a world which had come
to associate all kinds of special powers and effects with the use of a
great variety of divine names, the prayer of Jesus uses only a title
which displays a remarkable and inclusive simplicity. This has a far-
reaching bearing on the understanding of prayer itself, which takes
on through this form of invocation, the character of a relationship
defined by the nature of human relationships. Prayer is thereby lifted
out of the range of religious practices which have so often bordered
on the semimagical and the impersonal. Nothing that dishonors or
debases or in any other way detracts from the personal nature of our
human existence can be a worthy and effective means of communion
with God. In this regard it is paradoxical and regrettable that in the
course of Christian history the recitation of a "Paternoster" has at
times been allowed to slip to the level of an impersonal and unthinking repetition. At times it has itself been regarded as empowered to
exert a special "pull" upon God. The recognition that God is to be
thought of under the analogy of a human father, emphasizes the essentially personal nature of religion.

We ought not, simply on account of the historic and respected
place which this prayer has within the Christian faith, ignore altogether objections which can and have been raised against this central
feature of Christian prayer. The portrayal of the ultimate Source and
Ground of all reality under the image of a father clearly cannot say
all that needs to be said regarding God. It may, and sometimes has,

encouraged a false and illusory familiarity with God which can easily border on the ridiculous. If it is allowed to encourage the idea that God has little to do other than to make life comfortable and enjoyable for each of us individually, it could only be judged as a cruel misrepresentation of reality. Yet this is certainly not a necessary inference to draw from such a title, which must rather be seen as a most valuable rescuing of the notion of deity from confusion and disarray in a world which had come to know a great variety of gods. It may be objected also that the kind of trust implied by faith in God as Father marks a lowering of the level of human responsibility by leaving all initiative with God. If at times the Christian religion has been guilty of encouraging such an attitude, then it can hardly be said to have been due to an undue emphasis on the idea of divine "Fatherhood." Rather we must insist that it is this analogy that has acted as a barrier against such attitudes of religious irresponsibility. No father worthy of the name leaves his children unprepared or untutored for the demands, responsibilities, and decision making that growth and maturity in a family context require. Where at times such irresponsibility has emerged it has arisen from too great a concern with the "childlike" nature of trust in God. We must, in any case, recognize that no one single analogy can possibly be expected to convey a full and completely balanced picture of God. Even the best and most valued analogy can only be a partial expression of the whole truth.

This too must certainly be said in regard to a very much discussed feature of the modern world. The image of God as "Father" inevitably lacks the sensitivity to those "feminine" aspects of deity which the modern feminist movement has seen as of so great importance. No doubt this is true, but equally we can hardly have expected that the situation would be otherwise. During its history the Christian faith has, in other ways, given more place to the "feminine" aspects of the divine Creator than the use of the invocation "Father" properly demands. The Lord's Prayer is necessarily bound up to a certain extent with the first-century social world of Palestinian Galilee.

This prayer of Jesus has become one of the most central and valued treasures of the Christian church. Where institutions have so often proved divided and divisive and where even the great historic creeds of Christendom have failed to elicit unfettered support from

all Christians, nevertheless this prayer has acquired a claim upon
every Christian. It is a prayer that unites, and it is entirely fitting that
this should be so. In calling upon God as Father we are each drawn
into a familial relationship to other Christians, no matter how incomplete and distant that relationship may appear to be. The prayer
which Jesus gave to his church, and through that church to all people,
is therefore a never failing reminder of the reconciling and unifying
power of the knowledge of God. In the concluding admonition which
Matthew's Gospel brings to the prayer this point is given added emphasis. How can men and women be forgiven, if they themselves are
unready or unwilling to forgive?

23
Another Prayer of JESUS

Luke 10:21–24

Jesus; the Man of Prayer

Besides The Lord's Prayer, several other short prayers of Jesus are recorded in the Gospels, and that which we are now to look at is very distinctive. It is not a "pattern" prayer in the manner of most of those prayers we have considered, and it belongs quite uniquely to the person of Jesus of Nazareth. In fact it is a prayer which offers an intimate disclosure of who Jesus is and why he is unique. It is not in the more familiar sense a prayer which we can use and follow. However, it is a "prayer about prayer," since it provides an answer to the question why Christians offer their prayers "in the name of Jesus" and why we may believe that praying to God through the mediation of Jesus Christ is a unique Christian privilege.

We may note at the outset therefore two important factors which make a special examination of this prayer instructive. The first of these concerns the fact that throughout the Gospels Jesus is presented as a man who was much given to prayer and whose relationship to God was one which was established and maintained through prayer. It might appear on a superficial reflection that, as the Son of God, Jesus would have felt himself to have been so uniquely "at one" with God that he had no need of prayer as others do. Nothing could be further from the portrait of Jesus which the biblical record offers. So far as the life of Jesus is concerned communion with God was a communion that found its realization in and through prayer. In his search to do the will of God, in his seeking to experience the power and support of God, and in his anguish to fulfill the purpose of God at whatever cost to himself, Jesus resorted to prayer. In his doing so he undoubtedly set the activity of prayer at the top of all that he had to teach concerning the life of the spirit.

A second unexpected feature in this particular prayer of Jesus has a bearing upon Christian faith and practice. It might appear to the casual observer that prayer is the most private, intimate, and direct form of communion between humans and God. In fact in the language of much religious thinking prayer has often been presented in this guise as "being alone with the Alone." No mediation whatsoever is required between the human soul and the eternal spirit of God. To a certain extent this is undoubtedly true, but ultimately all faith and spiritual insight are dependent on the experience, teaching, and guidance of others. Were it not so the history of religion would have been very different from what it has been. Religion, including especially prayer, is dependent not only on God but on the lives and experience of other men and women. Uniquely for the Christian, therefore, this means a dependence on the life, teaching, and ministry of Jesus Christ. It is this point that is brought home to us so emphatically in this prayer of Jesus. In it he places himself and his teaching uniquely in the center of the Christian's knowledge and experience of God. Without the mediation of Jesus, Christian prayer would be no different from that of any other form of religion. Prayer "in the name of Jesus" becomes vitalized and directed through all that Jesus means and has meant for the Christian church. The prayer in Luke 10:21–24, therefore, is the Christological prayer *par excellence* of the Gospels, since it lifts the figure of Jesus to the most central and indispensable place in all Christian understanding of God. Furthermore, it makes prayer a part of the experience of Christian discipleship and Christian discipleship a necessary part of the experience of prayer.

It is a concern with the issue of what it means to follow Jesus which provides the immediate context for this particular prayer. Its form is that of a thanksgiving on the part of Jesus to God for those who had become his disciples, followed by an invocation of blessing upon them. What they had experienced was a disclosure of the grace of God's wisdom, and this same wisdom was now working to extend its riches to others. The followers of Jesus were becoming teachers of a fuller understanding of God, which exceeded that previously given even to the kings and prophets of Israel.

Luke 9:51 introduces the reader to a series of encounters between Jesus and intending disciples which highlight what discipleship called for. In the first of these James and John were tempted, when a Samaritan village refused to receive Jesus, to invoke the fire of judgment down from heaven, in the manner of Elijah (cf. 2 Kings 1:9–16). Such a vengeful attitude was entirely contrary to the reconciling and forgiving nature of Christian discipleship. Three further incidents then follow in which potential disciples begin to learn the level of commitment that is required of those who would be followers of Jesus. No considerations of personal comfort or even personal or family loyalty were to be allowed to stand in the way. These incidents are then followed by a mission in which Jesus sent out no less than seventy of his followers into the towns and villages of Galilee, thereby anticipating the great Christian mission which did not begin until after his death and resurrection. In this mission too, essential guidelines and truths were laid down for Christian discipleship. The disciples were to accept the hospitality of the towns and villages to which the message of the kingdom was brought, and this hospitality was to be held as sufficient for Christian need. Even more pertinently, the attitude shown by a community towards the missioners sent by Jesus was to be interpreted as their attitude towards the hope and message of God's kingdom. By acting in this way the disciples of Jesus were to learn that they had a constitutive role to play in the work of the kingdom of God. No longer was it to remain in the sphere of hope and anticipation, but it was to be seen as already breaking in through the mission of the seventy sent out by Jesus. This was a particularly intense period of activity, therefore, in which Jesus lifted the position of his disciples from that of being simply listeners and learners about the kingdom of God into being its agents and heralds through the authority that he had given to them.

It is instructive to keep in mind this special background to the prayer of thanksgiving offered by Jesus since it shows the intimate link between prayer and discipleship. Being a disciple of Jesus centers upon an understanding of who he is; yet acquiring this understanding of his person is very different from the kind of understanding that pertains to knowledge of other things, and differs too from the pursuit of wisdom and learning that colored so much of the religious life of his time. It is an understanding that is direct, committed, and intuitive—given by God—rather than based on assembling and comparing a vast collection of facts. It is the kind of understanding that can be reached more truly through prayer than through the academic pursuits of the learned scribes, who were exercising an ever more dominant role in the life of contemporary Jewish faith. Theirs was a piety and a knowledge of God that was based upon the learning and traditions of scribes and religious scholars, where even the role of the priest was receding into a more secondary position. Against such there were others who viewed the knowledge of God's kingdom as essentially a pragmatic and even violent involvement in the political realities of a people smarting under centuries of foreign imperial rule. Such were the Zealots who were already making their mark in Galilee in the days of Jesus and who were destined in the near future to play a fateful part in the catastrophic Jewish war against Rome. The followers of Jesus were not drawn either from the especially learned and erudite ranks of the scribes nor yet from the eager political activists whose piety was coupled to the sword. In the eyes of the world those who were rallying to the message and call of Jesus were mere "babes"—simple, trusting, and committed men and women who heard in the message of Jesus about the kingdom of God a truth that was able to transform them and their society.

It would have been easy for those questioning and uncommitted men and women who watched the spread of the influence of Jesus and the growth in the number of his followers to object that what they saw was attractive and interesting but not the promised coming of God's kingdom which the Scriptures foretold. They preferred to adopt an attitude of waiting to see how the mission of Jesus fared before embracing a more clear-cut and decisive attitude towards it. To such people also the prayer of Jesus is a remarkable response, since it affirms that ever since the days of the kings and prophets of Israel the work and wisdom of God had been recognized by only a few. A kind of spiritual principle had emerged in which only a faithful remnant had grasped the significance of what God was doing in their days. Now something greater, fuller, and more enduringly significant was taking place in Galilee than any of these kings or prophets had witnessed. It was an incomparable privilege therefore for the few who followed Jesus to have secured the most honored places in God's kingdom, not as their just reward, but as God's free and unconditional gift.

Jesus' Prayer of Thanksgiving

This prayer of Jesus is in two parts, the first of which (Luke 10:21–22) is in the form of a thanksgiving to God for his disciples and their privileged position in the kingdom of God. The second part (Luke 10:23–24) is not strictly speaking a prayer as such but a pronouncement of blessing upon his disciples. We have already seen in similar pronouncements of blessing, as in the cases of Jacob and Moses, that these should be seen as essentially prayerful invocations of blessing upon specific persons. This blessing from the lips of Jesus shares this same character as an invoking of God's blessing upon his followers. Much discussion has taken place about whether the two sayings of Jesus concerning his disciples, his thanksgiving to God for them, and his pronouncement of blessing upon them were originally separate or whether from the outset they belonged together. Probably no completely final verdict on this question can be reached, and the view taken here is that the two parts are to be taken together. Certainly in content they reflect two aspects of the same truth—the centrality of Jesus for Christian faith and the knowledge of God.

> In that same hour he rejoiced in the Holy Spirit and said, "I thank thee, Father, Lord of heaven and earth, that thou hast hidden these things from the wise and understanding and revealed them to babes; yea, Father, for such was thy gracious will. All things have been delivered to me by my Father; and no one knows who the Son is except the Father, or who the Father is except the Son and any one to whom the Son chooses to reveal him."
>
> Then turning to the disciples he said privately, "Blessed are the eyes which see what you see! For I tell you that many prophets and kings desired to see what you see, and did not see it, and to hear what you hear, and did not hear it."
>
> (Luke 10:21–24)

The form of the first part—the prayer of thanksgiving—follows quite closely that of individual thanksgivings, such as we find in the Psalter. The second part—the blessing of the disciples—is also quite straightforward in its form and must echo closely the kind of blessing formula which the head of a family or a teacher would have employed in pronouncing blessing upon the family or pupils. It is attractive to speculate that it was probably quite common for a teacher to offer some formal blessing upon his pupils as a way of encouraging them and in order to keep before them a sense of goal and direction. It is not in any formal features therefore that these two sayings of Jesus are remarkable. Rather it is in their content and in the extraordinary way in which they place Jesus in a central and indispensable position as the Mediator between God and humanity.

So far as the thanksgiving for the disciples is concerned we must recognize that it represents one of the most memorable and astounding sayings from Jesus concerning his unique relationship to God. It represents a "Christological" confession that Jesus is the "Son of God" in a way that can be said of no other human being. Moreover it interprets what this Sonship means not in the terms of his sharing a common "substance" with the Father—a form of theological understanding that became necessary in the midst of later controversy—but in terms of his mediating a unique revelation of God. We may look at the individual parts of this great prayerful confession.

It begins in a rather unexpected fashion with the recognition that God has hidden "these things" from those who are wise and understanding and that he has instead disclosed them to "babes." In this the prayer follows a characteristic theme that is to be found in contemporary Jewish writings from this period that true wisdom is something that is hidden from the great mass of the human race, but can be easily found by those who are prepared to trust in God. In the pages of the Old Testament the most beautiful expression of this theme is to be found in Job 28. In this the poet, after surveying all the possible avenues and sources of wisdom, recognizes that it can only be found through a simple and obedient trust: "Behold the fear of the Lord, that is wisdom; and to depart from evil is understanding" (Job 28:28). Now Jesus discerned that it was precisely the essential core of this truth that was showing itself through the experience of his disciples. Those who were blessed with a great tradition of learning and who spent their lives in the study of the Scriptures were failing to discern the action of God in their own day. Their eyes were in a sense fixed on the past so that the work of God was hidden from them. Contrastingly those who were mere "babes" in their religious and educational attainments were responding eagerly to the message and mission of Jesus, and in doing so, finding a truth about God which no book learning could ever provide. We can see that by his reference to "these things" in his prayer Jesus was referring to the experience of the disciples and especially to the mission of the seventy which Luke's Gospel reports as the context.

The second part of the thanksgiving affirms the uniqueness of the knowledge of God the Father, enjoyed by Jesus, and in a corresponding fashion, the unique knowledge of the Son—Jesus—possessed by the Father. Jesus occupies the central position in human knowledge of God, and yet men and women themselves do not fully know the fullness and mystery of the person of Jesus. That he was the long awaited Messiah, the Son of Man who was destined to play a leading role in the establishing of God's kingdom and the Son of God in a sense that could not apply to other men and women as "sons and daughters" of God, was only just beginning to become clear to those disciples who responded to the challenge of the Galilean mission. What is important in the thanksgiving therefore lies not simply in its uncovering of the true identity of Jesus but in its affirmation of the sharing of the knowledge of God which Jesus grants to his disciples. Therefore a kind of paradoxical contrast appears between the mystery and hiddenness of God and the freedom with which God was now being revealed to men and women through the simplicity of faith. Against a background in which "no one knows who the Father is," a situation had now arisen in which this knowledge could be shared by "any one to whom the Son chooses to reveal him."

In a sense the blessing of the disciples follows directly from this thanksgiving from the lips of Jesus: "Blessed are the eyes which see what you see!" Those who had committed themselves to Jesus and who had responded to his message of the kingdom of God now found themselves more privileged than even the kings and prophets of the Old Testament Scriptures. These latter had looked forward to the future coming of God's kingdom in hope and patience. Now even the poor and underprivileged people of Galilee were enjoying a greater spiritual experience, since they were living within the power and riches of God's kingdom. The joy which Jesus felt in seeing the fruits of this first Galilean mission spilled over into a joy which he could not but share with his disciples.

The Significance of the Prayer

We may single out a number of features concerning this prayer which have a bearing upon the way in which we ourselves offer our prayer. It should be said at this point that the central importance of this short thanksgiving from Jesus in the Gospel story reaches way beyond the confines of a concern with prayer alone. It provides one of the most central Christological affirmations which the biblical record gives to us, and certainly deserves major consideration. Jesus is presented as the Son of the Father in a manner which fully emphasizes the uniqueness of what this meant, and in a way which clearly places Jesus in a category apart from other men and women—even Moses and the Prophets—as the One through whom a knowledge of God is revealed. Moreover it achieves this in disclosing to us something of what we can only describe as the "mind" of Jesus. Central to our modern attempts to understand and interpret the uniqueness of the person of Jesus has been the awareness that this must necessarily have involved an inner subjective consciousness of God, of which we know very little. Understandably the Gospel records tell us much of the work of Jesus and not a little of his teaching. Yet in our quest to know the true mystery of his person, and the manner in which he was different from other humans, we are perplexed and often disappointed because they tell us so little of the inner consciousness and "mind" of Jesus. Often, for instance, we can only guess at what his feelings and intentions were on a particular occasion. Even his purpose in going up to Jerusalem for the Passover celebrations which eventually led to his death are described only very briefly.

It is very fitting therefore that this great silence regarding the inner thoughts and feelings of Jesus should be broken in the disclosure of this short prayer of thanksgiving. Prayer is undoubtedly a form of our thinking and reflecting in which such ideas as "meaning, purpose, and destiny" come to the fore. Prayer uncovers the awareness of ultimate meaning and purpose. A truth of lasting importance was disclosed, therefore, in Jesus' simple thanksgiving for the success of his disciples in their mission. The sense of his "Sonship" to God which Jesus experienced was altogether unique.

Another aspect of this prayer also has considerable significance for us in the modern world. It brings to the surface a tension which reappears several times in the Bible and which has continued to demand attention and rethinking ever since. In this prayer Jesus contrasts the fact that the truth about God is often hidden from the minds of those who regard themselves as wise and understanding while those who are "babes" can receive it as a gift and do so with simplicity. Such a contrast raises two issues which cannot be dealt with in any very simple fashion. The first of these concerns the place that learning and the pursuit of wisdom have, and should have, in Christian spirituality. It would be easy to allow this, together with other biblical sayings, to lead us into a false and dangerous anti-intellectualism. The pursuit of wisdom is certainly not something wrong in itself, and to accept Christian truth "on trust," without ever examining it with a critical and careful mind, is undoubtedly a most dangerous proceeding. It often has left the well-intentioned Christian open to all kinds of false and misleading ideas. If nothing is critically examined then all kinds of nonsense and error can be passed off as Christian truth. A right and proper use of reason and a healthy respect for wisdom are essential to growth in Christian spirituality. It must also be noted that the pursuit of wisdom in itself, however, can lead to a certain detachment and lack of trust and commitment which mean a failure to enter fully into Christian discipleship. The least we know from long human experience is that the pursuit of wisdom can lead to the display of a certain intellectual pride which is unhealthy and offensive. It is undoubtedly this side of the concern with wisdom which stands in the forefront of Jesus' confessional thanksgiving. Galilee did not lack for scribes and learned people, both those who cherished the traditions of Jewish scribal learning and those who favored the philosophizings of the Greeks. Often those who nurtured the pursuit of either were tempted into feelings of superiority and intellectual pride. The teaching of a Jewish leader from Nazareth, therefore, whose followers were made up of fishermen and others from Capernaum, did not seem in their eyes to be worth serious argument and attention. Through their very wisdom, they allowed the kingdom of God to pass them by. Such intellectual pride therefore can have no secure and rightful place in the Christian spiritual life. An immense amount of vital understanding about life and about God appeared to Jesus, as it has appeared to many since, to be ignored by those who regarded themselves as wise and understanding. By comparison even Christian "babes" appear more knowledgable.

In a second way, however, this prayer concerning what is hidden from the wise and understanding and yet is known to babes has influenced Christian thinking. Its contrast between those who seek wisdom and those to whom wisdom is revealed has pointed many to a belief in an insurmountable barrier between the way of the world, which is one of seeking to discover knowledge by honest human endeavor, and the way of faith, which is one where knowledge is revealed. Certainly there are valuable and important factors to be borne in mind on both sides of this debate. Nor can there be any serious questioning of the fact that both Christian and Jewish religion has, in keeping with most other religions, leaned heavily on the concepts of revelation and revealed truth. It has proved dangerous to press this too far, however, since truth itself is of many kinds and all too often different kinds of truth have been lumped together in unhelpful ways. Ultimately all truth is one, since the world itself is a unity and we experience it as such. Yet we know that the artist and the scientist will view the same object in very different ways and will discover differing emphases in their appreciation of it. Similarly the religious mind will respond to life and its challenges in ways that may be different from the scientist and the engineer. It will remain essentially the same world and the same life-situation which each encounters. Certainly too each has a rightful place. While it is often true in a practical and experiential way that the knowledge that the scientist or philosopher seeks to attain will be different from that offered by "revelation" to the mind of faith, this can imply no absolute separation between the two. To carry further the examination of such a question would go far beyond the confines of a reflection on this particular prayer of Jesus, and no completely satisfying resolution of the contrasts has appeared. What has become evident however is that the revelation of the truth of the knowledge of God which Jesus was conscious of possessing and teaching was not intended to set aside the right and proper use of human reason in the service of God.

We may conclude our reflection by returning to the recognition that this particular prayer of thanksgiving on the part of Jesus is not a "pattern" prayer which we can readily adapt for our own use. It is, in a very prominent way, a "prayer about prayer," since it points us to the most central feature of Christian devotion. Christians pray "in the name of Jesus" not because this offers some more meritorious or influential way of getting God to hear our prayer. Rather it is because through Jesus we are able to enter more fully into a knowledge of God as "Our God" and thereby direct our prayers more intelligently and constructively towards the purposes of God's kingdom.

24
A Prayer of PAUL

Ephesians 3:14–21

Paul the Missionary

The letter of Paul to the Ephesians is regarded as one of his later "prison" epistles, and although in a number of ancient manuscripts, it is addressed to the Christians of Ephesus, in others it has no specified addressee. It bears all the marks of being a "circular letter" addressed to Gentile Christians in the Roman Empire and expressing a concern that they should recognize the fullness of their heritage within the purpose of God. It is consequently very much in the nature of a letter of reassurance to Gentile Christians, reaffirming the fact that they truly are "fellow heirs" with Jews in the Christian church and fully partakers with them of the riches and promises of the gospel. If we are to reconstruct the kind of situation in which the first recipients found themselves and to understand the worries and anxieties that were robbing them of their confidence and joy in Christian living, then we must look more deeply into the missionary background of the work of Paul and consider its presuppositions.

We read of Paul's own experience in establishing the Christian church in Ephesus in Acts 19. Some quite unexpected and surprising features are drawn to our attention. When Paul arrived there, Ephesus was a flourishing Greek city which evidently had a well established and prosperous Jewish community with a synagogue where Paul was at first given complete freedom to speak. There were also disciples who knew of the baptism of John the Baptist and who had submitted to this with all that it implied concerning repentance: a renewed cleansing in which Jews submitted to the same rite of purification as did Gentile proselytes and the awaiting of the coming of

God's kingdom. Yet such men and women apparently knew nothing of Jesus as the expected Messiah nor of the gift of the Holy Spirit. After enjoying the freedom of preaching in the synagogue for three months Paul was banished from this, taking the disciples with him, and thereafter continued his preaching work in the hall of a certain Tyrannus. Therefore the Christian disciples separated from the older established Jewish community, a pattern which was to become increasingly common as the Christian gospel spread. Eventually church and synagogue were to become identifiable as quite separate religious institutions.

To appreciate fully the significance of the spread of the Christian gospel among the non-Jewish peoples of the Mediterranean world and the developments which led to the Christian church becoming a truly "universal" church, we must examine more closely Paul's missionary work. In doing this we must certainly bear in mind that the developments which occurred among the first-century Christians resulted in the Christian faith becoming the first truly "universal" religion of humankind. Of course, since the size and range of the inhabited world was not at that time properly known, the full implications of the universality of the Christian faith could not immediately be fully explored. Nevertheless the essential steps in the realms of faith and ideas had been taken which were to be among the most momentous steps ever taken in history. The vision of one world, the creation of one God, and one universal faith made possible in and through the name of Jesus of Nazareth now emerged.

We are tempted, when reading the New Testament, to think of the Christian church as a new foundation which began with the work of Jesus and which could trace its birth to the first experience of the Holy Spirit at Pentecost (Acts 2). This was certainly not how Paul viewed the origin of the church nor how the earliest Christians, whether they were of Jewish or Christian origin, would have looked at themselves. Our word "church" is a translation of a Greek word *ekklesia*, meaning "assembly, those who are called together." As such it was used frequently but not uniformly to translate older Hebrew words of the Old Testament which our modern English versions have more often translated as "congregation." It is not the linguistic usage that need especially occupy our attention, except for the fact that in reading the Scriptures in Greek, Paul and other Greek-speaking Christians like him would have recognized that God's "church" (*ekklesia*) had existed since the days of Moses. Even the generation that came out of Egypt with Moses could be seen as the "fathers" of the Christian church (cf. 1 Cor. 10:1). This is important for reasons that have already become plain through the varied and painful history of the people of God during the Old Testament period. From being a nation, Israel had become divided into two nations, and then had suffered an even more serious breakup in being scattered among the nations of the world as a Diaspora, a situation that has prevailed among Jews to the present. All of this had both a positive as well as a negative side. Negatively, this scattering was seen as a judgment of God which seriously impaired the purity and wholeness of Jewish life and worship. Positively, it had the effect of compelling loyal Jews to be witnesses among the nations to the one God and to the purity and integrity of faith in this one God. As a consequence many Gentiles, as Paul well knew, had by his day become adherents—proselytes—to Judaism. Others adopted a less fully committed position and associated themselves with Jewish faith and worship as God-fearers, without embracing the whole Jewish faith. Therefore, by the time of Paul's missionary work, an aspect of Jewish life prepared the way for it, even though it was not truly "missionary" in the full sense. Only a few from among the Gentiles were welcomed fully into the fold of the people of God, and then only on conditions which were difficult and which tended to alienate such converts from their erstwhile neighbors.

If a certain Jewish "preparation for mission" already existed among the Gentiles of the Hellenistic-Roman world by the time of Jesus and Paul, then this was certainly every bit as evident in the intellectual sphere. The cultural achievements of Hellenism combined with the administrative power of Rome had brought about among the Mediterranean peoples a remarkable leap forward in the quality and character of life. The better educated people of the city readily saw the retention of crude and outmoded beliefs in magic and ancient gods and goddesses to be false and dangerous. Paul's experiences while preaching in Ephesus highlighted some of the consequences of the changes taking place. On the one side a cult based on fear and claims of magic was practiced by seven sons of a Jewish high priest, and on the other the silversmiths who fashioned images of the locally venerated Ephesian goddess Artemis all suffered loss and discrediting through the preaching of Paul. Intellectually the Greek world was growing up and becoming more and more aware of the spurious hold of magic and crude religion. Paul preached the clear and intelligent message of how the one God, the Creator of heaven and earth, was not represented in simple images, however costly, but had spoken to men and women decisively through God's own Son—the man Jesus of Nazareth! Such a message was itself a triumph for reason, integrity, and love, over the false claims of fear and superstition.

Not only in the dangerous and forbidding subculture of local religious traditions and leaders, however, but more generally also, the world of the Roman Empire was ready for a message concerning the oneness of God and the oneness of all true faith and religion. For more than a millennium the Near East had flourished as the cradle of civilization, at least so far as our own Western world has experienced it. Within this, religion had played a decisive role, and yet it had become confined within the limits of its own origins. The many gods which had at one time been primarily understood and worshiped in local terms, had slowly risen to the level of becoming "national" gods. We find this situation reflected quite extensively in the Old Testament, where the nations of Egypt, Moab, Edom, Syria, and then Assyria, Babylon, and Persia, had all worshiped their own national gods. Yet in the Hellenistic world which was brought into being in the wake of Alexander the Great such national gods had become outmoded. By the time of Paul the very idea of national or local gods and goddesses, such as Artemis of the Ephesians, was a mark of inadequate and outmoded religious tradition. Faith itself had not moved forward with the times sufficiently to enable religion to remain credible and convincing in a world that had changed so rapidly. The Jewish faith, which many saw to be both intellectually and morally more convincing, could not freely and unreservedly welcome Gentiles to its truth. Therefore, to a degree that it is hard for us to appreciate, the Roman world to which Paul came with his good news was ready to hear and to respond to the gospel.

The Prayer

The prayer which is contained in Paul's letter to the church in Ephesus is, as was probably also true of the letter as a whole, concerned with the position of all Gentile Christians. It is a simple prayer of intercession which reads as relevantly and as impressively today as it must have done when first it was penned. It is in every way a most fitting tribute and memorial to the figure who has been remembered as the great missionary apostle to the Gentiles. That Christian evangelists may often have used it and have encouraged others to use it, appears highly likely, for it is a prayer about the goal of Christian living.

> For this reason I bow my knees before the Father, from whom every family in heaven and on earth is named, that according to the riches of his glory he may grant you to be strengthened with might through his Spirit in the inner man, and that Christ may dwell in your hearts through faith; that you, being rooted and grounded in love, may have power to comprehend with all the saints what is the breadth and length and height and depth, and to know the love of Christ which surpasses knowledge, that you may be filled with all the fulness of God.
> Now to him who by the power at work within us is able to do far more abundantly than all that we ask or think, to him be glory in the church and in Christ Jesus to all generations, for ever and ever. Amen.
> (Ephesians 3:14–21)

The prayer is a straightforward intercession for the Christian church, and its significance rests much less in any special feature of its form than in the theological and humanitarian ideas to which it gives expression. It is on this account that it remains as relevant and as exciting today as it did in the first century. It is evidently a prayer specially applicable to Gentile Christian churches, but in fact it is equally applicable and meaningful for the entire universal Christian church. It is a prayer that is both "catholic" and "ecumenical" in the proper literal meaning of these adjectives as descriptive of the church which exists "universally" across the world and which constitutes the whole "household" of God. We may examine in detail the particular benefits which it seeks from God.

First, fundamental to its entire character is that it is addressed to the One who is properly known as "Father." Here the remarkable, and world-embracing, simplicity of the Christian designation of God provides a verbal image not only of the warmth and nearness of God to every human being but also a corresponding image of the oneness of the entire human race—they are a great family, divided up into a countless host of small families spread across the surface of the earth. No single part of the human race can any longer be dismissively labeled as "sub-human," or "less than human," since by their common origin from the one Father all people share the same privileged status. In one single sweeping divine ascription "to the Father" the prayer establishes a visionary image of the oneness of the whole human species so that those who are properly to be prayed for, as well as the One to whom the prayer is addressed, are seen to possess an inalienable common relationship. If God is "Father" then not only those who choose to recognize this fact, but all owe their own existence among one of the many human families to God. By such a simple ascription therefore the prayer establishes a truth that cannot be too often emphasized or repeated. Faith, if it is truly to be faith in the One God, must be a conviction and an experience that reconciles and unites, not one that divides. The world to which Paul carried the Christian gospel of reconciliation had hitherto known religion only as a feature of life that divided and separated people from each other. Especially in its demarcation between Jew and Gentile had this colored the early upbringing and life of Paul but also in different ways and with different religious traditions, such division and religious labels were an everyday part of life throughout the Roman Empire. What god or what worship men and women adhered to marked them off for who they were and what their place in society was to be. Now a much richer and worthier insight had been given to faith highlighted under the simple and familiar words "Father" and "family."

The second feature of the prayer is that the specific benefit sought for Christians is that they may be "strengthened with might through his Spirit in the inner man," which is particularly interesting in view of the fact that Paul had encountered in Ephesus disciples of John the Baptist who knew nothing of the gift of the Spirit through the name of Jesus. Here we are face to face with the great gift that new life through the reconciling power of Jesus makes possible for Christians—an inner renewal which recreates the "inner being," conferring personal spiritual resources that are otherwise undeveloped. Such a renewal of the "inner being" is tantamount to Christ himself dwelling in the hearts of men and women through faith. In this fashion the entire outlook, attitude, and personal will of the man or woman who embraces the Christian faith is refashioned and recreated.

Third, what such a total inner transformation of life is to mean and how it is to be built up on entirely new foundations is then set out very clearly in the phrase "being rooted and grounded in love." Love is to be the foundation and solid base for the rebuilding of the human personality which faith in Christ has made possible. Salvation and justification are not therefore a complete end in themselves but only the beginning of the refashioning of the inner life, which the Holy Spirit will nurture and develop towards a God-intended fulfillment. It is this fulfillment which represents for the Christian a goal of perfection, or more properly "completion," of the new life that has begun.

Fourth, the filling out of the picture of what this goal for Christian living means is spelled out with remarkable images which convey a sense of the limitless possibilities that the experience of new life has opened up. First, it is to be a progressive searching out of the "breadth, length, height, and depth" of the love of Christ. In one sense we recognize that such spatial terms are not strictly applicable to such a quality as love, which does not have physical or spatial boundaries. The imagery is all the more meaningful on this account, however, since the Christian knows that no finite boundary exists to the range and extent of the love of Christ but instead an endless exploring of its possibilities. Second this goal is to be a paradoxical "knowing" of the love of Christ "which surpasses knowledge." What precisely is intended by this expression has been much discussed, since it has a strikingly undefinable character. In one sense it recognizes that an experience of the love of Christ can reach beyond the boundaries of reason and human understanding, which is certainly true. The Christian must also recognize that what he or she knows of the meaning and power of the love of Christ will be subject to continued expansion and extension. It will open out into an ever richer understanding of its potentialities to transform human life and human society. Thirdly, and as a kind of triumphant concluding image, the final goal of life for the Christian is described in terms of being "filled with all the fullness of God." Such an expression affirms with extraordinary boldness the truth that, through faith in Christ, the ultimate possibilities for humankind are without limit. God's work as Creator will be continued in and through the life of men and women to achieve new heights of excellence and richness.

Fifth, in its final ascription of praise, the prayer employs an expression which has become a model for all our thinking about God and about the meaning and worth of prayer. God is portrayed as One "who is able to do far more abundantly than all that we ask or think." In one sense it is a most remarkable challenge to all our religious thinking and devotion. Inevitably, in our thoughts, as well as in the patterns and programs of our Christian living, a fundamental fixation and hardening process sets in to establish the boundaries of our understanding and expectation. These boundaries become the goals and concerns which we set for ourselves and through which we believe that we can express Christian faith and love. They will not be the whole truth about the way God has worked in our lives, however, and inevitably they will present only a very circumscribed and limited picture of the power and purpose of God. A fundamental feature of prayer and Christian reflection therefore must represent a lifting of the horizon to see a little further and to try to "take in" a little more of what it is that God has made possible for us through the gift of life, and the transforming of that life, through Christ. "A man's reach must exceed his grasp, or what's a heaven for," as Robert Browning wrote.

The Significance of the Prayer

Most Christians would certainly accept that they ought to pray and would probably admit to the feeling that they ought to pray more than they do. Although it is superficially easy to account for our failure to do so on the grounds that "there just isn't time," in reality it requires a rather deeper analysis. A major reason why we do not pray very much lies in a deep uncertainty about what to pray for. If this is true to some extent when applied to our own selves in respect of petitionary prayer, then it is certainly even more true when applied

to others in respect of intercessory prayer. It is difficult enough thinking what we should be spiritually concerned about for ourselves,
without being either trivially mundane or positively selfish, so that
to extend this to others becomes almost impossibly demanding. In
any case it raises a quite fundamental question about religion and the
understanding of God, since it is basic and axiomatic to faith that
God more truly knows our needs than we possibly can. One consequence of this is markedly evident, especially where the need and
occasion for free public prayer is present. This is that, as a kind of
all-inclusive last resort we simply ask God to "bless" all sorts of
people. What this will actually mean for them, how it will take effect,
or even how we ourselves might possibly take some part in assisting
to realize this "blessing" is left indeterminate. We would prefer to
leave that side of the question to God and trust God to find appropriate ways by which to carry our prayers over into effective results.
All of this stems from an overpreoccupation with what we may describe as an immature and unbiblical picture of divine causation as
the model for our prayers. We trust that in some mysterious fashion
our prayers will cause God to act in a manner that God would not
otherwise have done. This is, however, deeply contrary to the richer
biblical insights concerning the nature of the divine initiative and the
power and role of God as Creator. Much closer to the biblical perspective would be the analogy of a designer who has created a vast
and wonderful machine. For reasons of their own ignorance and in-
competence those who have acquired this machine neither use it
properly nor realize its full potentialities. As they begin to appreciate
the extent of their own folly and inadequacy they realize that it would
be very much to their advantage to explore a little more extensively
the possibilities of their machine, and most of all, to consult the
designer in pursuing their intentions. Our lives are received as a gift
from God and the world in which we can develop and exercise that
life is also part of this gift. At no point does God ever cease to be the
Giver and to retain the initiative. We can learn to appreciate more
fully the extent of the divine gift and the possibilities it opens up.
Prayer is therefore a path to discovering that life is essentially a gift
and a returning to the Giver in order to discover what the full range
and possibilities of this gift are. If this can provide some practical

insight into the reasons why we might pray, then it also suggests some important things we can fittingly pray for. It still remains easier to fulfill such a task in a purely personal and individual direction, but it at least opens up the realization that there are a number of things that we can sensibly pray for in an intercessory way. More than this, we should certainly reach a point of recognizing that our own lives will be seriously impaired and restricted if we do not at some point reach out in our thinking and praying for the needs and aims of our fellow men and women.

This remarkable prayer of Paul's set in the epistle to the Ephesians is invaluable as a guide to the nature and purpose of Christian intercession. In the use of two simple words—"Father" and "family"—it establishes the nature and character of life as a gift, and our place as recipients of such a gift. We neither chose our parents nor our family but were given them by right of birth and enjoy our place within the family as a gift. Others also share the same family heritage. Even more memorable and instructive, however, are the contents of the prayer and the manner in which it sets out a sequence of word-pictures of what the meaning and goal of life can now be through the reconciling power of Christ and the renewing work of the Holy Spirit. More than anything else therefore this prayer provides a pattern of instruction, since it shows us what we can pray for.

Beyond this, such a simple and short prayer of intercession achieves far more than offering to God a lengthy catalog of persons and their needs. In a real sense it discloses the fact that it is not only the hungry, the impoverished, and the oppressed who are in special need of God's care and help. To some extent all of us stand in such need, since no one has fully explored the potential of what it means to receive new life and renewing power through Jesus Christ. However much we may already have achieved, it will still not be the fullness of what remains possible for God's children.

Seen in such a light this invaluable prayer shows that a major part of the purpose of praying is that we might lift our horizons a little further and set our ambitions a little higher in the service of God. It also draws our attention to a further aspect of the biblical understanding of life. Sin, in such a context, is not the rather naively pictured "breaking the rules" of the world that God has made. It is a much deeper and more devastating malaise, for sin exists wherever we fail to realize the full potentialities of what God's gift of life means. It is a failure to become what we were first created to be. Now, through the reconciling work of Christ and the renewing power of the Holy Spirit, the way lies open to the fullness of this possibility of life. Paul's prayer sets before our minds a goal to strive for for the whole human race. It is a goal that might be overpoweringly beyond our grasp were it not for the knowledge that God is able to achieve in us and through us "more than we can ask or think."

25
Another Prayer of
PAUL
Colossians 1:9–23

Paul the Apologist

We have already noted that there was considerable intellectual ferment in the Hellenistic-Roman world to which the Apostle Paul brought the Christian gospel. The reasons for this are not at all difficult to see, since from Spain in the West to as far as Syria and Persia in the East an extraordinary encounter had taken place of peoples from widely differing ethnic origins and traditions. Also from Britain in the North to the shores of North Africa the same mixing of peoples and the same surprised encounters with traditions, customs, and ideas from parts of the world which had lost their previous isolation was taking place. If Rome supplied the military, political, and administrative power that enabled this to continue, the intellectual ideas and stimulus had come more directly from Greece. In a very profound sense, then, it was a "Hellenistic" culture that pervaded the Roman empire, and it was the teachings and enquiries of the greatest of the Greek philosophers which lay at its root. From the fifth century B.C. outstanding figures had arisen in Athens, most eminently Socrates, Plato, and Aristotle, who had turned the world of human thinking upside down and who had established new principles of reasoning and research that had enabled succeeding generations to pursue further the quest for truth these leaders had so profoundly guided. A very significant and vital aspect of the Graeco-Roman world was to be found in its pursuit of knowledge and learning. Even relatively minor cities, far removed from the location of the original public squares of Athens and Rome, had their own preachers and philosophers, ever eager to teach and discuss their ideas and pursuits.

Judaism had had to come to terms with this new learning before the time of Paul, and it had done so in various directions. It too had a tradition of wise men, besides the great figures of Moses and the prophets, whose teachings bore comparison with the popular traditions of the learned men of Greece. We find a number of Jewish writers in the two centuries before the birth of Jesus occupying themselves with admonitions and instructions, especially addressed to young men, very much along the same pattern as other new cities of the Hellenistic world.

It is not difficult to see how valuable such a pursuit of learning and knowledge could be in the Roman Empire. Such a large and complex world demanded a host of administrators, officials, and businessmen who understood Greek and Latin and who could serve as leaders and guides in this huge international scene. Learning became an avenue to success in a way that had not existed previously and the knowledge of Greek language and thought, in particular, became a sign of ability and culture. It is not therefore surprising for us to learn that young men of ambition of very diverse ethnic origins were tempted and even encouraged to shake off their roots and instead to pursue knowledge and wisdom and all things Greek.

However, as we can discover in looking at other periods of history, a strong and dominant culture may give rise to a curious and bewildering subculture. In the case of the Hellenistic world there are added reasons why this should have occurred. East had encountered West in a striking fashion, and within this encounter, ancient and mysterious religious traditions of the Orient had become mingled with the philosophies of Greece and Rome. The outcome was a host of bizarre and exotic cults and doctrines which displayed every sign of antiquity and learned respectability, but which were in reality an offshoot of the Graeco-Roman achievement. Among the most celebrated of these was the revival of the ancient Egyptian worship of deities such as Isis and Osiris, though far more complex and strange mixtures of religious tradition and ancient learning also appeared. The quest for the mastery of life, so dear to the aims of the Greek thinkers, was intermingled with the search to discover the secret of eternal life. The pursuit of knowledge, so characteristic of the philosophic mind, was identified with "enlightenment" so cherished by the religious mystic. Even terms such as "authority" and 'power" which carried such weight in the political sphere, came to be understood in terms of magical power and mastery of the spiritual world. The world to which Paul took the Christian gospel was eager to listen to new ideas and religious traditions emanating from the East. For a full century a rich traffic in such exchanges of ideas and traditions had been taking place. Under the titles of "Knowledge" ("Gnosis") and "Salvation" and "Power" the way to a successful life appeared to be freely offered by cults to those who were willing to embrace their teachings and submit to their rituals.

It was impossible for the early Christian missionaries to remain unconcerned and unaffected by this bizarre intellectual ferment. Inevitably on hearing the message of the Christian gospel, some would associate it with other forms of oriental teaching and mythology of which they had heard. In addition, it was not long before the Christian teaching concerning salvation and the role of Jesus as Messiah and Lord came to be linked with popular expectations concerning the coming to earth of a divine "Savior" and "Deliverer," who would bring "enlightenment" and who would overcome the powers of darkness and death. Thereby the biblical message of the divine promise of the coming of the kingdom of God, given through the prophets of the Old Testament, came to be associated broadly with more popular, and less biblically defined, expectations that God would intervene in the world to redeem and recreate the human race. As the gospel message spread among Greek-speaking, non-Jewish people, who had no prior knowledge of the Old Testament Scriptures, so did this broader understanding of hope appear more prominently in their thinking. From a Christian perspective, this was not a particularly bad thing since the universal relevance of the Christian gospel was confirmed and enhanced by it. Yet it is clear that there were dangers, the most obvious of which was that, as the gospel message moved further away from its Judean and Jewish origins, so it would become subtly transformed until it appeared as just one other form of oriental speculation and religious ideology among the host of others that flourished in different parts of the Roman Empire.

All of this posed a difficult task for the earliest Christian evangelists, who certainly did not want to discount those aspects of human

life and thinking which expressed so vividly and relevantly the longing of the human heart for God. At the same time they did not wish
to present the message concerning Jesus and the kingdom of God in
such a fashion as to allow it to become transformed into a mysterious
oriental cult, competing for popular support. Jesus had to be presented not simply as Deliverer, but as *the* Deliverer. The teaching of
the gospel had to be understood not simply as wisdom but as the
decisive *Wisdom* of God. Faith had to be understood not merely as a
path to "enlightenment," but as the decisive and sole, God-appointed
way to salvation. There can be no doubt that the Christian church in
Colossae had been much affected by teachings drawn from these
pseudo-oriental cults and doctrines which promised enlightenment,
salvation, and new life. Paul's prayer for the church was, quite
understandably didactic in its purpose, seeking that these young
Christians might be filled with a sincere love for and understanding
of Jesus as the Lord. Most especially he was concerned to seek that
they might be able to grasp fully and permanently the complete suf-
ficiency and finality of Jesus for faith. He was not to be trusted and
revered as one Deliverer among a number. Nor was the salvation that
he offered a blessing that might be set alongside other forms or avenues which promised new life and new experiences of divine enlightenment. Jesus was the one full, complete, and sufficient way to God,
and the revelation to humankind given in him by God was a full and
complete disclosure of the reality and purpose of God. Unless these
truths were grasped, which may appear in the modern world to be
almost self-evident features of the gospel message, then the entire
way of salvation given in the gospel of Jesus Christ would be distorted so seriously as to destroy its central character.

The Prayer

The remarks of Paul set out in Colossians 1:9–23 refer to the
substance of his prayers which were concerned to set out essential
truths about God's work in Jesus as Lord and Savior. In a sense
therefore we can see how these remarks have been affected by the
needs of the church in Colossae. As remarks they are addressed, not
to God, but to a specific audience. However, to disregard their importance as a guide to the substance of Paul's prayers on this account

would be a mistake. When uttered publicly there is an inevitable subjective element in all prayer, since it cannot but be affected by the needs and awareness of its human audience. Prayer is a way of mediating between God's all-sufficiency and those who are aware of their insufficiency. Therefore, Paul's remarks concerning his earnest intercessions to God for the church in Colossae open our eyes to a special need of the church there, and incidentally to a need which, in varying degrees, remains a need of all Christians. We need to know more of God and the divine will, yet the quest for such knowledge can never be a purely "academic" pursuit, even though it cannot dispense with such an academic understanding either. Ultimately a deeper knowledge of God must be a deeper knowledge of the fullness of the revelation that God has given to us in Jesus Christ:

> And so, from the day we heard of it, we have not ceased to pray for you, asking that you may be filled with the knowledge of his will in all spiritual wisdom and understanding, to lead a life worthy of the Lord, fully pleasing to him, bearing fruit in every good work and increasing in the knowledge of God. May you be strengthened with all power, according to his glorious might, for all endurance and patience with joy, giving thanks to the Father, who has qualified us to share in the inheritance of the saints in light. He has delivered us from the dominion of darkness and transferred us to the kingdom of his beloved Son, in whom we have redemption, the forgiveness of sins.
>
> He is the image of the invisible God, the first-born of all creation; for in him all things were created, in heaven and on earth, visible and invisible, whether thrones or dominions or principalities or authorities—all things were created through him and for him. He is before all things, and in him all things hold together. He is the head of the body, the church; he is the beginning, the first-born from the dead, that in everything he might be pre-eminent. For in him all the fulness of God was pleased to dwell, and through him to reconcile to himself all things, whether on earth or in heaven, making peace by the blood of his cross.
>
> And you, who once were estranged and hostile in mind, doing evil deeds, he has now reconciled in his body of flesh by his death, in order to present you holy and blameless and irreproachable before him, provided that you continue in the faith, stable and steadfast, not shifting from the hope of the gospel which you heard, which has been preached to every creature under heaven, and of which I, Paul, became a minister.
>
> (Colossians 1:9–23)

We can see that this is not, in the strictest sense, a prayer at all, but simply an intimation to the Christians at Colossae of those spiritual benefits for which Paul regularly prayed on their behalf. He wanted them to know that he regularly prayed for them and what the things were that he was especially concerned that they should receive. In fact this amounts to a declaration of essential truths that they must know and adhere to, if they were to grow at all as Christians. These were combined with certain basic guidelines showing how the Christian life should develop towards the realization of its God-given possibilities. In one sense it is true that, on becoming Christians, they have passed from one life into another and from one world into another. This does not mean that everything is now complete and final so far as Christian living is concerned, however. On the contrary this new life has only just begun and it opens up a whole new realm of possibility for growth and development in Christian experience and understanding. Although, as we can see by the explicit address to the church in Colossae, this passage is about what he regularly prays for, rather than a transcript of such a prayer, this information from Paul is very much concerned with the nature and content of Christian prayer. As we have noted in regard to other prayers of the Bible, people often give up praying simply because they feel that they no longer know what to pray for. We learn here some basic essentials of what Christians can and should pray for.

It is not at all hard to see how the opening section of Paul's remarks reflect the distinctive intellectual ferment which formed the environment of several of the earliest Greek-speaking Christian churches. Men and women were very much aware that through their religious allegiance they sought to acquire "knowledge," "power," and "the strength to endure." All of these were very much a part of the proffered benefits of the mystery cults and doctrines of "Knowledge" (Gnosis) which they in their pagan environment so eagerly canvassed. All of these were wholly and truly theirs in Christ, however, so that there could be no need or excuse for abandoning commitment to Christ in favor of some other cult. All worthwhile riches of knowledge and wisdom were available to them in Christ. More than this, the very "worthiness" of such knowledge and wisdom could be seen and tested by the worthiness and goodness of the life to which it led. By such means the wholesomeness and morality of the Christian message could be readily distinguished from the perverse and often spurious claims to enlightenment and wisdom which misguidedly persuaded some to abandon all moral and social responsibility. The Christian had truly been delivered from "the kingdom of darkness," but this did not mean, as some speculative claims of the "New Knowledge" would have it, that the new person was thereby free to ignore moral demands and responsibilities, with obligations to family, to work, and to society.

The following section of Paul's remarks centers on the fullness and all-sufficiency of the person of Jesus Christ. Drawing upon his Jewish background and his knowledge of the Old Testament Scriptures, Paul sets out a catalog of the completeness of the revelation given in Jesus as Christ and Lord. He is the image of the invisible God, the first-born of all creation, before all things, the head of the body, the first-born from the dead, and the dwelling-place of all the fullness of God.

We could easily elaborate on the way in which Paul amplifies each of these confessional statements about the fullness and finality of the revelation of God in Jesus and on the way in which they shed light on the teaching to which the church in Colossae had been subjected. Undoubtedly these doctrinal assertions show that Paul, the missionary and man of prayer, was also an apologist—a defender of the faith. He was concerned that the Christians of the Gentile world should not be misled into thinking that they could embrace the Christian gospel alongside other forms of religion and knowledge. However much these other religious cults displayed their spurious attractiveness, and however much they might lay claim to some new excellence or teaching, the Christian must recognize that the Christian gospel offered all that was necessary for a full and sufficient knowledge of God and of the divine will. There was no need at all therefore for Christians to suppose that they could augment their faith or their armory of spiritual blessings by joining some other sectarian group. Prayer did not need to be offered to God through many names of lords and spiritual authorities in order to be heard. The name of Jesus was all-sufficient.

We can even probe further into Paul's comments and sense the plausible temptation that existed for the young Christians of Colossae to elaborate upon the mysteries of their newfound faith, with its focus upon a Jewish carpenter from Nazareth, by speculations about new life and the power to conquer death. All spiritual riches, Paul insists, were theirs wholly and conclusively in and through the salvation and forgiveness given to them through Jesus. The Christian gospel was the true and full "enlightenment" which conquered death and the powers of evil.

Paul's comments in his letter to the Christians of Colossae concerning the nature and substance of his prayers on their behalf reveal some of the most central truths of the Christian message, and especially of the centrality of the figure of Jesus of Nazareth in this message. Christianity is a way of living in, with, by, and through Jesus Christ as Lord.

The Significance of the Prayer

We may begin our further reflection on these remarks of Paul about the contents of his prayers for young Christians, by noting afresh their heavily didactic intention. In praying for the Christians of Colossae Paul was not at all reluctant to make it plain to them that he was giving them guidance and instruction. This may at first appear a little surprising, and even strange, since we are usually very conscious that prayer and teaching are two separate functions of the church and of the Christian minister. Yet public prayer must inevitably instruct, and it must, by its very nature, rest upon a sound basis of Christian instruction. Nothing can more readily bring dishonor and disrepute upon the Christian understanding of God than to address the deity in a misleading or unworthy fashion. Just as so much Christian teaching is "acquired" almost unconsciously through hymns, so the way in which we think about God, the way in which we picture to ourselves God's attitude towards us, and not least the way in which we sense that God wants to enrich and enhance our lives, will derive from public prayer. Prayer is in a very real sense "theology in action," putting into practical effect the understanding that we have adopted concerning ourselves and our place in the created scheme of things. It matters greatly then that public prayer is not undertaken lightly, and we can, no matter how free and sincere we wish our entreaties of God to be, recognize the reverent caution which led the Fathers of the church to prepare collections of prayers for public use. Recognizably these can also have their limitations, easily becoming archaic and all too readily uttered from the lips and not from the heart. Certainly the truth is that public prayer is not easy. It would not be exaggerating to claim there is no guarantee that all public prayer to God fulfills all the requirements of relevance, truth, adequacy, sincerity, and intelligibility. At its best it is always a compromise, adjusting truth to what its human hearers can understand, and stretching sincerity to ask a little higher and more nobly than the average worshiper really wants to! If prayer is to be freed from the restraints of a printed page and the conventional wisdom of ancient liturgists, however, it must be most carefully thought about and prepared beforehand. It is not too harsh a judgment either to claim that men and women, tired of hackneyed and slipshod generalities, may be inclined to give up praying altogether if they cannot match the intensity of their ambitions with the integrity of their thinking. Prayer has to be thoughtful, so that there is a very real place for exploring the riches and resources of our theology—our thinking about the nature and activity of God—with our natural preoccupation with ourselves and our desire to worship God and to enrich our lives. Prayer can and should quite properly be an instructive exercise in thought.

A second feature also strikes the Christian very forcibly when considering the contents of Paul's prayers for the Colossian Christians. As modern scholars have rightly seen and demonstrated, although what he has to say about the centrality and unique status of Jesus in the Christian faith is drawn from the Old Testament, Paul's christological assertions in Colossians show a deep awareness of the new doctrinal speculations that were rife in the young Greek churches. He has undoubtedly gone some way toward meeting the intellectual concerns of Gentile Christians in a manner which interpreted the gospel in a new framework of ideas and assumptions drawn from the Hellenistic world. In doing so he has certainly been concerned, not only to defend the Christian faith against those who were claiming to possess superior versions of it, but also to stress its richness and appeal in a very distinctive intellectual context. He displays a very strong awareness that in every human mind the desire to know the truth about the world, to understand one's own place within it, and also to obtain some mastery over it and the threatening face which it often assumes, are legitimate concerns. This very sense of need and of intellectual curiosity are part of the preparation for the receiving of the gospel. This can also be recognized as true when the modern day Christian is made very forcibly aware that many other powerful and appealing religions exist in the world. All too often the sincere Christian has been led into adopting a very negative and hostile approach to such religions, seeing in them competitors and rival claimants to truth. Assertions about their false and misleading claims are given the maximum degree of emphasis, showing them to be inimical to the Christian faith. Such is not the attitude of the Bible, however, nor even of Paul, who rightly recognizes that God has left witnesses among all the nations of the world. In this way, when boldly and prayerfully understood, Jesus can be presented and understood as the true fulfillment and satisfaction of those many and varied speculations and longings to know the nature of reality. Furthermore, it is not wrong to seek power and the mastery of life, when these aims are seen in a properly spiritual perspective as the seeking after a truly moral and spiritual power.

The true Christian response to a searching and enquiring quest for truth is not to resist and to deny any place for such a quest but rather to direct and focus it upon the person of Jesus Christ.

It is also instructive for us to note another aspect of Paul's remarks about the content of his prayers which has a direct bearing upon the way in which we ourselves pray. Even in the English translations of his remarks, a certain touch of rhetoric and verbal extravagance cannot be mistaken. Paul insists that, in and through Jesus Christ, all things were created, and then he proceeds to spell out what "all things" must include—things in heaven, things on earth, things visible, things invisible—and so on, to reach also to include thrones, dominions, principalities, and authorities. It all sounds very contrived and strange, and yet it must match closely the titles of the various agencies and powers which had come to exercise such an appeal to the minds of the Christians of Colossae. They had been tempted into believing that there was some special path by which they could give added power and effectiveness to their prayers by appealing to special forces and agencies in the spiritual world. All of this Paul rightly saw to be a nonsense, which would, if allowed to continue, result in the falsifying of their entire spiritual life. God had revealed to men and women love, forgiveness, graciousness towards humankind, and a willingness to hear prayer through Jesus Christ. No spiritual agency could make God's love more readily attainable or prayer more effective than already existed in Jesus Christ. Paul's rhetorical flourish therefore reflects an attitude which had arisen among the Colossian Christians, and which, in varying forms, has constantly reappeared since in one guise or another. This lies in the belief that there is some special trick or name or form of words which will enable prayers to "get through" to God more readily and easily. It is the mistaken belief that some unique "hot-line" to God exists, of which the enlightened worshiper can make use. Any such belief represents a most fundamental distortion of the spiritual life. At best it may be no more than an innocent misconception, but at worst it can become a deeply unsettling illusion which can replace genuine faith with what is no better than a superstition. True faith must recognize the essentially spiritual quality of all human communion with God, and it is precisely that spiritual quality which is revealed and upheld for every Christian by the knowledge of Jesus Christ. To pray to God in and through the name of Jesus, therefore, is to open our lives in a genuinely spiritual fashion to God's creative and renewing Spirit.

26
A Prayer of
THE CHURCH
Revelation 5:9–14

St. John the Divine and the Book of Revelation

The Christian Bible concludes with a book which stands apart in a number of respects from the rest of the New Testament. This is the Revelation of St. John the Divine, which, so far as its literary character is concerned, has its closest counterpart in the book of Daniel in the Old Testament. It is a book of "apocalyptic," a form of writing which emerged as an exclusively religious form of Jewish literature and which was taken up and developed further in Christianity. It is a type of literature which is full of symbolism, and as such it explores and gives permanent expression to an aspect of religion which has, since prehistoric antiquity, enjoyed a very prominent place. Religion employs symbols, makes strong practical use of them in worship, and seeks through its teaching and instruction about symbols, to affirm the reality of the transcendent world. Such symbols may often be of the simplest kind, such as the Christian cross, with which we are most familiar. Yet even such crosses take different forms and shapes, often elaborated into highly ornate crucifixes, and at other times being no more than two pieces of wood joined together or a sign scratched onto a piece of wall. All such symbols have meaning, and the basic symbols are usually readily grasped and understood by even the most untutored initiate. More complex and advanced symbols require more complex teaching and instruction.

Words can be used as a form of symbolism, so that with these too a whole host of meanings can be vested in a simple title or phrase. Once words are more fully developed in holy writings or elaborated in descriptions of dreams and visions, then the way in which such symbols can point to the transcendent realm and mediate between the seen and the unseen becomes greatly extended. Apocalyptic writing is a literature of this kind, structured around the use and elaboration of certain symbols, which for the most part antedate the written document by some centuries, and combining these to form more complex symbols in the form of visions and their interpretations. In this fashion the apocalyptic writings become witnesses to the transcendent realm which lies beyond the visible world of reality. It is therefore a type of literature which aims to draw our attention to the ultimate meaning of things and to the ultimate issues.

Another feature is also evident. Such apocalyptic writings represent a kind of "crisis literature," very conscious of the fragile and dangerous world in which we live, aware of the insecurity and threats which destroy the peace and stability of society, and most especially of the titanic forces of evil which threaten so often to overwhelm the love and loyalty of devout men and women. It is not difficult to see why the need to resort to a complex range of word-symbols and visions should have occurred in times of special danger and threat. Already with the book of Daniel we have noted how this was true at the time of the Maccabean uprising of pious Jews in the second century B.C. Later similar political and social tensions reappeared in both Judaism and Christianity during the first Christian century.

The author, John the Divine, of the book of Revelation in the New Testament is usually regarded by modern scholars as distinct from the author of the fourth gospel and the epistles of John. Certainly this appears borne out by the fact that the style, character, and themes of the separate writings are very different. The author of Revelation was imprisoned on the island of Patmos (Rev. 1:9) as a consequence of his loyalty to Jesus Christ. Throughout the book John writes of Christians suffering persecution and being forced to examine themselves and the extent of their Christian commitment, with the realization that they may soon have to face the prospect of martyrdom. It was clearly a far from happy or secure time for the Christian church, and its grimness is made all the more poignant for us who know for how long the fires of persecution were kindled against the Christian church. For more than another century there were steady and relentless outbreaks of hostility against Christians which did not cease officially until the time of Constantine (A.D. 274–337) in the fourth century. Most scholars have concluded that the book of Revelation was probably composed during the reign of the Roman emperor Domitian (A.D. 81–96), when a very alarming period of persecution took place.

When we come to ask why Christians were persecuted we do not find simple or wholly straightforward answers. Most evident was an element of political suspicion which attached to Christians when they met together in relatively small groups for worship and instruction. Their close fellowship could easily be misunderstood as the mark of political activists, so that Christians could readily be mistaken for social malcontents, bent on overthrowing the local pattern of government which was established under Roman administration. Such suspicions could be confirmed when Christians refused to take an oath of allegiance to the Roman emperor as God, an act normally readily performed by the token offering of sacrifice without prejudicing a person's other religious loyalties. For Christians, however, such an action could not be undertaken without impugning the Lordship of Jesus Christ.

Undoubtedly, another factor was engendered by the measure of social alienation which befell the Christian churches of the Roman Empire. Without endorsing the rather extreme caricatures of the moral and social life of men and women in the first century A.D. which have often been canvassed as a kind of "counterfoil" to the Christian message of love, purity, and social responsibility, it is clear that a very notable difference emerged between the habits of those who were Christians and those who were not. Inevitably a measure of social separation occurred when the newly converted Christians sought to live out the reality of the gospel of love, which aroused resentment and suspicion on the part of those who resisted its claims. Such an element of social "stigma" attaching to Christians has frequently reappeared since, when the standards and conduct of society have been far removed from those of the gospel. It was a peculiar and painful privilege therefore that Christians should have to suffer for the sake of a message of love and goodwill. It was seen as a part of the mysterious ordering of divine providence that men and women, inspired by a message of love and reconciliation, should undeservedly find themselves opposed and rebuffed by their resentful neighbors. Such experiences readily deepened suspicions that were levelled against Christians on other grounds, however, and inevitably fanned yet further the fires of hostility and persecution of the church.

In addition, we cannot altogether ignore other factors which, from time to time, could add to the burden of pain and suffering which the Christian church had to face in the first century. Rivalry between Jews and Christians was rife, as each religious community became more fully conscious of its own separate identity. Even within the Christian church, the emergence of differing doctrinal and sectarian movements gave rise to jealousy and recriminations which could all too easily result in hostile denunciations and controversy. By such situations the very essence of the gospel of love was undermined.

All of these circumstances had clearly emerged by the close of the first century so that the thrilling story of success and the spread of the gospel throughout the Gentile world which we read of in the book of Acts had undergone significant changes. It is such changes which the Revelation of St. John brings to our attention, and in a reawakening of the symbols and intricacies of apocalyptic writing it shows the resources with which the Christian can confront them. It is therefore an example of "crisis literature," and its theme is the Lordship of Jesus Christ. With the use of imagery which can for the most part be readily traced back to the Old Testament and especially to the book of Ezekiel, it displays the immensity of the riches of Christ and the glory which the Christian possesses even when, in the eyes of the world, he or she is despised and persecuted.

The Prayer of the Church

One of the most striking features of the book of Revelation is that, in its portrayal of the triumphant church in heaven, it echoes much of the worship and prayer-life of the church on earth. Therefore, we find a number of brief expressions of praise to God and to Christ which must have derived from the patterns of emerging liturgy which had by this time developed among the churches. Through its worship and prayer-life the oneness of the whole church could find expression, making use of the same words and images. It is as if,

Sunday by Sunday as the Christians came together, frequently not knowing what new perils and dangers the coming week held in store for them, they experienced some brief foretaste of what the final glory of the church in heaven would be. Their minds and hearts could then be raised to a fresh contemplation of ultimate issues. If they were tempted to waver and to consider again whether it was worth going on with a commitment which was continually fraught with danger and anxiety, they were reminded that what they were expressing was "worthship." This is, in fact, the word from which "worship" has derived, and it is noteworthy that the key phrase with which the hymnic refrains of the visions of heaven in the book of Revelation begin, affirms: "Worthy art thou." Even though to the modern Christian a preoccupation with the themes of martyrdom and persecution can often seem a somber and rather forbidding reminder of the darker side of life, yet they necessarily bring out something essentially religious. Who is ultimately "worthy" in life of receiving loyalty and allegiance? What are those issues and causes in life which are so vital and important that they are worth dying for? In the end the Christian can only feel sorrow and pity for the man or woman who has found nothing in life worth dying for. It is when we do discover persons and causes that are "worthy" of such commitment that we know we have found some of the most valuable treasures of life. We can then read the succession of ascriptions of praise to God and to Jesus, of which the visions of Revelation are furnished, with a deepened awareness of how their affirmations of "worthiness" touch upon our lives:

> *To God*:
> "Holy, holy, holy, is the Lord God Almighty,
> who was and is and is to come!"
> "Worthy art thou, our Lord and God,
> to receive glory and honor and power,
> for thou didst create all things,
> and by thy will they existed and were created."
> *To Jesus*:
> "Worthy art thou to take the scroll and to open its seals,
> for thou wast slain and by thy blood didst ransom men for God
> from every tribe and tongue and people and nation,

and hast made them a kingdom and priests to our God,
and they shall reign on earth."

"Worthy is the Lamb who was slain, to receive power and wealth
and wisdom and might and honor and glory and blessing!"

To God and Jesus:

"To him who sits upon the throne and to the Lamb be blessing
and honor and glory and might for ever and ever!" And the four
living creatures said, "Amen!" and the elders fell down and
worshiped.

(Revelation 4:8, 11; 5:9–10, 12, 13–14)

These brief ascriptions of praise to God picture the final triumph
of the church and the triumphant worship which they and all the
heavenly host—"every creature in heaven and on earth and under
the earth and in the sea, and all therein" (Rev. 5:13)—offer to God.
In one sense it is rather simplistic with its portrayal of a never-ending
chorus of sound declaring the praises of God and of Jesus Christ the
Son. Yet this would be to misunderstand the symbolic nature of the
book of Revelation, which is concerned rather to portray through
images and symbolic titles truths which are otherwise inexpressible.
The truth that is presented here is of the complete "worthship" of
God and of Jesus. All that the resources of language will allow can
only declare a small part of the truth of the complete and absolute
"worthship-fulness" of God. To any who may have felt themselves
to be wavering in their Christian allegiance, or who felt appalled at
the prospect of undeserved suffering and possible martyrdom for the
sake of the gospel, the message was unmistakable. Right and love
would triumph because they already had triumphed in Jesus Christ
and because they alone were worthy of the ultimate victory. The
vision is a supreme and magisterial declaration of faith and commitment, and it discerns the vital truth that worship itself is indissolubly
linked to that commitment. In presenting the great "Amen!" uttered
by the four living creatures in heaven, John is giving voice to the
great and final "Amen!" of the entire church. This brief Hebrew
word, which simply means "So be it!" is the response of personal
involvement in, and assent to, the words that have been expressed.

It has become a normal part of all Christian worship to conclude
any public prayer, and for the majority of instances any prayer at all,

with the one word "Amen." Thereby the prayer is affirmed to be complete and offered to God. More significantly, however, by uttering this word the worshiper affirms that what has been prayed truly is his or her prayer. This is what the worshiper wants to present to God, to ask of God, or as the case may be, to assert as true about God and about the world. "Amen" is the biblical formula for commitment. We can see this most strikingly and instructively if we look back to the pages of the Old Testament. The book of Deuteronomy contains a series of curses upon miscreants who perpetrate certain offenses undertaken in secret against the community or against God. They are cursed because their offense may not be discovered. To each of the uttered curses, declared publicly by the Levites, the entire assembled congregation responds "Amen"—"So be it!" Thereby the entire people take upon themselves a solemn commitment and responsibility. On the one hand they declare their intention never to do such things as have been cursed and on the other they fully endorse the verdict so that any offender who suffers as a result of the curse will have brought misfortune upon his or her own head. By using this one simple word, which has become a constituent feature of all biblical prayer, the hearers affirm that this is what they truly know and intend to be the case.

The somber situation which surrounds the use of the formula "Amen" in Deuteronomy 27 is transformed to one of joy and thanksgiving when we turn to the great psalm of praise to God offered by the Levites for the bringing of the Ark into Jerusalem by David in 1 Chronicles 16. Here it is a joyful note of praise to God which is endorsed by the people with their great shout of "Amen" (1 Chron. 16:36). However, in all the many biblical examples of the use of this simple affirmation in prayer we find that it has essentially the same purpose. It is a formula by which the worshiper identifies himself or herself with the prayer and makes known that this is what is understood to be true and what is truly desired of God.

We know as we survey so many of the great prayers of the Bible and as we search our own hearts in prayer, however, that this one simple word can be the most difficult one of all to utter with that level of sincerity which we understand to be the heart of genuine prayer. The complaint of the prophet Isaiah that Israel honored God with their lips, while their hearts were far from God (Isa. 29:13) is a stricture that can inevitably be applied to so much of our human prayer. If only it were possible to utter the Lord's Prayer with the degree of sincerity and longing that it properly demands then we know that our whole lives would have been transformed. Prayer is the education of desire, teaching us to look and long for that which is truly worthy. The conclusion of a prayer with the word "Amen," enables us to remain aware of the gap that exists between what we see that we should pray for and that which we know, deep down, we only half-heartedly desire.

The book of Revelation can then picture the ultimate goal of worship in heaven, and the discovery and enjoyment of the true "worthship" of God and of Jesus Christ, by picturing a spontaneous outburst of the four heavenly creatures with the word "Amen!" No doubt it is significant also that one of the symbolic titles that it employs, alongside Lamb and Lion of the tribe of Judah, to describe the person of Jesus is that of "the Amen" (Rev. 3:14). In the obedience of Jesus to submit to the humiliation of the cross, the longing for God and the desire to do God's will have found their fullest expression. Jesus is the Alpha and the Omega, the Beginning and the End, the One in whom men's and women's constant striving to say "Amen" to God, has found its ultimate fulfillment.

The Significance of the Prayer

A first reflection on the way in which the book of Revelation pictures the final triumph of the church and the true worshipfulness of God must rest in a reflection upon the nature of the book itself. Symbols and symbolic language are richly meaningful and inseparable from the inner character of religion. Yet they are also dangerous and discomforting if pressed in an unthinking or overliteral fashion. Undoubtedly the history of the Christian church has witnessed good cause for caution in the way in which the book is and has been interpreted. Symbols can be interpreted and understood in many ways, and all too often, sincere Christians have wrestled with the symbols in an effort to elicit some final meaning from them and have, in consequence, arrived at dangerous and disruptive ideas. Not realizing that in interpreting the symbols and images of the book, they have set out limited conclusions of their own, they proceed to act as though it were actually these conclusions that are set out in the book. In this way the book has acquired a disturbing reputation because of the disturbing interpretations which have mistakenly been derived from it. All kinds of millenarian movements, social revolutions, and conclusions regarding the imminent threat of the ending of the world and the destruction of the universe have become associated with interpretations of the visions of the book of Revelation. The discerning Christian and prayerful worshiper can readily feel nonplussed and insecure in the face of such seemingly urgent forewarnings of God's purpose. Such is neither the true character nor the spiritual purpose for which the book was composed. Rather it sought by bringing together a host of images and themes already well established in the Old Testament to show the true Lordship of Jesus Christ and the way in which the purpose of God has been and will be fulfilled in Jesus. It is a vision for a time of crisis which seeks to show how such critical moments in history may serve to highlight the ultimate issues which we face. It is a writing that sincerely endeavors to penetrate through the mists and shadows of agonized human experience of history and to show that beyond it lies a more ultimate and more enduring reality. It calls for decision and commitment so that, rather than submit to the forces of evil and injustice that were temporarily prevailing, men and women might fix their gaze on the ultimate end of things. By its symbols it declares that Christians should not forsake all that is worthy, true, and good in the face of the almost intolerable pressures that may threaten to engulf the Christian church.

The portrayal of the worship of the church triumphant in heaven given in Revelation 5 is also memorable because it views that worship as ultimately one of glad and unrestrained praise. It pictures every creature of the entire universe struggling with the inadequacy of language and the poverty of ideas to express the majesty and power of God. Only by heaping up a sequence of more or less synonymous words—honor, power, majesty, glory—can the true worthiness of God to receive our praise be voiced. The ultimate splendor and greatness of the Creator can only be understood beyond the limits imposed by the inadequacies and partial vision which is the best that this world enables us to achieve. The sheer unimaginable vastness and wonder of creation points us to contemplate the even more wonderful majesty of its Creator!

It is however only in relatively few of life's moments, and even then only in a very imperfect fashion, that we can direct our minds and thoughts sufficiently towards the Creator to feel a tingling thrill of excitement that we are God's creatures and that the greatest thing is to know the Creator. Our minds are so preoccupied with our own affairs and with a concern to obtain our share of things that the ultimate Source of life is beyond our horizon. "If the day comes when all the desire in my soul is detached from the things of this world and directed wholly and exclusively towards the good, then on that day I shall possess the sovereign good" (Simone Weil, *Gateway to God* [London: Collins 1974] 45). Prayer has a part to play in the true shaping and forming of our lives, then, since prayer is essentially the education of our desires for God. When we begin in prayer by petitioning God to give us things or to order events so that they may work out to our advantage, we begin to discover two things: first that God does not necessarily want to give us "things" at all but has some higher and more enriching purpose in store for us; second, we discover, by comparing our needs with the needs of the world and by seeing how many good and worthy things could be achieved in it, that we do not very much desire these worthier things. Yet we feel that we ought to pray for them, so that slowly, and often painfully for our own peace of mind, we discover that we are at least beginning to desire them. We are moving forward sufficiently in prayer to realize that it is not God's reluctance that is making prayer difficult but rather our inability to seek those things that God is desirous of giving. It is not God who is a reluctant Giver, since that would be a contradiction of the essential divine nature and of God's work as Creator. Rather it is that we are reluctant recipients of the Creator's gifts.

Seen in this light, a great and resounding "Amen!" marks a very fitting portrayal of the ultimate goal and purpose of all the prayers of all God's creatures. It is only in God's very presence that our desires for God can be fully complete. Only when we discover the fullness of what it means for God to be God can we also say with a full and unrestrained sincerity, "Amen!" Before that transforming experience prayer must always remain a discomforting process. We find our wayward desires constantly in need of redirection and our innate capacity for praise and adoration fastening onto less worthy and less satisfying objects. Only when we discover that they are less than the total worthiness of God and that they are less good than the absolute Good that God alone can offer, do we return to prayer with a renewed questing for our Creator.